Marines on the Beach

Marines on the Beach

The Politics of U.S. Military Intervention Decision Making

Christopher Paul

PSI Reports

PRAEGER SECURITY INTERNATIONAL
Westport, Connecticut · London

Library of Congress Cataloging-in-Publication Data

Paul, Christopher, 1971–
Marines on the beach : the politics of U.S. military intervention decision making / Christopher Paul.
p. cm.
Includes bibliographical references and index.
ISBN 978–0–313–35684–1 (alk. paper)
1. Intervention (International law)—Government policy—United States—Decision making. 2. United States—Foreign relations—1945–1989—Decision making. 3. United States—Foreign relations—1989—Decision making. 4. United States—Military policy—Decision making. 5. United States—Relations—Latin America—Case studies. 6. Latin America—Relations—United States—Case studies. I. Title.
JZ1480.A984 2008
327.1'170973—dc22 2008020454

British Library Cataloguing in Publication Data is available.

Library of Congress Catalog Card Number: 2008020454
ISBN-13: 978–0–313–35684–1

First published in 2008

Praeger Security International, 88 Post Road West, Westport, CT 06881
An imprint of Greenwood Publishing Group, Inc.
www.praeger.com

Printed in the United States of America

The paper used in this book complies with the Permanent Paper Standard issued by the National Information Standards Organization (Z39.48–1984).

10 9 8 7 6 5 4 3 2 1

To my wife, Melissa

Contents

Preface and Acknowledgments

This book is a reorganized, revised, and updated version of my dissertation, completed in 2001 in the University of California at Los Angeles department of sociology. The bulk of the empirical research was completed between 1996 and 2000; substantial revisions were made in 2003 (following the onset of U.S. operations in Iraq) and again in 2007 (following the agreement of a publishing contract with Praeger).

My thanks go to my orginal dissertation committee, Richard Rosecrance, William G. Roy, David Lopez, and Michael Mann, Committee Chair. Special thanks are owed to Mick, whose consistent quality criticism and tireless patience with iteration allowed me to arrive at a product both he and I are happy with. I extend my gratitude to other colleagues who read, discussed, or otherwise contributed to the development of earlier drafts: Bill Domhoff, Laura Miller, Nick Wolfinger, Sean Edwards, Cathie Lee, Susan Stockdale, and Anne Holohan. My thanks go, too, to my RAND colleague Maria Falvo who helped me update and reformat the considerable volume of citations throughout the book.

I owe an enormous debt to my wife (first my girlfriend, then fiancé during the course of this effort) and partner, Melissa Tabbarah. Without her love and support, many things in my life would be incomplete. I appreciate the contributions of Praeger Security International's Adam Kane, especially his helpful suggestions and guidance through the publication process. Errors, omissions, and incongruities remain my responsibility alone.

1

Introduction: The Politics of Military Intervention

Force, particularly overt force, is the most solemn, and potentially the most costly, instrument of power that a state has at its disposal.

—*Stephen Krasner*

The United States has a long history of sending troops to intervene in other nations. This book concerns itself with how those decisions are made and what factors beyond the events occurring in the target country affect the outcome of the decisional process. The deployment of armed forces in a foreign sovereign country is one of the most grave decisions that can be undertaken on behalf of a nation, yet a RAND study prepared for the United States Army characterizes U.S. intervention decisions as "relatively unpredictable."[1]

Military interventions hold a prominent place in U.S. history and seem likely to maintain that place in the future. The consequences of military interventions are sometimes staggering in their scope and encompass many levels: consequences for the invaded country, consequences for the region in which that country is located, consequences for the shape of geopolitics for years to come; at home, there are electoral consequences, consequences in public opinion, consequences in business, and consequences for U.S. military personnel.

Given the continued salience and considerable consequences of U.S. military interventions, "relatively unpredictable" leaves something to be desired. This multiple-case study increases our understanding of how and why U.S. military intervention decisions are made by examining the four U.S. military interventions in the Caribbean and Central America since World War II: the Dominican Republic (1965), Grenada (1983), Panama (1989), and Haiti (1994).

INTRODUCTION TO THE STUDY

When we start to think about the politics of military interventions, at core we want to know who makes these decisions, and in whose interest. While the question of who makes the decisions is an empirical question and a question about process, the question of interests cuts toward a deeper question about *governance.* In this book I pose that question: Which model of governance best describes the way in which the United States makes military intervention decisions: the class model, the pluralist model, the elite model, or some hybrid? The first major contribution of this volume is to adjudicate among these existing theories of governance (which are elaborated in Chapter 3) for U.S. military interventions. While this study finds that elite theory provides the best general model, the notions of both the pluralist and class positions contribute to a complete explanation, and sometimes in an unexpected way.

This book is also concerned with the factors that affect the decisional outcomes that policy makers reach. Do decision makers rationally pursue the interests (the *national interest*) provided to them by the "correct" model of governance, or are they influenced or constrained by "structural" or institutional factors? The second major contribution of the volume addresses this question, usually referred to as the "agency-structure" debate (elaborated in Chapter 3). Findings demonstrate considerable contribution from and constraints by institutional sources. However, far from finding that institutional factors are wholly deterministic (a pure "structure" answer), this research offers support for a "choice-within-constraints" model, as advanced by researchers in a new strand in neoinstitutionalism.[2]

Chapter by Chapter Introduction

In what follows, I introduce the central questions and primary findings of each chapter. Each contributes in some way to the testing of the competing theories of governance and to a resolution of the agency-structure debate.

Chapter 2

Chapter 2, "Case Histories: U.S. Military Interventions in Central America and the Caribbean since 1945," gives details of case selection and tells the story of each of the four interventions and the decision process leading to them. This chapter provides short, clear historical backgrounds for the cases: what actually happened in the target country, what U.S. decision makers did in response, and when.

Chapter 3

Chapter 3, "Theoretical Issues and Concepts: Governance and Context," returns to the theoretical issues introduced in this chapter. The chapter reviews the major theories of governance (pluralism, elite theory, and class theory) and the ongoing structure-agency debate, setting the stage for the analytical chapters. The chapter also contains notes regarding data sources and methods of data collection.

Chapter 4

Chapter 4, "U.S. National Interest and Foreign Policy Making," explains what the national interest is and what interests were pursued in these four military interventions. The whole notion of the "national interest" is central to the question of governance. The national interest (however constructed) has to do with the reasons that the United States undertakes military interventions (the actual substance of

American foreign policy), rather than the determinants of the military intervention decision-making process.

I find all of the existing notions of the national interest to be unsatisfactory, in that they all maintain a "unitary" conception of the national interest, supposing that it is a single, definable set of interests. In opposition to that unitary character, I advance a tripartite model of the national interest, which proposes that the national interest is socially constructed and that it is socially constructed at three meaningful levels: the public national interest, the calculated presidential national interest, and the legitimation national interest. As I have argued elsewhere in the case for state autonomy, the national interest is a property of a situation.[3] Sitting around and enumerating the national interest in the abstract is a fool's errand. Only when contemplating a real situation can the calculus be done, and then only the president's national interest calculations really matter. In the last instance, this conclusion supports the premises of elite theory; however, the existence and consequences of a public national interest allow for some contribution from pluralism (though not one proposed by the pluralists), and the way in which presidents reach their definitions of the national interest suggests the class-elite model is not without merit.

Chapter 5

In as much as the chapter on the national interest speaks to the question of governance with regard to military interventions, Chapter 5, "The Decision-Making Process: Who Participates, and How?" is the core chapter of the volume. This chapter directly addresses the way in which U.S. military intervention decisions are made and explains who participates in the decisional process. I find that the general character of intervention decision-making processes is determined by two sets of primary characteristics: whether an intervention is a response to a crisis or is premeditated and whether an intervention is decided in secret or in the public eye. Within the general character defined by these primary characteristics of the situation, intervention decisional processes are heavily influenced by elements of the bureaucracy, the salience of the events and of the intervention target, and a considerable set of contingent factors.

Findings indicate that intervention decision processes are affected by factors whose influences run from the bottom up and also from the top down, specifically that decision making takes place within a framework of "structured contingency" bounded by the institutional conditions and organizational rules in place and that the decisional process is highly dependent both on the consequences of the very personalist American presidency at the top and the state bureaucracy at the bottom (and middle).

Chapter 6

Chapter 6, "The Legacy of Previous Military Interventions for Decision Making in Subsequent Interventions," begins with the notion of path dependence and explains why "generals always fight the last war." The chapter argues that each military intervention leaves important institutional policy legacies for the interventions that follow. While the strongest legacy effect is realized on the immediately subsequent intervention, legacies continue from case to case and are slightly modified by each one to form extended legacy chains.

This legacy chain analysis speaks both to the question of governance and to the structure-agency issue. The legacy chain argument suggests that, in part, states do what they do as a product of what they have done before, trying to repeat successes and avoid failures. Findings indicate that policy legacies can affect both the decisional process and the outcome of that process. Legacies are embodied in two kinds of institutional changes: changes in the perceptions and "taken for granteds" of decision makers and the public, and changes in formal procedure, law, or rule.

Chapter 7

Chapter 7, "The Legitimacy of U.S. Military Interventions in Central America," connects the broad levels of the question of governance as addressed in Chapter 4 on the national interest with the more specific "how and why" questions focused on in Chapter 5's discussion of process by examining the process of military intervention legitimation. The chapter explains what military intervention legitimation strategies are likely to work in which situations and why legitimation is necessary in the first place. The analysis proceeds by detailing specific legitimations that were used in these four cases and then explains their use in terms of the logics of the specific legitimations, their normative appeal, and their possible position in the decisional process.

The chapter argues that legitimation is imperative in the American political system and draws an important analytic distinction between decision-maker *motives* and decision-maker *claims* that parallels the distinction between calculated presidential national interest and legitimation national interest discussed in Chapter 4. As in Chapter 4, the end of the Cold War is an important empirical turning point for legitimations. With the loss of unitary black and white goals associated with the end of the Cold War metanarrative some legitimating strategies lost normative force and thus declined in likely use and success. Findings show that legitimations are reflexive, tactical, and part of the decision-making process.

Chapter 8

Chapter 8, "Conclusions: Governance, Institutions, and Future U.S. Interventions," is the closing chapter of the volume. In it I reprise the general themes and findings of the whole enterprise. The chapter considers intervention cases outside of the four core cases of the book in order to argue that the findings of this research generalize beyond its own bounds. In that same section, I discuss cases in which intervention was considered but discarded in an effort to further validate my findings. The conclusion revisits the existing theories of governance and the agency-structure debate (introduced in Chapter 3) in light of the analyses in the substantive chapters.

Finally, while ongoing operations in Afghanistan and Iraq are not core cases in this research (they are not in Central America, much of the process data are still classified, and military action is still under way at this writing), the 9/11 attacks and the subsequent U.S. military interventions have an impact on several of the implications of this book. Given the high salience of these events in current public consciousness and discourse and since the analyses of this volume have a contribution to make to understanding the ongoing decisional processes for the "war on terror," I have included some discussion of the impact of 9/11. I try to point out where the war on terror impacts my analysis, where the findings of this study generalize to current events, and how the context in which military intervention decisions are made has been changed by the attacks.

2

Case Histories: U.S. Military Interventions in Central America and the Caribbean since 1945

This chapter provides a brief summary of the action of each of the four U.S. military intervention cases informing this analysis: the Dominican Republic (1965), Grenada (1983), Panama (1989), and Haiti (1994). The discussion includes some of the general historical background and a rough chronology of the events leading up to the intervention.

CASE SELECTION

The focus of the empirical inquiry is decisional processes that result in U.S. military interventions. To limit the number of possible cases, I made both a regional and a chronological restriction when selecting cases: U.S. military interventions in the Caribbean/Central America since World War II. In addition to constraining the total number of possible cases by restricting the analysis to Central American/Caribbean interventions, I hoped to maximize comparability across cases by assuring maximum homogeneity (to the extent that Caribbean/Central American countries share certain common characteristics and to the extent to which this region is squarely within the "U.S. sphere of influence," dating back to the Monroe Doctrine). This is comparability of decisional process outcome; while each of these processes resulted in an intervention in this region, the decisional processes may well have been very different indeed.

Definition of Intervention

I define a U.S. military intervention as a significant invasion or occupation of foreign territory that is conducted by U.S. troops and that is planned and commanded by U.S. personnel. By defining intervention in this way, I hope to capture what most people think of when they invoke the phrase "U.S. military intervention" and to exclude small-scale surgical strikes, covert operations, or U.S.–supported military actions conducted primarily by non–U.S. military personnel. While I exclude U.S. interventions in other parts of the world and U.S.–supported invasions and actions in Central America from full consideration as cases, many of these events have important policy legacies that influence the cases receiving full treatment (for example, the desire to "avoid another Cuba" in the rhetoric of the Dominican invasion decision and the acknowledged legacy of Vietnam in deciding the overwhelming force deployed in the Panama invasion). I have made no attempt to divorce my cases from their context as part of series of interventions and other military/paramilitary activities by the United States the world over. This case selection logic and case definition led me to the four cases examined here: the Dominican Republic (1965), Grenada (1983), Panama (1989), and Haiti (1994).

These four cases constitute the universe of U.S. military interventions in Central America since World War II, with military intervention defined as specified above, so there is no "sample" of cases within the population of possible cases; given the case selection criteria, these are all of the possible cases.

There are quite a few cases of U.S. involvement in military actions in the region that I examined in some detail before concluding that they did not meet my case selection criteria; these included the invasion of Guatemala in 1954, the failed "Bay of Pigs" operation against Cuba, and U.S. involvement in both El Salvador and Nicaragua.

While these events do not constitute cases of military interventions (as I have defined them), they are certainly cases of *something*, and a very relevant something at that. While I do not directly analyze these events, I do acknowledge their historical impact on the context in which the decisions considered here were taken, as well as their constitutive role in the institutional trends in the legitimacy of U.S. military action that took place over the time period considered. Intervention of one form or another outside of my central cases receive some attention in the chapter on policy legacies (Chapter 6).

Political sociologist Steven Lukes has observed the importance of nondecisions and agenda setting to political power and decision making.[1] It is methodologically problematic to evaluate cases that did not become intervention candidates (or even to evaluate candidates that were considered and discarded so quickly or briefly that no records of the decisional process exist). I have constrained my cases to "positive cases" of decisions resulting in a U.S. military intervention. I acknowledge that this has prevented me from asking comparative questions of the form "why did the U.S. intervene here rather than there?" but does not problematize the questions I do answer, namely, "what is the character of the processes that result in U.S. military interventions?" and "how do they differ from one intervention to another?"

That said, I acknowledge the value of counterfactuals and believe there is something to be learned from occasions that resulted in the consideration of, but did not result in, military intervention. While I do not include these instances as formal cases, I have found accounts of intervention candidates that were considered but not realized and collected some information about these "negative" cases. While I do not bring the full weight of comparative historical methods to bear on any of these discarded interventions, the insight available from casual comparison makes them interesting nonetheless. I return to these negative cases in my overall conclusions (Chapter 8).

Dominican Republic Narrative

On April 24, 1965, there was an uprising of rebel Dominican army officers against the existing "triumvirate" government. The resulting civil strife led to the U.S. decision to intervene, beginning on April 29. Within the first ten days of the intervention, nearly 23,000 American soldiers poured into the Dominican Republic, almost half as many as were in Vietnam at the time. How did this come to pass?

The United States has a long history of intervention and involvement in the Dominican Republic (DR). In fact, from 1916 to 1924, U.S. Marines occupied and administrated the country. Rafael L. Trujillo ran the country with a brutal dictatorship from 1931 to 1961. Because of Trujillo's anti-German position during World War II, his anticommunism once the Cold War began, and his willingness to coddle U.S. business interests, the United States overlooked his poor human rights record for a long time. In the late 1950s U.S.–Trujillo relations soured, as his oppression became more brutal and he became more and more disliked in other Central American countries. President John F. Kennedy saw three possibilities for the DR "in descending order of preference: a decent democratic regime, a continuation of the Trujillo regime, or a Castro regime. . . We ought to aim at the first, but we can't really renounce the second until we are sure we can avoid the third."[2] Trujillo's reign ended with his assassination on May 30, 1961, in a coup that the Central Intelligence Agency (CIA) at least knew about and in which it may or may not have had a more direct role.[3]

U.S. involvement increased as Kennedy pushed for democracy. While it did not become a direct intervention, part of the U.S. Navy's Caribbean Ready Group remained near Hispaniola (the island the Dominican Republic shares with Haiti) while two of Trujillo's brothers tried to precipitate a crisis in 1962. Under this thinly veiled threat and U.S. diplomatic initiatives, the brothers left the DR, and elections were held in December 1962; the winner was Juan Bosch.[4]

During Bosch's time as president, the Dominican Republic was Kennedy's "showcase for Latin American democracy." The United States remained heavily involved, counseling the new president and pouring U.S. Agency for International Development (USAID) money into the country.[5] Bosch was a mercurial and liberal president who was not a very effective coalition builder and thus a mediocre politician. Bosch wanted his country to be less dependent on the United States and on U.S. businesses. Bosch had considerable popular support, but little support among the business classes and the military. Though he (Bosch) was frustrating for the U.S. ambassador and the U.S. Department of State to work with, he was the democratically elected leader of the "showcase of democracy," so they tried to advise him, help him, and support him as well as they could, especially U.S. Ambassador John Martin.[6] After less than a year in office, Bosch was overthrown by a coup. The United States declined to intervene militarily, but did withdraw the ambassador and refused to recognize the new junta for the (rather short) remaining duration of the Kennedy administration. Bosch's short term had an important effect on the subsequent crisis in 1965. Historian Abraham Lowenthal observed:

> [Ambassador] Martin's own exasperation after months of dealing with the mercurial Dominican leader seems to have been very influential—together with the disenchantment of leading Latin American social democrat leaders with Bosch—in establishing a consensus view within the U.S. government that Bosch's own return should not be encouraged, a view that was to have an important effect on the 1965 crisis.[7]

Despite the initial nonrecognition of the new Dominican regime (originally a triumvirate junta that ultimately came to be dominated by Donald Reid Cabral after the other members of the triumvirate resigned), U.S. business again turned to the Dominican Republic, with U.S. direct investment increasing sharply.[8] Cabral continued Bosch's International Monetary Fund (IMF) approved austerity measures and tried to retain some of the limits on military corruption imposed by the Bosch regime. His support was weak, as there were many dissatisfied segments in Dominican society—just how weak would not become apparent until the coup in April 1965.

As noted, Cabral's triumvirate was not entirely popular, and there were many dissatisfied segments in Dominican society. To list a few, there were those who wished for Bosch's return as president, those who wished for a return to constitutionality with new elections (but supported Bosch for those elections), those who wished for new elections and supported Joaquin A. Balaguer, who was the last figurehead president under Trujillo, those who wanted a socialist or communist revolution, and those who just wanted a different junta so they could get on the gravy train. There were many different groups involved in (often overlapping) plots, none of which yet seemed ripe. On April 11, 1965, the CIA reported to Washington that Bosch's party, the PRD (Dominican Revolutionary Party), was plotting with military officers to overthrow Cabral.[9] This was, in fact, the group of plotters who would ultimately spark the uprising 15 days later. This was just one plot among several in the politically volatile country; while this news was a source of general concern, Department of State officials imagined that plotters would at least wait for election campaigning to begin (or fail to begin if Cabral prevented Bosch or Balaguer from returning to the country to campaign) as a possible excuse for a coup. That the U.S. government took the situation seriously but did not expect action as soon as it occurred is clear: U.S. Ambassador William Tapley Bennett, Jr. was called to Washington for high-level consultations in April. Bennett was visiting his sick mother in Georgia en route to Washington and was thus neither in the DR nor Washington when the crisis began on April 24.[10] Ambassador Bennett was not the only member of the U.S. Embassy "country team" who was out of the country: The USAID mission director, the Public Safety Adviser, and 11 of the 13 Military Assistance Advisory Group officers were also out of the Dominican Republic.[11] These absences left a lowly chargé d'affaires as the senior official in residence.

The uprising began on April 24, 1965, several days before the plotters had planned. Reid Cabral had discovered the identity of some of the plotters (officers at a nearby army base) and sent a loyal colonel to arrest them. The officers that the colonel turned to to help him make the arrests turned out to be in on the plot as well; they arrested the arresting colonel and sent word to their fellow plotters that the uprising must begin immediately.[12]

A coalition of dissatisfied army officers, pro-Bosch PRD activists, and others began their uprising. Forces marched from the army camp in revolt to Santo Domingo, the capital. A group captured Radio Santo Domingo for a while during the afternoon, and announced that Reid Cabral's government had fallen and that a return to "constitutionality" was under way. The government-controlled TV station subsequently announced that this was not so.[13] Nonetheless, the crisis was under way.

At this point, the U.S. decision-making process entered an "informational" stage, where it would remain for several days—arguably much too long. Attaché William Connett, the ranking U.S. Embassy officer, sent a "CRITIC" (the highest level of urgency) cable to the Department of State announcing the uprising.[14] After making several phone calls and receiving various reports about the uprising, the U.S. Embassy staff members remained unsure of the political ties and intentions of the coup makers; they reported to Washington that the situation was confusing, but that the insurgency was confined to a few army officers and that Cabral should maintain control.[15]

The Dominican desk officer at the Department of State acknowledged that there was a situation and accepted the U.S. Embassy's assessment. President Lyndon Baines Johnson claims in his memoir that Under Secretary of State Thomas C. Mann briefed him that evening, and he asked to be kept informed.[16] The presidential daily diary does confirm that he and Mann spoke on the phone at about 6 P.M., but does not indicate the topic. It is certainly possible that Johnson first learned of the budding situation at this point; in any case, he did not yet consider it critical (no one in Washington did), and he did not yet take an active role.

Early in the morning of April 25 rebel troops entered the capital, Santo Domingo, and sounded the sirens at the fire station.[17] After the Embassy informed Washington that the situation was deteriorating for the Cabral regime, a "Dominican Republic Task Force" was established at the Department of State Operations Center.[18] Ambassador Bennett requested immediate travel to Washington, which was arranged. Department of State Caribbean Country Director Kennedy M. Crockett requested (on a contingency basis, without informing the president) that the U.S. Navy's Caribbean Ready Group move toward the DR, but stay out of sight of land, in case it was needed.[19]

Reid Cabral contacted the U.S. Embassy and informed them the staff rebel soldiers had entered the city and that he believed communist activists were at work. He requested U.S. intervention at that time. In consultation, Connett and Crockett decided to back the formation of a junta, but to take very few steps to encourage it.[20] During the day on April 25, another major army camp joined the revolt.

The CIA reported that known leftists were participating. Throughout the crisis, CIA intelligence gathering focused more on the activities of known or suspected communists and less on the general events of the crisis.[21] No serious thought was given to supporting the revolt and encouraging Bosch's return, nor was the sustenance of the Cabral government seriously considered. Right from the start, avoiding a communist takeover and trying not to get too involved were the default positions of the U.S. government.[22]

The PRD again took over Radio Santo Domingo, announced that Cabral had fallen, and urged the public to gather at the national palace. Thousands of Dominicans crowded the palace plaza cheering for Bosch. Later in the afternoon, forces opposed to Bosch finally began to act. The Dominican navy shelled the palace and the Dominican air force strafed the crowd in front of the palace.[23] This was a major polarizing event, though its import was not realized by U.S. decision makers at that time.[24] Despite this increased resistance, Rafael Molina Ureña (the last remaining minister from the former Bosch government) was sworn in as provisional president.[25]

Gen. Elias Wessin y Wessin and Gen. Emilio De Los Santos (opposed to Bosch) informed the Embassy that they would cooperate to prevent Bosch's return. The country team encouraged the support of the Wessin–De Los Santos plan; the team maintained that, while it might lead to bloodshed, it would prevent the return of Bosch and would minimize communist risk, as Wessin and De Los Santos should have been able to win easily.[26]

U.S. Secretary of State Dean Rusk visited the Operation Center in the afternoon and inquired after the strength of communists in Santo Domingo, fearing a "second Cuba."[27] That specific language, fear of a second Cuba, pervaded high-level discourse throughout the crisis. At this point decision making was still in an informational stage, in which a situation of some kind was acknowledged, but the likely outcome of that situation was believed to be known, and U.S. action of any kind appeared unlikely to be necessary to meet the only stated U.S. policy goals: avoidance of a second Cuba and protection of American lives. Washington officials were still calm, believing, based on Embassy reports, that the Dominican military had the situation well in hand.

By nightfall, what began in the morning as a small military coup against the previous regime had taken on a massively populist character (many citizen residents were in the streets and armed). This uprising was no longer against Cabral, but against Wessin, and was rapidly developing toward a civil war, all without the understanding of the U.S. Embassy and thus without the knowledge of Washington officials.[28]

By the dawn of Monday, April 26, many Americans had contacted the U.S. Embassy to request evacuation.[29] The *New York Times* reported that approximately 500 out of 2,500 U.S. citizens in the country wanted to leave on April 26.[30] In contrast with its reports the night before, the U.S. Embassy reported that probably nothing short of major U.S. involvement could prevent Bosch's return.[31] Washington officials continued to assume that, given the chance, a military junta would form and restore order and that a cease-fire should have made that more likely. At this point the decision-making process had entered into a second, dichotomous, phase in which the in-country embassy staff had begun to realize the extent of the crisis and that the outcome was far from certain, but the Washington bureaucracy failed to appreciate the situation and was still collecting information rather than considering action.

Fighting continued in Santo Domingo throughout the day. Four times during the day anti-Bosch forces stopped their attack in response to Embassy pressure, but quickly resumed each time. Washington continued to request updates on communist influence. Embassy and CIA reporting focused more and more on the communist role in response, creating an informational self-fulfilling prophesy.[32] Ask about communists, and you will be told about communists.

The fact that the USS *Boxer*'s ready group (U.S. Marines Amphibious Ready Group) was in the area was common knowledge and was reported in the *New York Times*.[33]

By Monday night (April 26), both U.S. Embassy and Washington officials recognized that a cease-fire would not be easily achieved as the factions had become increasingly bitter (the growing consequences of the polarizing shelling and strafing of the palace the day before). Before midnight, the Department of Defense (DoD) alerted the Caribbean Ready Amphibious Squadron and part of the 82nd Airborne Division that they might be called upon for action.

Come Tuesday morning (April 27) Washington officials were willing to acknowledge the deteriorating situation and authorized the Embassy to take a more active role; the Embassy officers, however, had become skeptical that diplomatic intervention could succeed.[34] Thus the dichotomous second phase of the decision-making process was drawn out, with Washington's appreciation of the situation lagging critically.

Fierce fighting raged in the city through the afternoon as the anti-Bosch regular army units advanced into the city. Provisional President Ureña himself entered the U.S. Embassy about 4 P.M. to negotiate.[35] Bennett declined Ureña's invitation to accompany him to begin negotiations with anti-Bosch leaders.[36] Ureña took asylum in the Colombian Embassy shortly after this failed meeting.[37] *New York Times*' reporters interpreted this as the end of the revolt ("Dominican Revolt Fails after a Day of Savage Battle" was the headline), not realizing that significant elements of the armed population would fight on.[38]

A briefing prepared by the Department of State for the White House predicted (incorrectly) that General Wessin would soon control Santo Domingo. Johnson issued a news conference statement deploring the violence and disorder in the DR, announcing the evacuation of Americans wishing to leave, and hoping for a peaceful resolution.[39]

In the evening, Ambassador Bennett, having returned to the DR, told Washington that mop-up operations should begin soon; they may be rough, but he expected anti-Bosch forces to prevail.[40] Washington's concern at this point was to urge moderation on the presumed triumphant military leaders. Bennett was urged to get to the anti-Bosch leaders' headquarters (HQ) as soon as possible and urge them to avoid reprisals or atrocities.[41]

At that point, there was still no sense in Washington of "crisis." Johnson and Rusk attended the retirement party for exiting CIA Director John A. McCone, with no sign of concern about the DR.[42]

In the late evening, the military advance stalled and began to fail. Defections, desertions, and exhaustion were prevalent among the soldiers. Bennett's late evening reports indicated that radio broadcasts had a "definite Castro Flavor" and that well-armed and organized communist groups were moving to take advantage of the uncertain situation downtown.[43]

The next morning, pro-Bosch (henceforth "rebel") forces organized, increased their armament, and managed to capture an important police station. Radio San

Isidro (a station broadcasting from the San Isidro Air Force Base, the HQ of Wessin and De Los Santos) announced the formation of a new military junta of three colonels, each representing one service. During the course of the day it became clearer that the ability of the Dominican Armed Forces (henceforth "antirebels," as there is a new junta formed, and the pro-Bosch leaders have mostly left the rebel movement) to restore order was very much in question.[44]

The press was told that Johnson would leave Washington on Thursday for a long weekend at his ranch, more indication of the general failure in Washington to appreciate the extent of the crisis.

Throughout April 28, antirebel forces were demoralized and unable to advance into the city, perhaps unable even to hold their bridgehead. Antirebel leaders informed Embassy personnel that they did not have enough personnel to maintain order in the city or to guarantee the lives or property of foreign nationals and appealed for U.S. assistancc.

At 3 P.M. the antirebel junta Dominican Air Force Colonel Pedro Bartolomé Benoit contacted the U.S. Embassy and requested that the United States land 1,200 U.S. Marines to help restore the peace. Bennett relayed this request to Washington, adding that the antirebels would almost surely win if things were logical, but the situation was not logical and thus the outcome was in doubt.[45] Bennett did not recommend landing the marines at this time.[46] In the early afternoon, unarmed marine pathfinders from the USS *Boxer* measured the beach for a possible amphibious landing.

At 3:50 P.M. on April 28, Special Assistant to the President for National Security Affairs McGeorge Bundy called Mann to discuss Bennett's latest cable. They continued to oppose landing troops, but would consider it if the outcome were in doubt. They decided to brief the president, and did so at 4:45 P.M.[47] At that point the decisional process had finally passed through the phase of split perceptions and entered the third and final phase, with an almost fully shared understanding of the situation between the Embassy and Washington, a clear articulation of policy goals, and a willingness to make decisions to take action to pursue them.

At 4 P.M., Colonel Benoit (antirebel) submitted a written request (in English) for U.S. military support "to Prevent another Cuba," the text of which was cabled to Washington.[48] A rapid exchange of cables ensued. Washington informed Bennett it would not yet intervene. Bennett informed Washington that the situation had deteriorated. Bennett sent a CRITIC cable at 5:30 P.M. indicating that the country team agreed that the time had come to land the marines and that American lives were in danger. Bennett urged intervention.[49] Almost immediately after this cable, Bennett contacted the commander of the Caribbean Ready Amphibious Squadron on the USS *Boxer* and requested helicopters to pick up American evacuees and more marines to augment the marine guard at the U.S. Embassy by a platoon, so some marines were en route before the urgent cable requesting marines reached Johnson's desk. This time lag was considerable and is noteworthy. An attachment to the president's daily diary for April 28 indicates that the cable was sent from Santo Domingo at 4:40 P.M., but was not received by the White House until 5:23 P.M.

and was not delivered to the president until it interrupted a meeting in the Cabinet Room at 5:30 P.M.

Around 5:30 P.M. the president and his key advisors (including Rusk, Under Secretary of State George W. Ball, Secretary of Defense Robert S. McNamara, Bundy, and White House Press Secretary Bill Moyers) met to discuss Vietnam. During this meeting they received Bennett's cable; they authorized the request with very little discussion. After calling a few more advisors (including Mann and Deputy Secretary of Defense Cyrus R. Vance) Johnson authorized the landing of 500 marines, with rules of engagement (ROE) allowing them to return fire at approximately 6 P.M.[50]

After a short conversation between Bennett and the Ready group commander, 500 marines (in addition to the pathfinders, the extra U.S. Embassy contingent, and the helicopter/police crews already on the island or in flight) were dispatched to the island. Mann called Bennett and instructed him to obtain a written statement from Colonel Benoit asking for military assistance that specifically mentioned the need to protect American lives (instead of just the need to prevent another Cuba).[51] By the time an attaché returned with the requested statement, marines had already landed (the statement was transmitted the next morning at approximately 1 A.M. in Santo Domingo cable 24640).

At 7:30 P.M. on April 28, President Johnson briefed congressional leaders, the vice president, and others.[52] During this consultation, Senator Everett Dirksen (Senate Republican Leader) raised the question of communism (against the stated goal of protecting American lives). William Raborn (the new CIA Director) replied carefully that there were "7 or 8" possible communists in the rebel leadership, admitting that there was some concern of communism, but was trying to pretend that it was not the primary motivation; this began the slippery slope of legitimizing what was fundamentally an anticommunist intervention.[53]

Rusk, Bundy, presidential speechwriter Richard N. Goodwin, and Bill Moyers met to draft the presidential announcement of the landing. They were joined by Adlai Stevenson (U.S. Ambassador to the United Nations) and decided after argument and debate to mention only the need to protect American lives, with no mention at all of the communist threat yet.[54] While many people participated in the drafting of this announcement, Senator Mike J. Mansfield (Senate Democratic Leader) suggested a mention of the OAS (Organization of American States) in the announcement, which had been overlooked up to that point; it is interesting that the OAS, later to have a large role in trying to legitimize the intervention, was added as an afterthought.[55] Ball, Mann, Assistant Secretary of State for Inter-American Affairs Jack Vaughn, Robert Sayre (from the National Security Council Staff), Crockett, and Special Assistant to the Secretary of State Benjamin Read conferred with Bennett regarding the proposed announcement. Bennett agreed with the stated rationale.

Thursday, April 29, was the day the news coverage carried the first mention of communism as a possible motive for intervention, on the last page of Dominican coverage, in a speculative fashion. The entire text of the article read as follows: "ENVOY SEES RED PLOT—Washington, April 28 (AP)—The Dominican

Republic's Ambassador here, Jose A. Bonilla, said today that the strife in his country was a result of a communist attempt to take over the nation."[56]

Thursday (April 29) morning Johnson and his advisors urged Pentagon officers to review their contingency plans and to make sure there were enough troops in and near Santo Domingo for any necessity.[57] Colonel Benoit informed the Embassy that anti-rebel forces would again attempt a mop-up operation. Anti-rebel troops were exhausted and demoralized, but it was assumed that the rebels must also have been.[58] They were not, and mop-up operations did not get off the ground. Reports came in to the Embassy of alleged atrocities in the city and escalated violence (most of which ultimately turned out to be gross exaggerations). There was a severe limit to intelligence gathering because of the U.S. Embassy's refusal to deal with rebels and because of the obsession with gathering information about specific communists, rather than general situational intelligence. The U.S. Embassy had no firsthand information about activities downtown and no idea who or what the rebel leadership was at that time, but it had abundant information about the activities of known communists from CIA informants.[59]

U.S. Embassy reports indicated that antirebel forces were ineffective and that known communists may have been prominent in rebel activities. Johnson met with his advisors and asked for more information on Dominican communists. CIA Director Raborn and Federal Bureau of Investigation (FBI) Director J. Edgar Hoover both reported that communists were involved.[60]

McNamara and Gen. Earle Wheeler (Chairman of the Joint Chiefs of Staff) indicated that USS *Boxer*'s marine contingent was inadequate to perform operations against opposition and urged the deployment of troops that were on standby. After 2 P.M., following discussions with very little detailed situational information, Johnson ordered the debarkation of USS *Boxer*'s remaining marines (about 500 more men), apparently authorizing (if not yet ordering) an all-out military intervention. Here, the decision was taken, but it is practically inevitable at this point.[61]

Washington cabled the U.S. Embassy and USS *Boxer* requesting evaluations of the situation and the estimates of the necessity of U.S. intervention, pointedly observing that the situation could not be allowed to deteriorate so that a communist takeover occurs.[62] There was an evening consultation among Rusk, Ball, McNamara, Wheeler, and Raborn in Washington and Bennett, Connett, the CIA station chief, and the military attachés in Santo Domingo. They concluded that their desire was to avoid intervention if orderly forces can prevail, but to intervene to avoid a communist takeover.[63]

On Friday (April 30) there was still no mention of communism in official announcements (which was the same as the previous day), but the *New York Times* had mentions of the communist concern, no doubt "off the record" as the "officials" indicating that it was part of the motive were not named.[64]

Beginning in the small hours of April 30, U.S. forces began to pour into San Isidro airport. Within ten days, there were nearly 23,000 American soldiers in the DR. While still authorized only to return fire, the decision to intervene if "communist victory" appeared possible had already been taken.[65]

Grenada Narrative

On Sunday, October 25, 1983, U.S. forces executed Operation Urgent Fury, invading Grenada and putting an end, once and for all, to the popular revolutionary government that had begun in 1979. The New Jewel Movement had ended the dictatorial regime of Sir Edward Gairy on March 13, 1979, in a nearly bloodless coup, replacing it with a council that led the country as the People's Revolutionary Government (PRG), a government that would end with the U.S. invasion.

Relations between the PRG and the United States were never good. President Jimmy Carter's administration was alarmed by the leftist rhetoric of the PRG. Frank Ortiz, U.S. Ambassador to the Eastern Caribbean during the Carter administration, warned Grenadan Prime Minister Maurice Bishop not to seek assistance from Cuba or the Soviet Union, after offering a paltry U.S.$5,000 in economic aid.[66] The tenor of this warning, which Bishop considered an inappropriate dictation of policy to a sovereign nation,[67] coupled with the refusal of the United States to provide Grenada with development funds or assistance of any kind, led to Grenada accepting assistance from both Cuba and the USSR and the further deterioration of U.S.–Grenada relations. Throughout the four-and-a-half-year tenure of the PRG the United States failed to provide aid of any kind. Further U.S. package aid grants to the region (such as the Caribbean Basin Initiative) were written to exclude Grenada, and the United States used its influence to prevent Grenada from receiving funds from the IMF in 1981 and a World Bank loan in 1982.[68]

Under the Reagan administration, relations did not improve. President Ronald Reagan seems to have taken an immediate dislike to the Grenadan government, though his active posturing against it would wait until 1983. Upon his inauguration to the White House, Reagan received a congratulatory telegram from Bishop to which there was, as there would be to all other diplomatic efforts by the latter, a courteous but unsubstantial reply.[69] The proposed Grenadan Ambassador to the United States, Dessima Williams, was never accredited, and the Department of State did not commit an ambassador to Grenada.[70] When Bishop came to the United States in June 1983 and visited Washington, the president and all statesmen of any prominence actively avoided him.

In 1981 as a part of the second phase of the "Ocean Venture '81" training exercises, U.S. forces in the Caribbean conducted a practice operation called Operation Amber and the Amberdines, which simulated an invasion and restoration of democracy to a small island not entirely unlike Grenada (which is, incidentally, located in the Grenadine island chain). After this exercise the PRG announced that it believed a U.S. invasion was imminent and called up the militia and began round-the-clock watches. The Department of State asserted that Grenadan claims of an imminent invasion were preposterous, and, indeed, no invasion took place in 1981. It is unclear if the operation was, in fact, saber rattling directed at Grenada, or simply general U.S. saber rattling. The U.S. refusal to provide nonmilitary aid and threats of this kind drove the tiny nation into the arms of the Soviets both for military arms and economic assistance.[71] In June 1982, Congressman Ron Dellums's testimony before the House Subcommittee on Inter-American Affairs indicated that, after visiting the headquarters of the U.S. Atlantic Fleet, "Following extensive and comprehensive briefings, I came away with the absolute impression that nothing being done in Grenada constitutes a threat to the United States or her allies."[72]

Given that assessment, it is somewhat surprising the viperitude with which President Reagan attacked the tiny nation and its choice of allies in an address on March 23, 1983. In the same speech in which he revealed his plans for the Strategic Defense Initiative (the so-called "Star Wars" missile defense plan), he lashed out against communist influence in Grenada, revealing aerial spy-plane photography of a "secret" Grenadan "military" air base under construction by Cubans with a 10,000-foot runway, capable of handling the largest military planes. As a *New York Times* article not long after pointed out, the spy-plane photography was hardly necessary, as the construction site was open and picnickers and joggers from the medical school, as well as the general public, could walk by and take pictures if they were so inclined.[73] As for the alleged military nature of the airfield, the fuel storage tanks were visible above ground in the aerial photos, a fairly clear sign that it was a civilian facility, and the alarmingly long 10,000-foot runway was no longer than any of the runways of other airports in the region and is the length required to accommodate the largest airline passenger planes. Indeed, there were Cuban construction workers helping with the construction, but there was also a U.S. firm involved in the construction project, none of which was mentioned by the president or the reporters covering his address.

On October 12, 1983, the first signs of crisis began brewing in Grenada. Bishop and Deputy Prime Minister Bernard Coard had a disagreement and falling out, which led to Coard's resignation from his ministry and the government. The next day (October 13) the situation deteriorated. Bishop was placed under house arrest, but continued to hold the office of prime minister. The U.S. decision-making process began on October 13 following Bishop's house arrest. The arrest was reported to the Department of State by cable from the U.S. Embassy in Bridgetown, Barbados.[74] The Department of State began monitoring the situation, and, according to Secretary of State George P. Shultz's memoir, began drawing up preliminary plans for an evacuation of U.S. citizens, should that become necessary.[75]

Some might argue that the decisional process began considerably earlier, when Reagan began posturing against the tiny nation, or earlier still, during the U.S. military practice exercises of Ocean Venture's Operation Amber and the Amberdines. Several facts led me to discard this notion. First is the difference between premeditation and contingency planning. The U.S. government maintains a wide range of contingency plans. There were contingency plans for an invasion of Grenada to be "dusted off," but that is unremarkable. Consider instead what happened in Panama in 1989 (discussed later in the chapter) for an example of premeditation. Second, while Reagan was certainly glad to be rid of the leftist PRG, the decision was contingent. Other responses and a lack of response were considered. Third, the crisis was genuine. The government was toppled, people were assassinated, and there was chaos and uncertainty. Finally, the poor preparedness of the troops executing the invasion in terms of intelligence about the island precludes premeditation. None of the troops involved in Operation Amber and the Amberdines participated in Operation Urgent Fury. Most of the troops involved were diverted from reinforcements to the marine contingent then in Lebanon. Most telling is the fact that the map lockers on the ships used to carry the invasion force did not contain maps of Grenada. Maps had to be faxed and reproduced, and poor reproduction quality led to several near disasters.[76]

The decisional process, therefore, began on October 13, started by Ambassador Milan Bish (or some of his staff, but he signed the cable). We know from Shultz's memoirs that Bish was a hard-line anticommunist and refused to deal with communists at all, so he had no contact with the PRG and forbid his staff from traveling to Grenada, even for routine reasons.[77] This did not leave the Department of State with a good set of "regular channels" for information. Most of the Embassy cables throughout the rest of the crisis simply reported information gained through local news services and from members of governments other than Grenada or from civilians living on Grenada who had gone out of their way to contact the Embassy. It is unclear whether this cable report actually reached Shultz's desk on October 13 as anything more than an item on a list of possible concerns. Still, people at the Department of State's Central American desk, specifically Assistant Secretary Langhorne A. "Tony" Motley, were following the developing crisis and were aware that there were approximately 1,000 U.S. citizens, mostly medical students, in residence on the island.

On Friday, October 14, Constantine Menges, who was in his first week at the National Security Council (NSC) as the chief advisor on Central America (having just transferred from the CIA) took an active interest in Grenada. He was, by his own admission, very "Reaganite" and very anticommunist.[78] On October 14, he outlined the contours of a plan to invade Grenada and restore democracy. This seems a bit premature given the limited scope of the crisis. Menges did not present this plan formally to the hierarchy, but instead shared his ideas privately with two of his colleagues, Col. Oliver L. North (then Deputy Director Political-Military Affairs, NSC), for his military opinion, and Kenneth deGraffenreid, NSC Senior Intelligence Director.[79] North liked the idea, but was skeptical that anything like that would ever be done. DeGraffenreid was less supportive, suggesting that promoting the plan would be a quick way for Menges to lose his new appointment. In Grenada on October 14 there was continued confusion in the PRG. Radio Free Grenada (RFG, the official radio station of Grenada) announced Bishop's replacement by Coard; the announcement was later retracted. Coard announced his own resignation. Rumors and accusations flew over the next several days.

Little happened over the weekend in Washington. The situation continued to develop in Grenada, but the PRG remained in nominal control, and no deaths had occurred yet. On Monday, October 17, the Department of State convened a "restricted interagency group" meeting. The principal concern of the meeting was the possibility of hostage taking, with the recent Iran hostage crisis (November 4, 1979–January 20, 1981) on everyone's mind. The military favored a quick "in and out" rescue with elite forces withdrawing immediately to safety should action become necessary.[80] Following this meeting, Robert C. "Bud" McFarlane, National

Security Advisor as of that morning, informed President Reagan of the situation in Grenada.[81] The president authorized further contingency planning.

Secretary of State George P. Shultz authorized a special task force on Grenada within the Department of State headed by Tony Motley, promoting the developing crisis in importance. Shultz candidly admits that the Tehran hostage crisis was eminent in both his and Motley's minds.[82] In Grenada on October 18, most of the ministers of the PRG resigned. School children occupied the airport and demonstrated, shouting, "No Bishop, no school!"[83]

In Grenada on October 19, a crowd formed in front of Bishop's house, released him from his arrest, and escorted him to Fort Rupert (an administrative location, not a proper military fort). This release and this destination were somewhat suspicious.[84] Armored cars arrived at the rally at the fort and opened fire, dispersing the crowd. Bishop and other resigned ministers surrendered and were subsequently executed on the spot. A 24-hour shoot on sight curfew was imposed.

This was the day the situation in Grenada clearly became a crisis in the minds of U.S. decision makers. Milan Bish cabled that the prime minister of Barbados had requested U.S. assistance with regard to Grenada.[85] This first informal request for aid from the regional governments would help catalyze a shift in thinking from just rescuing hostages to a full-scale invasion.[86] While it is clear that certain people (Menges, for example) were already thinking invasion, the possibility of an invitation from other Caribbean leaders and the multilateral legitimacy that that would provide made invasion considerably more feasible. The restricted interagency group discussed contingencies, including a quick in and out operation to rescue the medical students.[87] Later on October 19, the Department of State tried to send officials to open negotiations, but they were not received by the Revolutionary Military Council (RMC).[88]

On October 20, Gen. Hudson Austin (head of the People's Revolutionary Army) announced the formation of the RMC with 14 members. Planning and discussion accelerated in Washington. The NSC crisis preplanning group (CPPG) on Grenada met; during the meeting, Menges argued that just in and out would be a mistake, leaving a hostile communist government behind. He proposed both rescue and restoration of democracy.[89] This CPPG referred the situation to the NSC Special Situation Group, which met later that day. Menges prepared the agenda and background brief for this NSC SSG.[90] Senior officials met for the SSG, and Menges reports that the discussion clearly led toward action, and the action most seriously discussed was the rescue plus restoration of democracy contingency.[91] If military action were to be undertaken, secrecy would be of utmost importance. With that in mind, all officials were encouraged to maintain the appearance of normalcy, so Shultz, Reagan, and McFarlane would all stick to their planned golf weekend in Georgia. During the meeting North suggested (and most others concurred) that the flotilla of marines en route to Lebanon be diverted to the Caribbean in case they were needed there. Despite the low risk of such a move, it was opposed by Art Moreau (Special Assistant to the Chairman of the Joint Chiefs of Staff), who refused the suggestion without a signed order from the Commander in Chief, President

Reagan.[92] It is unclear whether Moreau opposed the entire notion or was just covering all the bases and making sure the order came from the top. Shultz asserts that most of the opposition to the operation came from the joint chiefs and the secretary of defense, with objections based on the poor intelligence available, logistical concerns, and the short time available for planning. Shultz attributes this to "Vietnam syndrome," suggesting that the military is very hesitant to use force unless it is assured of the support and resources necessary to succeed.[93] Caspar Weinberger, the Secretary of Defense, makes no mention of opposing military action in his memoir, but does recall that he and the joint chiefs lamented the limits created by the lack of time for planning, intelligence gathering, and logistical arrangements.[94] At any rate, the order was quickly obtained, and the marines diverted.[95] McFarlane informed Reagan of the results of the meeting, and planning was allowed to proceed. These plans ultimately resulted in a National Security Decision Directive (NSDD), drafted by Menges, and signed and codenamed "Urgent Fury."[96] Pentagon planning proceeded as well.[97] Weinberger points out the difficulty of planning the operation on short notice, especially given that "we had spent the first two days looking at the matter in a more or less academic way to determine what we could do to evacuate American citizens."[98] Military plans can and do become much more cohesive once more extensive and final lists of goals become available.

In Grenada, on Friday, October 21, the curfew was lifted for four hours for citizens to resupply themselves with food and other essentials. Rioting ensued, but was denied on RFG. Also on October 21, the Organisation of Eastern Caribbean States (OECS; members included Antigua, Barbados, Dominica, St. Lucia, St. Vincent, Montserrat, and St. Kitts-Nevis [and Grenada]) met in Barbados. The OECS made a formal request to the United States for military assistance.[99] It is reasonable speculation, though no evidence exists, that Milan Bish encouraged this request to increase the legitimacy of U.S. action.[100] The actual letter requesting assistance is dated October 23, 1983.[101] This OECS appeal was used heavily in all the memoirs and in the public accounting of the decision as a major decisional factor and as highly legitimizing. According to the OECS charter (to which the United States is not and was not a party), a unanimous vote of the OECS members would allow them to intervene in each other's countries for the restoration of order. Despite the fact, therefore, that the invasion violated the OAS charter and several UN rules/resolutions, the OECS charter and its appeal were used as the principal legal justification for the invasion.[102] This justification was not accepted by the international community. It brought the condemnation of the OAS, the UN Security Council (where the condemnation was vetoed by the United States), and on the floor of the United Nations (where there is no veto), as well as by numerous individual countries, including several U.S. allies.[103]

Also on Friday, the restricted interagency group met. The Department of State took a very positive role in planning, due, according to Menges, to the fact that Shultz was very proaction on Grenada.[104] The CPPG met to prepare for the NSC meeting the next day.[105] On October 21, Grenada's Gen. Hudson Austin managed to contact the U.S. Embassy in Barbados and requested that the United States send a representative to "discuss the situation." The Embassy cabled the Department of State.[106] No reply was authorized or made (of which I could find record or mention).

On Saturday, October 22, Austin announced assurances that U.S. students were safe and that the RMC would be replaced by a civilian administration within 12 days. The morning of October 22, Vice President George H.W. Bush cabled that he had met with the spokesman of the OECS who made a personal appeal regarding U.S. support of its intervention, indicating the member countries would commit forces from their constabulary and that they would fail without U.S. support.[107] Later in the morning, there was a high-level NSC teleconference with the president. President Reagan, Shultz, and McFarlane were all in Georgia golfing; Vice President George H.W. Bush and a few other unidentified NSC staff were on the other end of the line.[108] At this point, the decision to intervene was taken. The Department of Defense cautioned against a hurried operation, wanting more time to prepare.[109] Precise details were not yet confirmed, and the decision was not necessarily final, but President Reagan made the decision and was decisive, according to both his own and Shultz's memoirs.[110] At a subsequent NSC meeting in Washington, the NSDD plan was refined to be the invasion with the multiple goal of rescue and restoration of order and government.[111] A phone meeting with the president following this meeting confirms the multiple goal.[112] After the decision had been made, word came from Gen. Austin Hudson through the Department of State, indicating that he wished to speak with U.S. representatives and that he would reopen the airport, offering assurances of the safety of the medical students and an intention to replace the military junta with a civilian government within 14 days. Two U.S. diplomats traveled from Barbados to determine the safety and the condition of the U.S. medical students.[113] Apparently, less than 10 percent of the students wished to leave the island.[114] Bridgetown cable 06547[115] contains a report of an offer to evacuate the American medical students on chartered flights. This offer was made by a private organization that specialized in "world wide emergency returns,"[116] acting on behalf of the parents association of the medical school. The group, the cable reports, wished to work closely with the Department of State for coordination's sake. I find no record of a reply, and no press coverage of the timing of this offer (or, had it been executed, its undermining effect on the White House legitimizing assertions about protecting American lives).

On Sunday, October 23, the island nation was quiet, with no violence. That morning President Reagan was awakened with news of the bombing of the U.S. Marine barracks in Lebanon. He returned immediately to Washington. Upon his return, there was an NSC meeting to discuss both Grenada and Lebanon. While the presidential daily diary does not allow us to discriminate between the two meeting topics, Shultz recalls all of the meetings that day and for the next several included both topics.[115] Reagan persevered with the plan to invade Grenada. He asserted that the barracks bombing had nothing to do with Grenada, and, if anything, was more of a mandate to demonstrate strength and resolve.[116] Assurances of the safety of the Americans on Grenada were rejected as not credible despite the assurance of the Chancellor of St. George's Medical School, Charles R. Modica, who claimed to have been in regular contact with the RMC and the Department of State.[117] After the big NSC meeting, Reagan met with John William Vessey (Chairman of the Joint Chiefs of Staff), Weinberger, McFarlane, Shultz, and a CIA representative, detailing the risks of the various Special Operations Forces.[118] Following all of this, Reagan signed the final plan.[119] This is the "end" of the decisional process; what follows is simply of interest to the outcome and some of the subsidiary aspects of the decision, such as its legitimacy and public opinion.

On Grenada on October 24, the curfew was lifted and approximately 70 percent of the island's population returned to work.[120] One might have imagined the crisis was over. Also on October 24, Bish cabled Governor General of Grenada Sir Paul Scoon's request for U.S. assistance in the restoration of order. Reagan met with the joint chiefs of staff (JCS) and the secretary of defense. The president polled each chief of staff and each confirmed for him that the plan would work, but each said he was concerned about the lack of time to get intelligence and to rehearse and practice difficult elements of the operation.[121] Although the decision had already been taken, it was not past the point of no return and could have been abandoned at this point (though that was very unlikely). Reagan spoke with British Prime Minister Margaret Thatcher, who attempted to dissuade him from his chosen course.[122] Shultz quotes House Speaker Tip O'Neill as saying, "Mr. President, I have been informed but not consulted" and promptly leaving when Reagan informed him and other congressional leaders of the impending invasion.[123] Special Forces operations to gather intelligence and to secure landing sites began on the island. In a subsequent NSC meeting, Menges noted that a colleague asked, "How are we going to sell this to the public?"[124]

On Sunday, October 25, U.S. troops landed in force on Grenada. No reporters accompanied the invasion force per the request of Grenada Task Force Commander Vice Adm. Joseph Metcalf, and none were allowed to land on the island by boat or air for several days. Weinberger claims the request was granted in part to not gainsay the commander in the field.[125] Reagan appeared with Dominica Prime Minister Eugenia Charles in a joint press conference. Reagan offered three reasons for the invasion: (1) to protect American lives, (2) to forestall further chaos, and (3) to assist in the restoration of law and order and governmental institutions.[126] Later, Reagan claimed it as a great victory over communism—"Major gain not only in political but in strategic terms."[127]

Panama Narrative

Just after midnight on the morning of December 20, 1989, U.S. forces began Operation Just Cause in Panama. Over 20,000 U.S. soldiers participated in the operation, which effectively eliminated the effectiveness of the Panamanian Defense Force (PDF) and ultimately led to the capture and arrest of Panama's "maximum leader," Manuel Noriega.

The history of U.S. involvement in Panama is a lengthy one and predates plans to construct the Panama Canal, which opened in 1914. U.S. ownership of the canal led to the establishment of a U.S. military base containing a standing force of considerable size within the confines of Panama. Panama's longtime strongman dictator,

Manuel Noriega, had relationships with the United States that differ considerably from those of most heads of state; he collaborated with a number of different U.S. agencies in their "war on drugs" and was on the CIA payroll until 1986 according to journalist and author William Blum.[128] The relationship began to sour in the late 1980s, with Noriega's civil rights records deteriorating, his contribution to U.S. policy goals waning, and his criminality and corruption increasing.

The Reagan administration concluded in the late 1980s that it would prefer to have Noriega retire. Diplomatic efforts were launched to arrange his retirement.[129] These failed, most likely because Noriega was still receiving mixed messages from different U.S. agencies (he was still on the CIA payroll until 1988 according to political scientist Margaret E. Scranton).[130] There was certainly little chance to remove Noriega while various U.S. agencies could not agree that it was a policy goal. Even when the end was agreed upon, the means remained contested. "[Secretary of State] George Shultz began pushing for aggressive action to remove Noriega, including U.S. military intervention. Frank Carlucci, then Secretary of Defense, and Admiral Bill Crowe, Chairman of the JCS, disagreed."[131]

Dissatisfaction increased, and pressure grew as time passed. On February 4, 1988, Noriega was indicted on drug trafficking charges in two U.S. federal courts.[132] Subsequently, retirement deals used the indictment as a bargaining chip; Noriega had to be careful with his foreign visits lest he be arrested under the terms of the indictment. The diplomatic offensive continued, when, on April 8, Reagan stepped up economic pressure, invoking sanctions against Panama.[133]

During this period of proposing deals and applying diplomatic pressures (before any more "active" solution had seriously been considered) Adm. William J. Crowe (Chairman, JCS at the time) ordered Gen. Fred F. Woerner (Commander, SOUTHCOM [United States Southern Command], in Panama) to revise contingency plans to include a broader range of possible military action in Panama.[134] While these preparations fell under the rubric of normal preparedness, they clearly paved the way for the possibility of a military intervention. Out of these plans came Operation Blue Spoon, a plan for a total takedown of the PDF, which, after several iterations and revisions, is the plan U.S. forces would execute in December 1989.

Throughout 1989, tension increased. In April U.S. Ambassador to Panama Arthur H. Davis, Jr. sent a strongly worded cable to the Department of State urging a more aggressive Panama policy to break the stalemate with Noriega.[135]

On May 7, 1989, Panama held elections. The elections seemed relatively free, and observers reported that Noriega's candidate was defeated. Noriega nullified the election and prevented the ballots from being counted. On May 10, Panamanian protests against the nullification of the election got international coverage when the "defeated" candidates were publicly beaten by Panamanian paramilitary "Dignity Battalions." That night, there was a White House meeting with President George H.W. Bush, Secretary of State James Baker, Admiral Crowe, and others. Bush indicated that he was fed up with Noriega and was looking for some action to take against him. They decided to use the election's failure to increase anti-Noriega sentiment. Bush released a mild statement condemning the violence. In the day following this event, Dick Cheney (then Secretary of Defense) and Crowe discussed options for the president. They urged the consideration of a contingent augmentation for Panama, but Woerner (the SOUTHCOM commander) did not want the implicit provocation. They ended up recommending sending 2,000 extra troops, and a secret compliment of SEAL and Delta Force forces, in case a "snatch" against Noriega became possible and desirable. On May 11, Crowe and Cheney briefed Bush on their recommendation, which he approved. Bush released a press statement announcing the addition of approximately 1,800 troops to Panama.[136]

On May 13, in a press question and answer session, Bush called on the people of Panama and the PDF to overthrow Noriega.[137] On July 17, Bush authorized a more aggressive assertion of treaty rights to conduct military exercises in Panama.[138] These exercises began shortly thereafter. Ultimately called "Southcom follies" by Gen. Thomas W. Kelly, these exercises never provoked any confrontations.[139] Noriega backed off, limiting the provocative behavior of the PDF. Intelligence reports indicate that Noriega had warned his PDF officers, "Don't piss off the Americans."[140] The Bush administration's desire to be rid of Noriega was at an all-time high.

The military option had crept on to the decisional plate. The process through which this occurred is unclear; it was probably just the culmination of continued frustration of policy and the increased salience of Noriega's removal as a goal. Panama was a plank in Bush's campaign platform. At any rate, changes began to occur to make the military option tenable. On June 13, 1989, Cheney and Army Secretary John O. Marsh, Jr. met with Gen. Maxwell R. Thurman, who was due to retire in two months, to size him up.[141] Thurman ended up replacing Woerner as SOUTHCOM commander; he was handpicked as an "action" general who would be able to "make it happen" when the time came. Thurman understood that he was probably going to Panama to make war. During his days between commands, he spent time looking over the contingency plans and was appalled to find that Operation Blue Spoon took five days to build up to sufficient force to execute. He began to work on revisions.

In August, Gen. Colin L. Powell, while waiting for his Senate confirmation hearings for appointment as chairman of the JCS, visited Gen. Carl W. Stiner at Fort Bragg and reviewed the whole PRAYER BOOK (code name for possible operations in Panama), including Operation Blue Spoon. They discussed the increased need for speed, flexibility, and the need to take advantage of U.S. forces' ability to operate at night. Stiner agreed and soon sent five of his best planners to Panama to work on important changes in the plans.[142]

The first certain acknowledgment I have that the decision to invade had been all but taken is based on a quotation from an account from a briefing in September. After a White House visit, Admiral Crowe told senior members of the joint staff, "I don't know when it's going to happen, I don't know what's going to precipitate it, but I am convinced that we are going to have to go in with military force into Panama to resolve the situation, and we need to be ready to do it."[143]

On September 30, 1989, General Thurman took over SOUTHCOM. The very next day brought a crisis that was revealing in terms of policy, preparedness, and decision making. Powell became Chair JCS at midnight, with events just beginning.

Briefly, what occurred was this: The CIA station in Panama reported that it had received information about a pending coup the next day. The coup makers intended to force Noriega to "retire" to the countryside. The coup makers requested that U.S. forces block two roads to prevent reinforcements from arriving at Noriega's headquarters.[144] This request went all the way up the chain of command.[145] The next day the coup was delayed by the coup makers for one day. Powell met with the president and his advisors and telephoned Thurman from the Oval Office for the latest news.[146] Powell comments in his memoirs on the odd institutional arrangement of the Bush meeting (but believes the correct decision was reached, ultimately):

> This was my first opportunity to see the Bush team in action, and I was surprised that critical deliberations were taking place with no preparation or follow-up planned. The PRG system that Frank Carlucci [Secretary of Defense from November 1987 through January 1989] and I had created had been dismantled by the new team. Brent Scowcroft [National Security Advisor], a sharp player, later diagnosed the problem and re-imposed order by reincarnating the PRG as a Deputies Committee, chaired by Bob Gates, his deputy. But all this was in the future. On this day, the Oval office debate was a free-swinging affair, and the freest swinger of all was the President's Chief of Staff, John Sununu. Sununu did not suffer fools gladly, or smart folks either, for that matter. He cut people off in midsentence and pursued his pet tangents, a behavior, I noticed which did not seem to bother the President. Bush listened, spoke little, and made sense when he did talk.[147]

The coup effort was considered "flaky." Talk ran up and down the chain of command; the ultimate decision was to accept Noriega as a prisoner if he was turned over to U.S. forces and to use routine military maneuvers to block one of the two requested roads (blocking the other being too obviously in support of the coup).[148]

The morning of October 3 the coup was launched and lost.[149] The Bush administration took considerable heat for not supporting the coup, despite how poorly executed it was—the coup makers left Noriega alone in a room with a phone; he called for reinforcements, and they came. After this "failure" Bush announced that "amateur hour is over" with regard to Panama. No subsequent opportunity would be allowed to slip by.[150]

Following the failed coup, there was a new set of attitudes in Washington, an increased sense of urgency, and a flurry of activity. On October 11, Thurman's request for an additional deployment of military police was approved.[151] Through October and November, Operation Blue Spoon plans were briefed around to senior defense personnel, revised, and ultimately signed. They were ready to go.

At that point the military had a plan it was happy with and was prepared to execute. While it would continue to make refinements and continue preparations, at that point the premeditation was complete; all that was required was a presidential decision to go, and all that required was a sufficient provocation or trigger to lend the invasion some kind of legitimacy. From there forward, the decision was almost anticlimactic, though the actors themselves try to lend it an air of drama in their memoirs.

Another development that increased the likelihood of exercising the military option was the issuance of a November 3 justice department memo to the White

House, indicating a change in a legal interpretation that allowed the military to make arrests abroad.[152] This would allow U.S. forces to arrest Noriega without needing to "detain" or follow him until an FBI or Drug Enforcement Agency officer could make the formal arrest as was previously the case.

The events that served as the trigger events for the invasion occurred in the middle of December 1989. On December 15, the Panamanian National Assembly made strong anti–U.S. statements, declaring Noriega maximum leader and announcing Panama to be in a "state of war" as long as U.S. aggression continued.[153] While the Assembly clearly was not making a serious declaration of war, its rhetoric did fire up the PDF and increased already high tensions. So high were tensions that the next day, December 16, some American officers who had taken a wrong turn panicked and ran a PDF checkpoint/roadblock. PDF troops fired on the retreating officers, wounding one, who died shortly thereafter. News of the shooting rocketed up the chain of command. Thurman was in Washington for consultations and, on learning of the incident, scheduled a 1 A.M. plane to return to Panama.[154]

By 6 A.M. the next morning (December 17), reports were coming in of a related incident involving a U.S. Navy lieutenant and his wife who were at the checkpoint at the time of the shooting. They were interrogated, the officer tortured, and his wife sexually threatened. The detention and harassment of the Curtises (the navy couple) were reported in detail to Powell and Cheney. Cheney called a meeting in his Pentagon office at 10 A.M. to review options. Cheney called Scowcroft and scheduled a meeting with President Bush later in the day. Thurman returned to Panama and went to his headquarters.[155]

While accounts in Bob Woodward's multiple interview study[156] and the various newspaper accounts and memoirs[157] indicate that this was the worst thing to have happened in Panama and was an inexcusable provocation, Scranton offers a different account:

> These incidents were like hundreds that had occurred during the last two years; many of those were minor, but some had been just as serious, including several beatings and one rape. The events of the December 16–17 weekend, particularly Lt. Paz's death, were perceived differently. They were interpreted in Washington as part of an increasingly threatening pattern, and, significantly, in the context of the National Assembly's declaration and Noriega's statements.[158]

Both in the context of the National Assembly's inflammatory remarks and in terms of having an operation against Panama ready to go, awaiting only a sufficient trigger event, these provocative actions were lent considerable gravity.

At 8:30 A.M. on December 17, Powell met in the Pentagon with Kelly and the crisis action team. Kelly reported that Noriega was trying to blame the incident on the Americans by claiming that they fired on the Comandancia (his headquarters) and then sped away. Kelly reported that the men involved had been fully debriefed and that Noriega's claims were totally unfounded. U.S. SIGINT (Signals Intelligence—radio/cell phone/phone/transmission monitoring) teams had intercepted calls in which Noriega himself was trying to arrange the cover-up and attempted blame shifting.[159]

Powell called Thurman. Thurman said he saw three options: (1) do nothing, just protest, (2) execute some portion of Operation Blue Spoon and try to capture Noriega, or (3) do the full version of Operation Blue Spoon. Thurman recommended the full version of Operation Blue Spoon.[160] Powell met with Cheney just before 10 A.M. They spoke briefly before being joined by Henry S. Rowan (Assistant Secretary of Defense for International Security Affairs), Richard Brown (Adviser for International Security Affairs at the Department of Defense), Pete Williams (Assistant Secretary of Defense for Public Affairs), Adm. William A. Owens (Senior Military Assistant to Secretary Cheney), David S. Addington (Special Assistant to Secretary Cheney), and General Kelly and Adm. Ted Sheafer (both Joint Chiefs of Staff). The civilians were especially uncertain that this was a sufficient catalyst event. Williams indicated he had spoken with SOUTHCOM's public affairs office and reported that the navy lieutenant (Curtis) was coherent and could go on TV and recount what happened to him and his wife. Cheney decided not to do that. Cheney said he wanted Williams to draft a statement saying precisely what happened to the men at the road block and the Curtises, and that he wanted to see it before it was released.[161]

Cheney and Powell talked more after others left. They realized that at that time Americans were in danger in Panama. Both agreed that the removal of Noriega and the destruction of the PDF were the best course of action. Powell indicated that he intended to contact the joint chiefs and get their views.[162]

Powell met with the chiefs at his home at 11:30 A.M. Chief Carl E. Vuono said that Operation Blue Spoon was a good plan and advocated using it. He urged that any attempt to dilute the plan must be resisted. He recalled Vietnam, where civilian leadership had been unwilling to commit the necessary resources and did not want to see that happen here (a legacy acknowledgment—see Chapter 5 on legacy chains). Chief Robert T. Herres agreed. All five of the joint chiefs advocated execution.[163] Chief Larry D. Welch pointed out that there were downsides, which they should accept, but with their eyes open. These downsides were (1) other Central American countries would not like it, (2) the PDF might be more resistant than expected, and the cost might thus be high in men and materiel, (3) critics would say the DoD was running out of enemies and was using this as a demonstration of the need for the maintenance of military force, (4) the David and Goliath problem—the media might portray Noriega as the little guy, unfairly overwhelmed, and (5) they must be sure this is a sufficient and unambiguous provocation, not like the Gulf of Tonkin.[164] Armed with the universal if not unqualified support of the chiefs, Powell and Kelly headed to the White House for a 2 P.M. meeting with President Bush.[165]

The meeting with Bush was at 2:28 P.M. on the December 17.[166] This was the decision. Attending were (confirmed by the Presidential Daily Diary): Bush, Powell, Kelly, Cheney, Baker, Scowcroft, Robert M. Gates (Deputy National Security Advisor), and Marlin Fitzwater (Bush's Press Secretary). Kelly presented the events that had transpired. Powell presented Operation Blue Spoon. Bush asked why they did not just go and get Noriega. Powell explained that getting Noriega but leaving the

PDF was risky, and there was no certainty about getting Noriega, but if the United States took the whole country, it would not really matter if they got Noriega, but the likelihood of getting Noriega would be higher. Powell warned that American blood would be spilled, and he indicated that he needed 48 hours to set things in motion. Bush probed and asked lots of questions. Powell made a strong recommendation, for which Cheney gave his full support. Powell mentioned that the chiefs all supported the plan. Baker supported invasion. Scowcroft asked questions, perhaps taking the role of devil's advocate on Bush's behalf.[167] Bush decided to go. H hour would be 1 A.M. on December 20.[168] The *New York Times* reported that Cheney announced (on December 20) that this was the day the decision was taken.[169]

Later on December 17, Kelly received a call from Gen. James J. Lindsay, Commander in Chief of the Special Operations Command. Lindsay pointed out that Blue Spoon is an awful name for an operation. With Joe Lopez (one of Kelly's staff), they tossed around names and decided on Operation Just Cause. They passed it up the chain of command and received approval.[170]

At this point the decision had been taken, and the plan was already in existence. While the operation could have been canceled in the time between the decision and the execution slightly more than two days later, nothing indicates that was ever seriously considered.

On December 18, everyone went about their daily business, maintaining maximum operational security—not telling anyone about it.[171] The military side mobilized; the president had no detectable increase in advisor meetings or calls, or any obvious signs of discussion about Panama.[172] Bush released a statement deploring the incidents in Panama.[173] The *New York Times* ran an extensive article about the DoD's detailed report on the incidents of December 16.[174]

On December 19, Bush met again with his major advisors in the afternoon. In the evening, Bush made calls to congressional leaders, informing them of the pending action.[175] After 9 P.M., Bush made calls to various heads of state.[176]

Just after midnight on the morning of December 20, Operation Just Cause began. During the day, the Soviet Union condemned the invasion in the strongest terms, as did most of the countries in Central America.[177] Baker asserted at a news conference that the UN Charter, the Charter of the OAS, and the Panama Canal treaties served as sufficient legal basis for the U.S. intervention.[178]

On December 22, after debating through the night, the OAS passed a resolution criticizing the U.S. invasion as a violation of international law and the principle of nonintervention. Scranton notes that similar resolutions had been attempted after the Dominican Republic intervention in 1965 and Grenada in 1983, but on those occasions the United States had prevented the resolution. This time the United States stood alone, outvoted 20 to 1.[179]

Haiti Narrative

The Haitian crisis, as it is referred to in the literature on the topic, began with the September 29, 1991, coup overthrowing democratically elected Haitian President

Jean-Bertrand Aristide, almost three full years prior to the U.S. military intervention on September 19, 1994.[180] This three-year period constituted the decision space for the intervention. The process spanned two presidential administrations, and, unlike any of the other cases discussed here, was extensively and publicly announced, considered, and discussed prior to the intervention's execution. While there is an extensive record of the public discourse on the topic, there is precious little in terms of behind-the-scenes recordings of the decisional process available as of yet. At the conclusion of my data collection, the U.S. president involved was still planning his presidential library, many of the relevant decision participants were still active public figures and had not yet produced memoirs, and all of the relevant records were still classified. At that time, the case was only accessible at all because so much of it was discussed (and contested) publicly.

Aristide was elected president on December 16, 1990.[181] After less than a year, the populist former Catholic priest was ousted by a coalition of generals, headed by Gen. Raoul Cédras. Aristide fled the country in exile, arriving immediately in the United States. International response to the coup was swift and negative. In early October, the OAS met in emergency session, ultimately condemning the coup and voting for an embargo against Haiti.[182] On October 4, President George H.W. Bush signed an executive order declaring a trade embargo on Haiti in protest to Aristide's removal.[183] These sanctions were tightened by a subsequent executive order later in the month. On October 11, the United Nations imposed sanctions against the renegade Haitian regime. Most of the world failed to recognize the new Haitian junta in a formal diplomatic sense.

Given the range of possibilities, initial efforts to restore Aristide were not particularly extensive. Aristide was a populist reformer with fairly radical ideas, no experience in government, and of mercurial temperament. "Aristide's background helps explain why first Bush and then Clinton gave him such lukewarm support. In fact, by May 1994 Bush was publicly arguing that the US should no longer support the restoration of Aristide to power."[184]

Very shortly after Aristide's overthrow, there was a dramatic increase in the number of Haitians fleeing Haiti. As this flow of émigrés and asylum seekers increased, it increased pressure on the processing capacity of the immigration and naturalization service and increased political pressure from and in Florida, where residents feared the immigration explosion would adversely affect their economy. In response to this increasing pressure, President Bush issued executive order 12807 on May 24, 1992, authorizing U.S. Coast Guard vessels to repatriate Haitian boat people who had not been granted asylum through the U.S. Embassy in Haiti.[185] Then presidential candidate Bill Clinton condemned this policy as inhumane during his campaign.[186] Candidate Clinton vowed a change in this policy when elected and promised support for Aristide's return. In fact, when inaugurated, Clinton would leave the Bush administration's policy of summary repatriation in place.

On January 14, 1993, the Clinton administration made its first official statements on Haiti, announcing the following major goals: the restoration of democracy, the saving of human lives, and establishment of a system of fair treatment of refugees.[187]

In March 1993, Clinton met with Aristide and pledged that the United States would contribute its share to a $1-billion multinational aid program for Haiti. Also in March, Clinton named Lawrence Pezullo as his special advisor on Haiti.[188]

Working in concert with "the friends of Haiti" (Canada, the United States, France, and Venezuela), on April 23, 1993, President Clinton announced a plan to send a multinational police force of 500–600 to help professionalize the Haitian military.[189] On July 3, 1993, the Governors Island Accord was signed by President Aristide and General Cédras agreeing to restore Aristide on October 30, 1993.[190] The agreement, while it was publicly heralded as a success, was known to be problematic, with the different sides (Aristide and the coup generals) thinking they had agreed to slightly different things: "Worse yet, the two sides had completely different interpretations of what had been signed. The central problems were papered over and the Clinton administration's announcements of a foreign policy achievement were premature. In fact, U.S. policy was at an impasse."[191]

On September 23, 1993, the United Nations passed a resolution authorizing an expanded mission to support the transition from Cédras to Aristide. On October 11, 1993, in an attempt to fulfill this role of transition support, a contingent of lightly armed American and Canadian military engineers and military police arrived in Port-au-Prince on board the USS *Harlan County.* The ship was turned away from Port-au-Prince by an armed civilian mob on the docks. The Haitian armed forces failed to keep order; this was heralded as U.S. cowardice and as a violation of the Governors Island Accord.[192]

With the breakdown of the Governors Island Accord, U.S. policy was derailed and there was no immediate alternative. The United Nations reimposed its trade embargo against Haiti on October 13, 1993, and the Clinton administration took unilateral steps to impose travel restrictions and freeze the assets of certain military leaders and their supporters. The "four friends of Haiti" condemned Haiti for failing to comply with the agreement. The Clinton administration still hoped for a diplomatic resolution, but the Congressional Black Caucus (CBC) and Aristide called for a complete embargo and blockade or other drastic action.[193]

After the Governors Island Accord had failed, it became clear that the U.S. approach for removing the Haitian regime was not working. On December 14, 1993, John Shattuck, Assistant Secretary of State for Human Rights and Humanitarian Affairs, called for a review of U.S. Haitian policy.[194] On January 15, 1994, Aristide increased pressure on the Clinton administration by calling on foreign governments to help him return to office by February 7. He received strong support from the Rev. Jesse Jackson and the leaders of the CBC, who urged that the United States consider using force to dislodge the military leaders who ousted Aristide.[195]

In March and April 1994, domestic pressure on administration policy reached a fever pitch. On March 18, Aristide relaunched his refugee-based offensive, calling Clinton's refugee policy "racist and criminal" at a meeting of the CBC in Miami.[196] On March 22, the CBC sent Clinton a blunt letter saying that the administration's Haiti policy "must be scrapped" in favor of far tougher efforts to restore the nation's exiled president to power.[197] On April 12, TransAfrica Forum's Randall Robinson, after strategizing with Aristide and the CBC, launched a 27-day media intensive hunger strike to urge Clinton to change his repatriation policy.[198] On April 14, prominent Congressmen condemned the Clinton policy and called for the invasion of Haiti and removal of its leaders. Administration officials admitted that they were reviewing their Haitian policy, amid pressure from many of Clinton's traditional allies, including the CBC, some human rights groups, several Hollywood stars, labor leaders, and prominent democratic Senators.[199]

Finally, on April 26, Clinton responded by ditching Lawrence Pezzullo (his special assistant on Haiti) and replacing him with former representative William H. Gray III (head of the United Negro College Fund) and announced a change in the asylum screening process.[200] On April 28, Clinton admitted that the administration Haiti policy had failed and confided that he and his team had been working on little else for the previous ten days.[201] Pezzullo complained in an open letter that administration policy had failed because the administration failed to back his more conciliatory approach and, as a result, the United States was now "heading irrevocably" toward a military intervention.[202]

As of April 28, 1994, Clinton and Aristide had met three times, but had never agreed on a common strategy.[203] The Pentagon steadfastly opposed the involvement of the American military. Pezzullo often worked by himself and put too much trust in the Haitian military leaders. More importantly, until that point, Clinton and most of his team had focused only episodically on Haiti.[204]

> In early May 1994, however, the Clinton administration seemed to make a dramatic policy shift. To begin with, Lawrence Pezzullo, Clinton's point man on Haiti, was replaced by special envoy William H. Gray III, a former ranking member of the Congressional Black Caucus with no previous foreign-service experience. Whereas senior policy advisors had argued earlier that the embargo against the military regime in Haiti was "stronger even than that against Cuba," Clinton was now proposing to give the blockade real teeth by including the previously exempt U.S.-owned assembly plants, sealing Haiti's border with the Dominican Republic and freezing the assets of Haitian military leaders. The same advisors had also claimed that the in-country asylum review process was safe and effective. Clinton was now proposing to allow offshore hearings to ensure due process for applicants. Furthermore, only three months prior to the policy shift, the very idea of using military intervention to restore democracy to Haiti had been categorically dismissed. Now, in what appeared to be the most substantive shift, military intervention—albeit as "a last resort"—was openly proposed.[205]

As part of the new policy, which included the promised changes in refugee screening and increased sanctions, on May 3, Clinton warned Haiti's leaders that "it's time for them to go" in a press conference.[206] On May 5, Clinton administration officials indicated that if the next round of sanctions failed, the administration would face the unpalatable choice between using force to restore Aristide and opening the door to Haitian refugees.

On May 24, the House of Representatives approved a "sense of Congress" amendment by a 223 to 201 margin stipulating that "the United States should not undertake any military action against the mainland of Haiti unless the President first certifies to Congress that clear and present danger to citizens of the United States or United States interests requires such action."[207] While this amendment was removed in a separate vote on June 9, 1994, it is clear evidence of the conflict in American politics on the Haiti question and its very public nature.

On June 1, 1994, Gen. John M. Shalikashvili, Chairman of the JCS, formally requested, via a planning order, that USACOM (United States Atlantic Command) conduct additional preparations for operations in Haiti. This request resulted from the understanding that the president finally viewed military action as a possible tool for resolving the situation.[208] Until then, all the planning (which had been considerable) had been just "on a contingency basis" to make sure that the options were there if needed, not at the formal request of the administration.

On June 9, encountering more opposition than it expected on the prospect of a military intervention in Haiti, the Clinton administration sought to signal a shift in policy by voicing a new confidence in economic sanctions at a press conference. One administration official said that the increased emphasis on sanctions and decreased emphasis on intervention was a "tactical shift."[209]

On June 24 the Clinton administration disclosed its support for a UN peacekeeping force of 12,000–14,000 multinational troops, with the United States providing 3,000 of the total.[210] This is not what ultimately happened, but was part of a campaign of saber rattling to try to dislodge the Haitian regime and part of testing the waters to see what intervention opponents would do in response. On July 14, 1994, Madeline Albright, Ambassador to the United Nations, announced that 11 nations had pledged support for the multinational force (MNF) to be placed in Haiti following the removal of the junta.[211]

On July 5, 1994, Clinton changed his refugee policy; Haitian boat people whom U.S. officials determined faced persecution would be sent to non–U.S. "safe havens" in the area, such as Panama.[212] On July 10, congressional opposition to invasion, or at least to invasion without congressional permission, was in the news.[213] On July 19, the Clinton administration announced that no invasion would be possible until September due to the time required to train the MNF, but it is clear that some sort of military option was still gaining momentum.[214] "The Administration went to great lengths to let the Haitian military leaders know that [military] preparations were continuing."[215] On July 20, Albright formally requested UN support for MNF operations.[216]

> On July 26th, the Haitian government began to organize a November election to choose a President as well as one-third of the senate, the entire lower house, and several local officials. This would, in effect, remove the Aristide government and, when the votes were collected, presumably justify the role of the junta in power. Unwittingly, by scheduling these elections, Haitian officials set a deadline for the initiation of operations.[217]

Soon after, on July 31, the UN Security Council passed Resolution 940, which gave the United States authority to carry out a military intervention in Haiti on the

United Nation's behalf.[218] The account by presidential scholars Edward R. Drachman and Alan Shank notes that the Clinton administration heavily facilitated the adoption of this resolution.[219]

On August 3, the Senate approved a "sense of the Senate" amendment (100 to 0) that the UN resolution did not authorize the deployment of U.S. armed forces under the constitution or the War Powers Resolution. Clinton denied that he needed congressional approval to invade Haiti.[220] This debate was prominently placed in national newspapers. Despite having won UN approval for an intervention, the Clinton administration was split over whether to set a deadline for carrying it out, according to a senior administration official.[221] The division became evident at a meeting of Mr. Clinton's top National Security advisors on August 2. Secretary of Defense William J. Perry opposed setting a deadline; Deputy Secretary of State Strobe Talbott, who has emerged as the Department of State's chief policy maker on Haiti, argued that offering incentives to step down to the coup leaders was morally repugnant and advocated an early invasion.[222]

On August 26, President Clinton reportedly agreed to the invasion plan that the Pentagon had prepared.[223] On August 27, 1994, Clinton issued the final go-ahead to the Pentagon to begin the countdown to a Haiti invasion.[224] On August 31, Talbott and Deputy Defense Secretary John M. Deutch stated that the United States would send troops to Haiti either to furnish security for Aristide's return or, if necessary, to force the junta out.[225] These announcements and the obvious training and preparation of troops for the invasion were designed, in part, to scare the Haitian regime from power.

On September 15 in a televised address, Clinton sternly declared that Cédras had to go.[226] Time was up, and all diplomacy had been exhausted. Later, at about 11:30 P.M., he called former President Jimmy Carter, who had offered to lead a delegation to Haiti, to allow him to do so.[227]

On September 17, Carter's delegation, consisting of Carter, Colin Powell (a private citizen at that moment), and Senator Sam Nunn, landed and began negotiations.[228] Carter had been instructed to leave the country by noon on September 18, deal or no deal. He requested and received a three-hour extension. In the morning on September 18, Carter, Nunn, and Powell visited the Cédras home. Carter gave Cédras's 10-year-old son a Carter Center pocket knife, making a personal connection with the boy and impressing Cédras and his wife. At 1 P.M. on September 18, with the delegation still in Haiti, Clinton ordered the invasion, scheduled to start at midnight. At 4 P.M., Powell called Clinton and urged him to accept the deal that Cédras was offering. At 5:30 P.M. one of the Haitian generals received reports that U.S. forces were in the air and tried to break off the negotiations; Carter managed to hold negotiations together. At 6 P.M., three hours after his mission's extension had expired, Carter called Clinton and informed him that the deal was almost there. Carter presented an amended agreement to provisional President Émile Jonassaint who accepted it, declaring, "We'll have peace, not war." At 6:45 P.M. paratroopers' planes launched from various U.S. air bases. At 8 P.M. Clinton endorsed the deal and recalled the planes.[229] On September 19, permissive invasion began.

Operation Restore Democracy was almost anticlimactic after months of Hamlet like indecision in the White House. Clinton's irresolution, in fact, detracted from what might otherwise have been a display of presidential power and decisiveness.[230]

On October 15, 1994, Aristide returned to Haiti and was restored to office.

3

Theoretical Issues and Concepts: Governance and Context

Men make history, but they do not make it under circumstances chosen by themselves, but under circumstances directly encountered, given and transmitted from the past.

—*Karl Marx*

The core theoretical question underpinning the empirical focus of this volume is whose interests are served, or whose will is followed, when the United Stated flexes its military might? Put differently, which model of governance best describes the way in which the United States makes military intervention decisions: the class model, the pluralist model, the elite model, or some hybrid? This chapter reviews three major theories of governance (pluralism, elite theory, and class theory) and the continuing structure-agency "problem," setting the stage for the analytical chapters.

SOCIOLOGICAL THEORIES OF THE STATE

If the question of governance is about how decisions are made and in whose interest (or at whose behest), then the classic answers of political sociology come from the pluralists, the class theorists, and the elite theorists.[1] These answers, caricaturized, include "as the result of fairly competing interest groups" (the pluralist position), "at the behest of, or in the interests of, capital" (class theory), or "through elite agreement" (elite theory). Of course, there are variations in individual theorists' positions, creating a variety of hybrid positions that cannot be fairly categorized in just one of the three ideal types. In the following sections, I briefly discuss each major position, its implicit explanation for military interventions as a state behavior, and any elements of an implicit theory of decision making.

Pluralism

Naive pluralism supports the naked rhetoric of democracy as an explanation for how politics actually works. In this view, individual citizens band together with other like-minded citizens on issues that are important to them, forming interest groups. These interest groups compete fairly for power within a state that is an arena rather than an actor. State decision makers are the effective representatives of the majority views of citizens, and state decision making processes are a benign black box.

The pluralist explanation of state military behavior would appeal either strictly to representatives choosing military action on behalf of their constituents or to some absolute notion of "the national interest," which all citizens want protected (see Chapter 4 for a detailed discussion of the concept of the national interest and its shortcomings).

More sophisticated pluralist arguments acknowledge the compelling central arguments of elite theory and recognize that leaders and elites have an important role in the political process. Political scientist Robert A. Dahl's notion of "polyarchy" allows for the existence of elites in the United States, but maintains that they are atomized and compete in such a way that mobilized publics can also participate and compete.[2] The core of pluralism, naive or otherwise, is a belief that in a democracy, strong and organized private interest associations can continually assert influence on the government.[3] Pluralism assumes *active* publics, engaged in public contestation. Throughout the book, I consider the observable influence the public has, and the role played by the public; in my conclusions (Chapter 8), I assess this role vis-à-vis the assertions of pluralist theory.

Class Theorists

Completely ignored by pluralism is the existence and role of nongovernmental power in society. Class theory argues that the real source of social power is capital, and state power exists, in one form or another, to protect capitalism. Class theory invokes the interests or rulership of the dominant economic class to explain state behavior. Some class theorists are "relative autonomists," allowing the state the freedom to choose *how* it will serve the interests of the ruling class, rather than simply being its tool.[4] With relative autonomy, the state will do what it does in pursuit of the interests of the dominant class; without relative autonomy, the state will do what it does at the behest of the dominant class. This tension between the state being structurally compelled to pursue the economic interests of dominant class and the dominant class also being an active "ruling class" has interesting implications for decision making.

Political sociologist G. William Domhoff's "class dominance" model is a fundamentally instrumentalist position. His theory contains a ruling business class and incorporates elements of elite theory and class theory, arguing for a ruling class that actively influences policy, as well as stacking the deck in its own favor in other ways in the policy arena.[5] Domhoff's ruling class is divided into "class segments" based on differences in their interests due to things such as region and sector of industry. The alliances of these different class segments and their work to influence and control policy making largely explains state behavior.

Domhoff's work is of particular interest because, unlike other sociological state theorists, he examines policy making and decisional process in considerable detail, allowing a theory of decision making to be extrapolated. Domhoff invokes the policy planning networks of a ruling class that mobilize influence based on business interests to influence policy that is important to them. Domhoff's method of demonstrating business class dominance includes finding data showing the influence and participation of individual members of the business elite; top decision makers do not make decisions favoring the business class just because "they rule," but because of the actions and active participation of business elites.

Sociologist Fred Block proposes a structuralist mechanism for capitalist influence on politics without assuming unified capitalist "class consciousness" or any real effort on the part of any capitalists.[6] He begins by pointing out the dependence of the state on a healthy economy, given the impact of the economy on state taxation revenues and citizen contentment during economic prosperity. Block argues that state policy that individual businessmen and investors consider threatening or concerning changes their behavior on an individual level. When aggregated, this "business confidence" (or its lack) can cause subtle but significant changes in a country's economy, worsening slowly but surely if business confidence is not restored. Block argues that state elites will act to forestall a loss in business confidence (and thus protect their country's economy, and its capitalists) or will end up being removed from power, "democratically" or otherwise.

A class argument would suggest, at its most basic level, that military interventions either serve the ruling-class interest or, at the very least, do not threaten its interests. Domhoff's argument is more subtle and involves business elite influence on the definition of the national interest, which plays an important role in motivating and legitimating the national interest. His argument receives attention in Chapter 4 on the national interest.

Elite Theorists

The central proposition of elite theory is that a few elites hold the power in, and make the major decisions for, society and that they are not accountable to the masses. Beyond that core consensus elite theorists differ widely on their specific claims. Classic elite theory holds that elites are powerful through their virtues as an organized few over a disorganized many.[7] C. Wright Mills argues (in a similar vein) that elites are powerful by virtue of their controlling positions at the top of society's major institutions.[8] Elite theorists differ on the extent to which elites are consensual and cohesive (and on whether they are consensual on the "rules of the game" while still not necessarily being in agreement on what policies they want enacted) and the extent to which elites act selfishly or in the interests of society or groups within society.

Like some class theories, one major strand within elite theory discusses the autonomy of the state. State autonomy (in an elite theory context) provides a slightly different answer to the question of governance (why do states do what they do?): states do what they do because they are acting in the state's own interests. All the state autonomy theorists admit that state autonomy is "potential autonomy" and that other groups in society can and do influence state behavior from time to time. Foreign policy, however, is one location that autonomy theorists hypothesize the most autonomy is likely, for reasons which will be discussed in Chapter 4.[9]

Elite theorists and state autonomy theorists would explain military interventions in one of two ways: either the state is acting in the interests of elites when it intervenes, or it is acting in the interests of "the state," which is, implicitly, an appeal to the same kind of absolute interests inherent in conventional conceptions of the national interest, just like the pluralists.[10] This book contains evidence with which to assess several of the core propositions of elite theory. With regard to military interventions, I examine whether or not the decision-making process is dominated by elites in general, whether these elites are accountable, whether they are cohesive, and whether they are autonomous.

The empirically tenable positions of all three major theoretical groups (pluralism, class, and elite) acknowledge elites, but differ on their importance and to whom (if anyone) they are accountable. In modern pluralism, elites are either the representatives of different societal interests that compete within the fair arena of the state or atomized self-seeking elites who are vulnerable to influence from organized publics. In elite theory, elites are either competing groups who agree upon the rules of the game (John Higley and Michael Burton's consensual elites[11]), consensual and unified seekers of their own interests, or autonomous leaders pursuing the interests of the state or nation. In class theory, elites are either instruments of the ruling class, structurally constrained to act in the interests of capital, or the representatives of various ruling-class segments.

The Structure-Agency Debate

The lead quote of this chapter is Karl Marx's famous aphorism from the introduction to the 18th Brumaire, oft paraphrased as "Men make history, but not under circumstances of their own choosing."[12] This quote points out two important facts of social reality. First, people (or *agents*) take consequential independent action. Second, circumstances (or *structure*) constrain the range of possible action, suggest certain actions, and make certain courses of action unavoidable. These truths impose demands on any social science theory: it must recognize the contribution of agents and the relevance of structure. "The 'agent-structure problem' refers to the difficulties of developing theory that successfully meets both demands."[13] This is the "chicken or egg" problem of social theory; many theories, intentionally or otherwise, afford primacy to either structure or agency in their explanations. The general consensus reached in the long-standing debate is that structure and agency should be considered to be "mutually constitutive." Realizing theory that genuinely satisfies this agreed-upon standard is more easily said than done.

The three major theories of governance that are the theoretical focus of this book do not match up perfectly with positions on the structure-agency continuum. To the extent that each camp does have a general corresponding position, they follow.

Pluralism requires a democratic structure to function; however, within that democratic structure, agents have surprising freedom to establish preferences and form interest groups to pursue or protect those preferences. At the policy-making level, pluralist elected leaders are prevented by the realities of the electoral structure from having any independent agency. Classic "rational choice" models (or even more sophisticated "bounded rational" models) consonant with pluralism are all profoundly *individualist* and thus agent centered.

Class theory, on the other hand, is almost always embodied in "structure first" positions. Class theory's founder Marx's "historical materialism" relates everything to economic constraints. Actors may have some agency, but in a profoundly structured context. Even the "relative autonomist" side of the Miliband/Poulantzas debate is a structuralist view; regardless of whether the state serves as an instrument of the capitalist class or the structures of capitalism, the core of the class view starts with the imperatives of the economic structure.[14]

Given the broad range of elite theories, it is not surprising to find elite theories that are both structure centered and agency centered. At its core, however, the kinds of propositions that allow for power to be concentrated in the hands of a few at the top of a social *structure* tend, as this sentence suggests, toward structural explanations.

This book intends to contribute to the ongoing work in "the new institutionalism." Findings here are consonant with the "choice-within-constraints" framework adopted by Victor Nee and Mary C. Brinton and their contributors.[15] Within the new institutionalism, a range of positions on the structure-agency debate finds representation. "Organizational" institutionalists such as John W. Meyer, John Boli, George M. Thomas, and Francisco O. Ramirez and Paul J. DiMaggio and Walter W. Powell leave little room for agency.[16] Institutions are powerful and deterministic; actors follow institutionalized routines, "scripts," rituals, or habits. A choice-within-constraints framework, in contrast, leaves more space for actors to behave in an intendedly rational way, constrained (imperfectly) by institutional forces.

"State actor" as it is used here does not denote reified states, but rather individual persons within the apparatus of that state, be it bureaucrat, soldier, or elected official. Scholars generally focus more on the state actors who are "core decision makers," but, as will be argued in Chapter 5, actors who are just "cogs" in the machinery of the state, or links in the chain of command, can impact state behavior in important ways.

For these actors institutions constrain choices in a path-dependent way; state actors follow their institutionalized scripts when they are able and implement solutions out of their cultural toolbox when they are not.[17] These institutions, writ large, act as constraints on the range of possible and conceivable actions state actors can undertake. However, in the interstices between these constraints, actors have some freedom to choose between institutionally and culturally viable alternatives. These spaces between constraints widen in unusual situations, where institutional scripts are not available (arguably the case, to some extent, in many situations leading to military interventions), leaving the purposive actor more freedom still.[18] Further, these actors are aware of some of the institutional constraints under which they operate (usually new formal intuitions, or recent and salient changes in cultural content) and may act in a reflexive way to attempt to influence the subsequent institutional context, attempts which may or may not succeed, and may or may not succeed in the way intended.

In sum, institutions and culture are powerful motive forces and nigh-deterministic constraints. However, actors are capable of surprising agency, and they are not totally naive to the institutional structures around them, but perceive them and actively attempt to alter them to some extent.

Institutions

Since several of the arguments in the empirical chapters rely on a specific notion of "institutions," this section clarifies what the term denotes here. I define institution quite inclusively. Following Victor Nee and Paul Ingram, "An institution is a *web of interrelated norms* [emphasis in the original]—formal and informal—governing social relationships."[19] For military intervention decisions, these institutions include not only the formal organizations and departments of the government, but the basic building blocks of the policy-formation process: the laws governing who participates in the policy process and the procedures that must be followed. More subtle factors in policy formation are also institutionalized: the relationships between different policy participants (for example, Congress and the White House, or the press and the military), taken for granted normative categories such as isolationism vs. interventionism, and the range of policies that are considered "legitimate" by the electorate and by other nations. The preferences, capabilities, and basic self-identities of individuals are conditioned by these institutional structures; if these individuals are part of the policy-making process, they can affect policy.[20] All actors are constrained by existing political institutions.[21] These institutions create and constitute the context (writ large) in which policy is made.

Institutional Context

I wish to argue that the actions of state decision makers are not sufficiently explained by pluralism, class theory, or elite theory. Throughout this book I examine the impact of historical institutions, institutional change, and institutional inertia on state decision making. I build my conception of the importance of the institutional context from two ideas existent in the sociological literature on the state: Kenneth Finegold and Theda Skocpol's notion of path dependence, and historical sociologist Michael Mann's notion of institutional statism.[22]

Path dependence is the observation that, like a cat climbing up the branches of a tree, the paths available now depend on the paths taken before. Previous choices constrain policy options either because of the structures and institutions now in place or because of the high cost (either in terms of capacity, power, or legitimacy) of "reversing direction" to reach previously cutoff options. Path dependence plays a role in several of the chapters and is discussed in detail in Chapter 6 on legacy chains.

Generalizing path dependency to the formal institutions of government leads toward Mann's notion of institutional statism. Mann observes that "states institutionalize present social conflicts, but institutionalized historic conflicts then exert considerable power over new conflicts."[23] These path-dependent legacies, I argue, leave an impression in the institutional context that constrains the policy options open to (or even conceivable by) policy makers.

There are several important legacies of the institutional context that led into the military interventions considered here. While I discuss these and other institutional legacies in Chapter 6, I want to present the strongest contextual affects here. First is the Cold War. I agree with Block's assertions of the U.S. state's dependence on the success of its capitalist economy; the threat of world communism, however, was an ideological threat that encompassed far more than its implicit economic threat.[24] American anticommunism was a far more powerful contextual factor than its longer-lived cousin, American procapitalism. Two of the interventions addressed here were taken within the context of the Cold War, while two were not. The institutional changes that accompanied the end of the Cold War receive attention in all of the substantive chapters.

The second major set of factors of initial institutional context has to do with the historical role of the United States in Central America. Dating back to the Monroe Doctrine, there is a well-established tradition of U.S. intervention in the Americas. Contextually, intervention is the normal, legitimate response to threats in the region. Given the magnitude of U.S. military might relative to other American states, intervention in the region has been comparatively "easy."

Finally, the tension between the U.S. role as a superpower and the premium placed on the lives of American soldiers acts as an important constraint in the institutional context. As a superpower, intervention and assertion of control in the international arena is very tempting. However, the unique view of the American "citizen soldier" (as opposed to the notion of "professional soldier" common in Europe) makes high costs in soldiers' lives institutionally unlikely unless the perceived stakes are very high. Again, these contextual legacies receive full attention in Chapter 6.

In addition to my focus on the path-dependent creation of institutional constraints, I propose a high degree of genuine contingency in the military intervention process. All of the existing theories I have discussed are overdetermined, offering an explanation of decision making or state behavior that does not include caprice, chance, or contingency. While the options available are constrained by a variety of factors, the actual outcomes within the constrained possibilities are highly contingent. Further, many of the constraints that occur in process that lead to a path-dependent restriction of options are highly contingent as well. This idea receives full attention in Chapter 5 on process.

In sum, my main focus is on the creation of constraints and the powerful residual contingency. The context holds a number of constraints, and more constraints are passed down in a path-dependent manner and held within the institutional state. This path-dependent constraint of choices puts policy possibilities within a "branch" (if one imagines a policy tree). However, the actual outcome within that branch is highly contingent on further (still path-dependent) events, decisions, actions, and *agency* at numerous levels of the policy process. Contingent cases build constraints for the future via a process of legacy chains (as discussed in Chapter 6).

INTRODUCTION TO THE STUDY

I have chosen my cases for regional and temporal comparability (see Chapter 2). A quick survey of these intervention decisions reveals some important differences that are focal threads in my research. The first is the distinction between premeditated interventions and crisis-response interventions. While the same sorts of questions are relevant to both types, the decisional processes differ in fundamental and interesting ways. The second major line of distinction is between Cold War and post–Cold War interventions. I argue that Cold War and post–Cold War intervention decisions follow very similar processes, but that the end of the Cold War forced a change in the way in which interventions were and are legitimated. Finally, each intervention decision chronologically follows the one before it. The extent to which the institutional legacies of earlier interventions and their decisional processes have important effects on subsequent interventions has important consequences for the analysis of decision making.

METHODS

This book is based on a descriptive and analytical multiple case study. While I do make comparisons across the cases, some of the formal requirements of the comparative method (namely, different outcomes on the dependent variable) are not available with this research design.

For each of the four military interventions under consideration, I have assembled a complete case history, detailing (to the extent possible) all of the relevant aspects of the decisional process. This includes the actual events of the intervention itself (what was decided); the chronology of decision-making, from first nomination as an intervention candidate, right up until the orders were signed; lists of decision participants from the various levels of decision making and throughout the duration of the decisional process; details about the backgrounds, affiliations, personalities, and relationships among those decision participants; details of the process history, including factors considered by the decision participants and the character of the discussions and meetings; other salient factors that might have been considered by the decision makers or otherwise have influenced the decisional process.

SPECIFIC DATA SOURCES

The following specific data sources have contributed to the development of these case studies: the National Archives and Records Administration holdings, including the National Archives itself, and the various presidential libraries; the holdings of the National Security Archive, news records, published memoirs of decision participants, and various secondary analyses of the interventions themselves. Below I detail the resources drawn from each of the sources mentioned.

National Archives and Presidential Libraries

The U.S. National Archives and Records Administration has several collections containing relevant data of which I have taken advantage. Most of the records after 1965 are classified, but are vulnerable to release by requests under the Freedom of Information Act (FOIA). I filed FOIA requests at the National Archives and at each of the three relevant presidential libraries. Holdings at the National Archives itself (located in College Park, Maryland) include largely complete Department of State records. These have furnished me with data such as original cable traffic between embassies, Department of State, and the White House, various "country reports" and other reports and briefings. The content and participants in cable traffic provided great insight into the flow of information in the decisional process for the Dominican intervention. Backlogs in FOIA requests and the general hesitancy of the Department of State to declassify documents that are less than 30 years old prevented me from including National Archive records for any case other than the Dominican intervention.

The Lyndon B. Johnson Presidential Library and Museum in Austin, Texas, has extensive records from the Johnson administration and regarding the Dominican intervention, of which I have taken advantage. The records include cable traffic (much of which is redundant with the holdings of the National Archives), various reports and briefs prepared for President Lyndon B. Johnson, meeting minutes, and schedules/appointment calendars indicating with whom the president met and when.

From the Ronald W. Reagan Presidential Library & Museum (located in Simi Valley, California), I obtained similar records regarding President Reagan's role in the Grenada intervention. Many of these records are still classified, so data available to me were more limited. Fortunately, at the time I began my research, another researcher had already filed FOIA requests for Grenada materials, so many had already been processed and declassified.

The George Bush Presidential Library and Museum (College Station, Texas) holds records regarding President George H.W. Bush's role in the decision to intervene in Panama. I filed a FOIA request, and have received information indicating that they are working on it; unfortunately, this case is still fairly recent, and progress may be slow and declassification less likely; as of this writing (2007), I have no direct archival material from the Panama invasion decisional process.

There was not yet a William J. Clinton Presidential Library at the time of my research, and a sitting president and his records are not vulnerable to FOIA requests (Clinton was president throughout the data-collection phase of my project), so NARA sources have not contributed to my final case, Haiti.

The archival materials I have used are largely Department of State cable traffic and presidential daily diary records. These data are excellent for establishing specific communications (the cables) and cross-confirming meeting participants and presidential involvement as claimed in various decision-maker memoirs (daily diaries). While these primary data have contributed considerably to my case studies and appear regularly in the case histories compiled in the narrative chapter (Chapter 2), their level of specificity is usually too high to appear in the analytic chapters, where I am painting with a broader brush.

National Security Archive

The National Security Archive (NSA), housed in the Gelman Library of The George Washington University, collects and archives national security-related materials from the FOIA requests of other scholars. My visit to the NSA turned up about 200 pages of material, mostly cable traffic, relevant to the Grenada intervention decision, some of which is redundant with materials from the Reagan library. The NSA does not yet have materials relating to the other interventions, but it will soon, as I plan to donate the results of my own FOIA requests to increase its holdings and increase the ease of public access to these materials.

Newspaper Records

Period newspapers, news magazines, and other periodicals have provided me with accounts of the actual interventions. Of more utility to me, however, have been the stories that detail the decision-making process, reporting on various press releases that are indicative of slightly changing administration positions from day to day throughout the decision process (as well as the public by-products of attempts to "spin" and legitimize the decision taken), and the opinion/editorial pieces that point out possible motives that are not present in official sources. I have examined the complete record of each case as made available in the *New York Times* and have examined some of the coverage from the *Wall Street Journal* and the *Washington Post.*

Memoirs

I have made use of the published memoirs of President Johnson, and President Reagan,[25] as well as the memoirs of various relevant secretaries of state and other administration personnel who make reference to my cases. While most of these are self-congratulatory in nature and tend to have qualities of hindsight that suggest that the final legitimizing logic was the motive for the decision all along, some of them contain wonderfully informative and candid bits of information or show aspects of the relationships between decision participants on wholly unrelated issues in a way that has helped me understand certain aspects of the decisional process. I have confirmed recollections by cross-checking them against as many other sources as possible, including confirming the attendance, duration, and dates of meetings claimed that involved the relevant president using the presidential daily diaries.

Secondary Sources

I have made extensive use of the work of other scholars. These secondary sources focus on a wide array of topics related to the interventions. Some are historical accounts of the events of the intervention and mention the decision only in passing. Some (few) focus specifically on the decision for a case, and these have been particularly helpful. Of course, since others' work on decision making is conducted from within their analytic paradigm rather than mine, it often fails to include details that are crucial to my analysis. The bulk of work done on these interventions is of purely historical character; histories of interventions that include decision chronologies are available for several of my cases. Also of particular interest among the secondary sources are polemic pieces that attack some aspect of U.S. policy related to the decision. These critical works often provide evidence of other possible decision motives that are absent from formal (or even just friendly) histories.

Recap of Sources Available for Each Case

Below I recap the materials that have constituted my research base for each of my four cases. Data sources that are obviously available for all cases (such as newspaper accounts) are not mentioned. Since some data sources are limited in their availability, I wish to make clear which sources I have used for each case.

Dominican Republic

Data for the Dominican case are extensive. Because these events occurred over 30 years ago, almost all of the relevant material is declassified and processed. I have used Department of States and White House records from both the National Archives and the Johnson library. I have examined LBJ's published memoirs, and several secondary sources that discuss the intervention and the decision in impressive detail. With the extensive primary records available and the rich secondary literature, the Dominican intervention is my strongest case.

Grenada

For Grenada, I have gathered significant primary material from the holdings of the National Security Archive and from the Reagan library. Additional materials have come from Reagan's published memoirs, from the memoirs of Secretary of State George P. Shultz, and from an exposé about power plays within the Reagan administration written by a member of the national security staff. There is a substantial secondary literature, including a number of works by indigenous authors, accessible to me because the national language of Grenada is English.

Panama

Primary archival materials for the Panama intervention are primarily still classified. Fortunately, the secondary literature on the Panama intervention is exceptional. One book in particular (Bob Woodward's *The Commanders*)[26] focuses in excruciating detail on the decisional process leading to the Panama invasion and is based on over 300 personal interviews by the author. While I did not have the resources (or connections) to replicate his effort, I have certainly taken advantage of his work. Coupled with the universally available resources (news and commerce records) and a modest collection of other secondary sources, my case for Panama is strong.

Haiti

Haiti is problematic; as it is so recent, virtually none of the records have been declassified, and even nonclassified government records have not been processed or otherwise made available. As we become more and more temporally distant from the intervention, the number of secondary sources increases, but my case is necessarily considerably less developed than the other cases. I knew from the outset that taking on such a recent case would be problematic, but I also knew that to satisfy the sampling requirements of my design I would need to include it. There are a number of secondary sources, one which details the formal and public aspects of the decision in a way that has helped frame my pursuit of the details of the decisional process. I feel comfortable with the paucity of data on this case only because it is so recent and because I have three complete cases with which to complete my analysis.

A NOTE ABOUT SEPTEMBER 11

The intervention in Afghanistan in response to the attacks of September 11, 2001, is not one of the core cases of the volume, nor are ongoing operations in Iraq, since neither is in Central America, almost all data are still heavily classified, and military action is still under way at this writing. Since these events are so salient in current public consciousness and discourse and since the analyses of this volume have a contribution to make to understanding the ongoing decisional processes for the "war on terror," I have included some discussion of the impact of 9/11, expanding and updating several of the chapters, and pointing out in the analysis where the findings generalize to current events, and how the context in which military intervention decisions are made has been changed by the attacks.

All of the research for this volume (and most of the writing) was completed before September 11, 2001, and the U.S. operations in Afghanistan and Iraq. As a consequence, I viewed events not just as another American interested in current events, but as another case of something on which I do research. I was pleased to see how my understanding of military intervention processes helped me frame and comprehend what information has been made available about the decisions taken and the claims made by the George W. Bush administration. I have also been gratified to see predictable shifts in the institutional context in which intervention decisions are made as a result of the attacks of 9/11 (see material added to chapters 4, 6, and 7 on legacies and on shifts from a post–Cold War context to a post-9/11 context). Finally, the discussion on generalizing beyond the core cases might help connect the analysis of military intervention decisions for Central America/the Caribbean to U.S. intervention decisions elsewhere.

4

U.S. National Interest and Foreign Policy Making

Our country! In her intercourse with foreign nations may she always be in the right; but our country, right or wrong.

—*Stephen Decatur*

INTRODUCTION

This chapter explores what the national interest is, and examines the interests that were pursued in the book's four military interventions. The whole notion of the national interest is central to the question of governance. The national interest (however constructed) has to do with the reasons that the United States undertakes military interventions (the actual substance of American foreign policy), rather than the determinants of the military intervention decision-making process.

What is the national interest? During data collection for the cases treated in this book, I found myself confounded by the inconsistent and unsatisfactory use of the term "national interest" made by both the decision participants in their memoirs and other historical records and by the scholars and analysts in the secondary literature. Ultimately, I came to reject any "unitary" conception of the national interest, and I advocate discussions of the topic that recognize the construction of the national interest as a social process whose *use* is also part of a social process; that is to say, the national interest is socially constructed, and the uses that are made of those social constructions are also negotiated through social processes. Further, I argue that there are three major different but overlapping constructions of the national interest, all with a reasonable claim to the label "the national interest," but all with notable differences in substance, and used for different things: *the public national interest, the calculated presidential national interest,* and *the legitimation national interest.*

Uses of National Interest

The national interest is invoked and is used for advocacy, analysis, assessment, and evaluation (among other things). Citizens at large use their conception of the national interest to evaluate whether or not a policy is "good" for the country, in some normative sense. Decision makers use their notion of the national interest to assess the options available to them and to help formulate goals in foreign policy. Finally, politicians use rhetorical constructions of the national interest to advocate and legitimize decisions they have taken or policies they would like to implement. Renowned international relations scholar Alexander L. George notes:

> The concept of national interest continues to be important to foreign-policymakers despite its limitations as a theoretical and scientific concept. They have used the concept in two different ways: first, as a *criterion* to assess what is at stake in any given situation and to evaluate what course of action is "best"; second, as a *justification* [emphasis in original] for decision taken. Particularly with respect to the latter use of national interest there is reason to be uneasy and dissatisfied.[1]

I wish to argue that the distinction between criterion and justification is not just a distinction in *use,* but a difference of definition; different constructions of the national interest are used for these two tasks. These two tasks constitute the primary distinction between two of the three "national interests" that I discuss in my tripartite model of the national interest, elaborated in what follows.

Inevitability of National Interest?

Conceptually, the national interest is problematic as a unitary concept. If one accepts a straightforward and absolute rational definition, "what is best for the country," there are two major problems with which to grapple. The first is specificity: what is best for *whom* in the country? (a question that cuts to the heart of the question of governance as posed in this book). Even if this problem is satisfactorily resolved (in either a utilitarian, democratic, or some new and genuinely clever way), the second problem is the absurd difficulty of calculating all of the impacts of a given possible policy on the interests of the nation.[2] For example, during American involvement in Vietnam persons who would be willing to agree on the same abstract definition of the national interest found themselves in sharp disagreement over which policies best served that national interest.

Regardless of the weaknesses inherent in the notion, it is here to stay. Foreign policy discourse will always contain discussions of the national interest in decision-making processes, and public discussions or contestations of foreign policy will always contain rhetorical appeals to the national interest. To contribute to the questions and goals of this volume, then, I want to clearly exposit the role the national interest plays in determining state military behavior and to encourage the best possible use of the term.

WHAT IS THE NATIONAL INTEREST?

In addition to being a fuzzy concept tossed across sound bytes and opinion pages by presidents and pundits, the national interest is a scholarly concept. I wish to argue that the national interest is something more than what politicians appeal to and that none of the existing scholarly definitions are fully satisfactory. The national interest is politically and socially defined and used in a complex way. In fact, I argue, the national interest has three main forms in American politics, and each form has slightly different content and is put to different uses.

The Tripartite National Interest

Various existing notions of the national interest contain several different ways to try to talk about what is ostensibly the same thing. I reject this unitary conception and argue there are three different national interests. I am not referring to three different specific interests, but rather three different major social constructions of what should be the same concept. They are all conceived similarly, undergo similar construction processes, and have considerable overlap in their content. However, their precise content, the use they are put to, and the users differ for all three. The three are (1) the public national interest, (2) the calculated presidential national interest, and (3) the legitimation national interest. The public national interest is the common sense consensual national interest that exists in public discourse; the calculated presidential national interest is the national interest as acted on by the president; the legitimation national interest is the national interest upon which the president *claims* to have acted.

The Public National Interest

The public national interest is impossible to ever *precisely* enumerate, as it assumes a nationwide consensus, but its construction does not include a tally to confirm the extent or existence of the consensus. It would not be unreasonable to suppose that every single U.S. citizen has a slightly different version of what is in the national interest, but that the important and substantial parts are either generally consensual or publicly disputed. Its bounds are never precisely defined, and much of its content is never explicitly stated. The discourse creating the public national interest takes place on television, in the opinion polls, in the appeals of politicians to their constituents, and in academic journals. The construction process is complex and is discussed in slightly more detail in the later section "The Construction of the National Interest."

The consensual extent of what is in the public national interest is only ever actually assessed by proxy in various public opinion polls. Because of this indefinite nature, the public national interest is almost wholly constituted in broad themes upon which almost everyone agrees. In practice, this will usually include things that scholars agree upon as "core" national interests, but will also include a wide range of broader and narrower normative issues. These issues are often ethical in nature and are not generally concerned with costs, but only with principles. They are usually fairly black and white, and many of them may be contradictory. When these interests come into conflict, one of them may grow in eminence and overshadow the other (for a time) in public discussion, and the conflict may ultimately lead to a consensual "sea change" in the public national interest, or the interests may return to their previous equilibrium after whatever event catapulted them to attention in the first place has passed.

Both the protection of democracy abroad and the protection of the lives of American soldiers are in the public national interest; when the two come into conflict, the discourse on the national interest heats up, but because the public national interest cannot be precisely assessed, the depth of the dispute is difficult to gauge, as is the strength and commitment of the opposed public positions. When this particular contradiction came into public discourse during the run-up to the Haiti intervention, public opinion polls and congressional opinion leaders leaned strongly toward the preservation of American soldiers' lives over Haitian democracy; the strongest evidence for my tripartite national interest argument is that the fact that the public national interest is clearly not THE national interest, because the president decided to intervene in Haiti anyway, and he was certainly acting in what he believed to be the national interest.

As a further example, consider the tension between civil liberties and protection of Americans against the threat of terrorism. Prior to September 11, 2001, these two interests were not seen to be orthogonal. Now, however, it is clear that they are in tension. In the months immediately following the attacks, the public national interest seems to have swung toward defense at the cautious expense of civil liberties. It will be interesting to see if the balance is restored in the years to come or if a more or less permanent sea change has taken place. Hot debate over the USA PATRIOT Act[3] and over the appropriateness of detaining designated enemy combatants at Guantanamo Bay is part of the contestation preceding whatever the new, durable consensus in this area will be.

The Calculated Presidential National Interest

In as much as the public national interest is the publicly semiexpressed consensual gestalt of every American's view of the national interest, the calculated presidential national interest is the private belief of just a few Americans: the president and (perhaps) a few of his closest advisors. As the national interest beliefs of (fundamentally) a single individual, the calculated presidential interest is much less likely to contain inherent contradictions. While the president is confronted by the same barrage of media attention to the national interest that constitutes much of the public discourse on the topic and has advisors who are concerned with and aware of the classic and contemporary scholarly work focused there, his conception of the national interest must be more precise than that of the average American by virtue of his position. The public national interest is, by nature, very general and is never specifically codified. The presidential calculated national interest, in contrast, starts with the general but traverses to the specific in the course of taking foreign policy decisions. This decisional imperative forces the calculated presidential national interest to a specific point. The president is forced to make value assessments and rank order the various possible interests that could be served through foreign policy, contradictory or not. Further, the president must consider interests that *are* for the benefit of the country, but are not necessarily normatively attractive (such as American business interests abroad at the expense of the well-being of citizens of other nations).

The president's national interest is, in many respects, the most consequential conception of the national interest, as it determines in large part what foreign policies will be pursued. Because of this gravity, the president's national interest is carefully calculated. When dealing with high-stakes normative contradictions and ethical trade-offs, decision making is conducted in an *intentionally* rational (as opposed to "truly" rational, which is never really possible) way. Put another way, when the chips are down, everyone wants to believe that they are, and are perceived as, thinking as clearly and rationally as possible. Even when the president is motivated by an ideological agenda or serving a normative interest, the president is likely to acknowledge that fact privately and fully consider the costs and benefits in terms of cold political reality. However, even if the decision taken is based on a dispassionate and pragmatic political calculation that is in some cold sense in the national interest, it is unlikely to be presented to the public in those dispassionate terms. Because of this, the content of the calculated presidential national interest may differ from the publicly stated national interest claims by a presidential administration. This leads to the following.

The Legitimation National Interest

One of the calculations that enters into presidential considerations of foreign policy and the national interest is undoubtedly an estimation of the impact of possible policy choices on presidential prestige. If the president wishes to pursue a policy that he truly believes is in the national interest but finds that that policy either involves one of the contradictions in the public national interest or, worse still, lies outside the consensual scope of the public national interest, this can be problematic. Because the calculated presidential national interest includes interests that are not necessarily endorsed in the public national interest, or serves interests that are among the contradictions in the public national interest, the real actual interests motivating a decision may not be particularly palatable to the bulk of Americans. The frequently adopted solution to this problem is for the president to pursue the policy, but to legitimate the policy with claims of motive that do not correspond precisely with the genuine motives (the calculated presidential national interest) but correspond instead with normatively attractive motives (likely to correspond to some aspects of the public national interest). In all four U.S. military interventions in the Caribbean since World War II, the genuine motives for intervention differed from the legitimation claims the administration made (see Chapter 7 on legitimacy, and see the case discussion later in this chapter for further details).

While the calculated presidential national interest proceeds from the general to the specific, the legitimation national interest proceeds from the specific to the general. Legitimations are targeted at specific policies, but appeal to broad interests contained within the public national interest. The legitimation national interest is rationally calculated either after the decision is taken, or simultaneously with it, so as to be as close to the calculated national interest as possible while fitting completely and compellingly in a noncontradictory way into the public national interest. Like the calculated national interest, the legitimation national interest is constructed within the president's inner circle, but instead of being based on careful interest calculations, it is based on political concerns and the understood public national interest and disinterest. In this way the legitimation national interest serves as a bridge between the public national interest and the calculated presidential national interest. While the public national interest certainly plays a part in determining the president's notion of the national interest, its direct effect on presidential calculations during decision making is unclear. However, because presidential calculations include the calculation of an acceptable legitimation national interest, a possible policy must be justifiable through some appeal to the public national interest, even if what is claimed is not the most central motive for the policy.

The Construction of the National Interest

My model of the national interest(s) relies on the sociological notion of the "social construction of reality."[4] Without the acknowledgment that the national interest is socially constructed, it is impossible to escape a unified conception of the national interest that relies on some reified external absolute national interest that scholars or decision makers could realize if only they could find the correct logical rules and be perfectly rational in their execution. By allowing that the national interest is defined through a social process, we can escape the not very fruitful unitary paradigm that surrounds much of the existing thinking on the topic.

Since the core of my argument rests on my assertion that the national interest(s) is (are) socially constructed, to make my argument compelling, I need to detail my model of the construction of the national interest. Each of the three elements of the tripartite national interest has slightly different constituent elements, but, since they share the same conceptual base and have considerable common substance, the principal differences in their construction stem from differences in the magnitude of contribution from each of the sources I mention here and the level of specificity required for their use, as detailed in the previous sections.

I identify five major spheres in which the social construction of the various national interests take place. In what follows, I detail the constituents of each sphere and the role they play in the process of definition. The five spheres are Academe, the elite foreign policy planning network, the government, the media, and the various publics.

Since the concept of the national interest already exists in the national discourse, it is pointless to talk about its origin in a system that is already in motion. That said, there are those whose business is much more directly wrapped up in the definition and use of the national interest, and that is as good a place to start as any.

Political sociologist G. William Domhoff argues very compellingly for a foreign policy planning network supported and controlled by the power elite and consisting of a network of academics hired by foundations, elites themselves in temporary government positions, and influential civilian councils, such as the Council on

Foreign Relations (CFR), that have (or make) the time and resources to give thorough consideration to the needs of the nation in a way that the federal government simply does not have the time or resources to do.[5] I join Domhoff in arguing that this network is the single strongest source in the ongoing construction of the national interest, having its strongest impact on the views of government officials, which will impact the calculated presidential national interest if these officials are presidential advisors, and can impact the public national interest if these officials make public advocacy statements or arguments. While the specific details of the participating individuals and foundations and organizations have changed since the postwar period that provided Domhoff with data for his analysis, the legacy left by that postwar CFR and the continued existence of foundation-supported think tank influence remains consequential.

Having identified the core network in the network of sources of participation in the definition of the national interest, I now turn to the sphere that performs almost as much thought and research as the elite policy planning network, but is not as actively influential: academic participation. The continuing buzz of scholarly debate on the national interest does have some impact on the definitions of the national interest. Most of the scholars studying the topic would, presumably, like for their discussion to have a greater impact. Scholars of foreign affairs are an important part of the recruiting ground for the academic portion of the elite planning network, but even those who are not chosen for (or choose to avoid) participation in that network can still have an impact on that network. There is an important interchange of ideas and personnel between the general academic discussion of the national interest and the foundation-supported think tank discussion of the national interest that is within the policy planning network.

The next major location of construction of the national interest is within the government itself. Certain agencies, notably the National Security Council and the Department of State, definitely include consideration of the national interest within their portfolios. Their need to manage crises and deal with routine affairs of governance leave them with fewer resources than the elite sponsored foreign policy planning network, so they generally welcome reports and personnel from that network, and a considerable degree of overlap results. Government decision makers of all sorts receive inputs to their conception of the national interest primarily from the elite foreign policy planning network, most often through papers, briefs, and reports produced either by civilian councils or the academics of the foundation-supported think tanks.

The national interest is of greatest concern to the president and his immediate advisors. As chief executive, the president is the final arbiter of the calculated presidential national interest, as he will decide, in the last instance, if a foreign policy lies sufficiently within the national interest to enact it.

Other agencies and entities within the government participate in the definition of the national interest. In addition to the executive agencies already mentioned, members of Congress often enter public discourse on the national interest, usually to advocate or oppose proposed policies. The two houses of Congress have several committees and subcommittees charged with the oversight of various activities of foreign policy. These activities can easily contribute to the views of citizens and thus to the public national interest; further, by framing foreign policy issues in national interest terms and indicating which position they advocate (as well as serving as a public pretest of these views), congressional discussion can contribute to the construction of the legitimation national interest (even if congressional leaders would prefer to have stronger influence on the calculated presidential national interest).

Another important sphere of contributors to the discussion of the national interest is the media. The mainstream media more or less apprehend the discourse on the national interest that becomes exposed during policy contests in the government and magnify and distribute discourses. This is one way disagreements between individuals and factions within the government over the national interest can receive a public hearing, and advocates and opponents of policy alike often seek to "take to the airwaves" and share their views. Additionally, politically motivated opinion pieces, especially from the fringe press (both left and right) aim directly at policy and use notions of the national interest taken from academic sources of one flavor or another and put them in a lay context for policy advocacy. The national interest rarely receives media attention unless it is attached to policy.

The media have their largest effect on the remaining sphere of contribution to the definition of the national interest, the public; the media also have an interesting feedback relationship with the government, which I elaborate shortly.

For the last sphere, I prefer the term "publics," plural, to the singular "public." Invoking the phrase "the public" is overly reductionist and begs the use of the term "masses," which is insufficient. While in the category of publics I do intend to include the uninformed or uninterested masses, the role they play in the definition of the national interest is minimal. Much more important are informed publics, and activist subsets of various informed publics, particularly those who are from, or are descended from, various countries around the world that are possible objects of foreign policy. While publics are never the source of a definition of the national interest, they are the source of *legitimacy* for the national interest (again, see Chapter 7 on legitimacy). Publics collectively and individually construct the public national interest. By acting as a sounding board through public opinion polls, demonstration, or mass action, publics can display aspects of the public national interest and perhaps impact the definition of the legitimation national interest.

The mechanism by which publics can influence the definition of the legitimation national interest involves the media. The ability of the media to apply pressure on the government is often discussed but not well understood. Moving toward a model of media pressure, media scholar Derek Miller proposes that the conventional model, in which the media alerts the public, the public protests, and then the media conveys public complaint and thus pressures the government, is incorrect.[6] Rather, he proposes that it is government anticipation of media exposure leading to public concern and protest, which, in turn, influences government leaders to act proactively when issues arise. The driving mechanism under this formulation is the strong desire of government actors to avoid public protest. While this part of the process may have little impact on the calculated presidential national interest, it has a significant impact on the legitimation national interest. Knowing that foreign policy requires presidential approval, and knowing that presidents crave public approval, foreign policy planners are likely to seek constructions of the national interest that are likely to be acceptable to the public, without ever being specifically asked to do so.

Other Theories of the National Interest

In this section I contrast other theories of the national interest with my own tripartite model. I focus particularly on the differences among them, taking care to point out what kinds of empirical observations would allow one to adjudicate among them.

With very few exceptions, theories of the national interest focus on the derivation or definition of the national interest, taking for granted that it is a single unitary definable thing, if only you approach it in the right way. Cold war historian Miroslav Nincic divides these definers into two major camps, those that define the national interest via an assumptive approach and those that reach their definition through an enumerative approach.[7]

Assumptive Theories

Under the assumptive approach some assumption or set of assumptions is made about the nature of international relations or the nature of states, and that determines the national interest. The best examples of assumptive theories come from IR (international relations) scholarship. IR theorists are usually divided into two categories (each with several subcategories): realists and liberals.[8] Realists start from the assumption of anarchy between states in international relations, which suggests that international cooperation is illusory, and that all interstate relations are about power maximization, which is fundamentally zero-sum. Liberals, on the other hand, start from the assumption that free market trade can result in a situation that is positive sum (all parties gain) and that this economic interdependence provides a foundation upon which international cooperation can be built. For liberals, ideology plays a huge role in understanding international relations, which are not necessarily either conflictual or cooperative by default. While different substrands among realists and liberals make slightly different assumptions and thus draw slightly different definitions of the national interest, for the present discussion, these caricatures will serve.[9]

By their very nature, assumptive theories are extremely limited. Anything that can be argued *a priori* about a nation's interests must apply to all nations and must speak to some fairly narrow range of issues and threats, saying little about how best to pursue or protect those interests and how to deal with foreign policy decisions that fall outside of core national interests, however defined. Specific assumptive theories can be discarded in one of two ways: either by finding comparative circumstances under which the assumed national interests for different countries (or even the same country at different times but under ostensibly similar circumstances) break down in a way that defies logic and clearly falsifies the assumption or by demonstrating that the national interest as defined assumptively has little or no bearing on actual policies pursued or actual policy discourse.

Expanding the definition of the national interest to include those who wish to assert that a nation may have its own specific national interests independent of the nature of international relations and the logic of the nation-state leads to enumerative theories.

Enumerative Theories

The second camp identified by Nincic is the enumerative approach, where some defined collection of things is taken to be in the national interest.[10] These can be either generic enumerations, such as survival of citizens, maintenance of internal norms, or maintenance of the economy, or things specific to a particular nation. Theories in this camp can come much closer to what actually happens in practice in the policy-making sphere, where the participants in the policy formulation process try to enumerate the national interest and then encourage policy in its pursuit (as I argue earlier in this chapter is the case for the formulation of the calculated presidential national interest).

The problem, Nincic argues, with the enumerative theories and with what happens in practice, is one of boundaries. "Efforts to establish a comprehensive catalogue of national interests can define the core but not the outer boundary of an inventory upon which general agreement could be reached."[11] Interests closer to the assumptive core are going to be easily accepted as within the national interest; the farther from the core and the more specific possible interests become, the greater the ambiguity or disagreement becomes. Of course, if one abandons the need to define the national interest in a unitary fashion and instead acknowledges the tripartite national interest model that I propose above, this problem becomes less problematic.

Enumerative theories have the potential to break down at the fringes, where definition of the national interest in a certain policy sphere becomes a matter of debate. At that point, one set of enumerations is either "wrong" or all of the competing sets of enumerations simply fail to acknowledge that the national interest is socially constructed and that their very disagreement may be part of that social process.

Further Theories

If one acknowledges a normative role in the defining of the national interest (as Nincic ultimately suggests) and the important normative role played by the national interest in its practical use, then other conceptions of the national interest become possible.[12]

Democracy

Nincic, after criticizing most of the conventional approaches to the definition of the national interest, proposes a definition based on democratic procedure.

His position relies "on an altogether different principle—the nature of the political procedure via which judgments about the link between foreign policy and national interest are made." He elaborates,

> I am suggesting that the rules for identifying the national interest are given by tenets of political process which have an independent normative value—specifically, the tenets of democratic procedure. Two assumptions are involved. First, that the national interest can best be identified when it resolves itself into a verifiable expression of the nation's preferences. Second, that the process by which preferences are defined is one that the national collectivity considers legitimate. For political democracies, this implies that the specifics of the process can be altered by society when it no longer produces an accurate representation of its interests.[13]

In the last instance, his theory reduces toward pluralism and is vulnerable to the same criticisms to which all naively democratic theories are subject. However, his position does make two important contributions. The first is the acknowledgement that, in practice, the national interest is identified by a political process and that scholarly theories of the national interest need to recognize how the national interest is actually defined in practice. Second, he ties the national interest to processes of legitimation and acknowledges that both the specifics of the process and the details of the resulting national interest can and do change over time. Both of these factors contributed to the conception of my tripartite national interest model.

While my model draws conceptually on Nincic's democracy model, the two models make very different predictions and correspond to different observable realities. For all its innovations, Nincic's model is still unitary: there is one national interest at the end of the democratic rainbow. If empirical examinations show that there is a difference between the national interest as pursued and the national interest as expressed to the democratic public (the difference between calculated presidential national interest and legitimation national interest) or if the political process is found wanting as a faithful translator of the national preferences, then Nincic's theory does not hold.

Krasner

International relations scholar Stephen D. Krasner rejects classical national interest thinking in favor of a definition that is analytically useful for understanding policy, in his case U.S. raw materials policy. For Krasner, the national interest is "defined inductively as the preferences of American central decision-makers."[14] His method is particularly well suited to discovering the preferences of decision makers, and he finds several interests that are pursued consistently over time. What is missing, however, is a solid theoretical reason to accept these decision-maker preferences as the national interest or any information regarding the way in which the preferences were determined. Nincic accuses Krasner of identifying the national interest with "whatever the government chooses to do" and asserts, "For Krasner the national interest is a datum, not a standard."[15] Domhoff takes issue with the lack of explanation for the origins of Krasner's preference-based national interest and instead painstakingly identifies the process by which U.S. primary foreign policy goals for the period in question were formulated, and how those goals resulted in the policy preferences Krasner observed.[16] Krasner's method may be well suited as a way to identify the calculated presidential national interest, but lacks a theory to support it.

Domhoff

In opposition to Krasner, G. William Domhoff argues that the national interest is defined by state leaders and private citizens alike, not by the goals of the state.[17] To demonstrate this, he shows that the U.S. postwar national identity that is central to Krasner's argument is actually the product of power elites and their hired academics, working through a private organization and temporary appointments within the federal government. Domhoff argues that the private Council on Foreign Relations, working closely with the Department of State, defined and articulated the U.S. national interest in the postwar era.

Domhoff's contribution, generalized to the discussion at hand, involves the details of how national goals and the national interest came to be defined by real persons through a social process in the United States in a specific era. Domhoff's larger theoretical project is labeled "the class dominance model," and Domhoff argues that, regarding the national interest, it is class elites and their hired academics, rather than policy makers (who are, by and large, too busy) or the general public (who participate only marginally in politics) who take the time to study and analyze possible policy scenarios and their implications for the nation and thus construct the national interest. While the specific theories and approaches to defining the national interest used by those elites and academics may correspond more or less with theories presented earlier in the book, it is the possible variance within that process and its translation to policy that is new and must be considered in effective discussions of the national interest.

Domhoff's model is potentially consonant with the tripartite model of the national interest. Domhoff would certainly allow for the interests pursued to differ from the claims made (the difference between calculated presidential interests and legitimation interests). One could easily imagine empirical reality following Domhoff's suggested path for the construction of the interests pursued *and* containing evidence of the multiple constructions of the national interest explicit in the tripartite national interest model.

Theories of Governance and the National Interest

Given the focus of this book on theories of governance, it makes sense to take a moment to make explicit the relationships among the three core models of governance discussed here (pluralism, class theory, and elite theory) and the various conceptions of the national interest. The three theories of governance discussed here are generalizations of numerous scholars' work and are sufficiently broad to not match up perfectly with theories of the national interest. That said, each major theory of governance has a set of theories of the national interest to which it is naturally disposed. The pluralist model, for example, is perfectly consonant with the democracy model posed by Nincic. One could also imagine a number of assumptive or enumerative models that could hold under pluralism; the fairly elected government pursues the (externally defined) national interest on behalf of The People. The class model has the potential to mesh with a variety of assumptive theories, provided that the interests assumed protect the interests of the capitalist class and state; the assumptions of either the realists or the liberals could produce national interests whose pursuit could be consonant with class theory. Class theory might also be used to suggest its own set of assumptive or enumerative interests that could be considered vital to the health of the capitalist state and ruling class. Domhoff's ruling class model has its own theory of the construction of the national interest, a formulation that is potentially consonant with this chapter's tripartite model. Several different conceptions of the national interest could be consistent with elite theory, depending on the strand or branch within the elite camp. "Responsible" elites could pursue assumed or enumerated national interests on behalf of the nation, as could autonomous elites. Autonomous elites or selfish elites could pursue complexly defined national interests as per Domhoff or through the tripartite model.

THE GENERAL SUBSTANCE OF THE AMERICAN NATIONAL INTEREST

In this section I paint, in broad strokes, a picture of the content and substance of the course of the American public national interest throughout the twentieth century. Where possible, I make reference to the different roles played in the construction of the national interest by some of the groups identified in the section above. I divide the twentieth century into four general periods: the prewar period, the postwar/Cold War period, the post–Cold War period, and after the turn of the century.

The Prewar Period

In this period, foreign policy was framed in terms of pursuing material betterment for the American people rather than in terms of pursuing the national interest.[18] American foreign policy was fundamentally isolationist, coupled with interventionism in its own region, with a particular focus on getting European powers out of the hemisphere. "From the start, Americans have constructed their creedal identity in contrast to an undesirable 'other.' America's opponents are always defined as liberty's opponents."[19]

The Postwar Period and the Cold War

The events of the two world wars clearly required a paradigm shift. The United States found itself more involved than ever in European affairs, and as the emerging hegemon of the "free world." During World War II, well before the Cold War was conceived, the elite foreign policy network began to operate. As Domhoff's detailed account shows, the Council on Foreign Relations mapped out a "grand area" necessary for American raw materials needs, markets, and economic prosperity.[20]

Domhoff argues quite persuasively that the Cold War did not really heat up until that grand area was threatened. In fact, Domhoff invokes the 1940s era grand area to account in part for early U.S. involvement in Vietnam.[21]

Domhoff argues that this new definition of the national interest founded by the elite foreign policy planning network in the 1940s was primarily economic in nature, in that it targeted the full functioning of the American capitalist system with minimal changes to it. This falls in keeping with the typical collection of core national interest values; if citizens and sovereignty are safe, the main interest that remains to be defended is economic well-being. The Council on Foreign Relations produced the outlines of a general world order that would satisfy that economic interest, and the U.S. government accepted that outline virtually wholesale. Throughout the period, the calculated presidential national interest shows continuous adherence to the defense of the grand area. Other scholars, however, ascribe much more importance to the ideological flavor of postwar foreign policy, specifically, the role played by the Cold War and anticommunism in general.

Domhoff argues that anticommunism as a key policy and its ideological consequences came about only after the grand area was threatened.[22] Without directly disputing that claim, other scholars ascribe importance to the Cold War all out of proportion to any thoughtful calculation about protecting economic interests. Krasner asserts that "[o]pposition to communism more closely resembles a millennial goal, a religious quest, than a logical or a rational strategy."[23] Krasner asserts that this ideological agenda is the primary characteristic of the postwar era. The details of the interplay between societal groups that brought about the Cold War and allowed anticommunism to force its way into the national interest and into every home in America is beyond the scope of this work. Political scientist Deborah Welch Larson offers an excellent account of the early construction of Cold War ideology and also acknowledges that the process was socially complex. She asserts, "Many historians have imposed a retrospective coherence on American foreign policy that simply did not exist at the time."[24]

While there are abundant outward signs of the ideological strength of anticommunism in America during the Cold War, there are certainly those who agree with Domhoff's ascription of motive and suggest that the elite foreign policy network continued to operate and participate well after the CFR's paradigm shifting work in the 1940s. Journalists Christina Jacqueline Johns and P. Ward Johnson note,

> The absence of true democracy in a Latin American country has never in and of itself determined U.S. foreign policy toward a government, nor has the existence of democracy ensured U.S. support. Guatemala had a democratically elected government in 1954, but because the United Fruit Company perceived its interests to be threatened by that government, the United States installed a military regime to replace it.[25]

They conclude that "[t]he concern of the U.S. policy elites is not, therefore, with the establishment or protection of democracy; it is with the establishment of capitalism worldwide and with the unimpeded control of resources and markets."[26]

Regardless of the underlying motive, the Cold War provided a powerful and unifying legitimation mythology. Anticommunism, even if selectively targeted for economic advantage, was a powerful force. For at least three decades after Castro's successful revolution in Cuba, the driving theme of American interventions and policies in the Caribbean basin and Central America was the prevention of "another Cuba" and the containment of Castro's influence.[27]

Through the 1960s, the degree of consensus on anticommunist ideology was nothing short of remarkable. With the exception of the extreme left, virtually all segments of the American population accepted anticommunism as the major parameter of American foreign policy.[28] In the 1960s and 1970s this consensus began to wear a bit thin,[29] but opposition to communist expansion or aggression would continue to be a powerful legitimizing tool until the Cold War "ended" in 1991.

The Post–Cold War Period

As the Cold War wound down in the late 1980s, Mikhail Gorbachev's advisor Georgiy Arbatov commented, "We are doing something really terrible to you—we are depriving you of an enemy."[30] The loss of an enemy, the end of the Cold War, leaving the United States as THE superpower, took the wind from the sails of anticommunism and, some would argue, from the sails of the ship of state with regard to foreign policy. The threat of communism during the Cold War had been twofold: first, the "Red Menace," the fear of an overwhelming "other" with different values, or mass destruction; second, the threat to business from leftist policies such as nationalization, labor laws, redistribution, or closed markets. The second kind of threat is much less normatively appealing, but, during the Cold War, was quietly able to hide behind the former in both the public national interest and the legitimation national interest. In the post–Cold War era, the Red Menace disappeared, but the calculated presidential national interest continued to include the protection of American business interests from leftist threats. Because the stalking horse of communism was no longer available to appeal to, presidents were forced to look elsewhere for effective legitimation national interests when acting to prevent leftist threats to business. President George H.W. Bush, as the first post–Cold War president, tried out the "New World Order" and the threat of "narco-terrorism" as replacements for the lost Cold War legitimating mythology, but what appeal they did have never approached the power of Cold War anticommunism.

With the loss of the single strongest defining element of, and source of legitimacy for, American foreign policy, the public national interest drifted. While the elite foreign policy planning network still exists (albeit in a slightly transformed form), the government has developed an improved capacity to do its own foreign policy analysis and long-range planning and has taken (and is likely to continue to take) a larger role in thinking about the national interest.

What really changed with the end of the Cold War, however, was not the process by which the national interest was constructed, but what substantial interests were likely to be in the contest for consideration for the national interest. With the dramatically reduced possibility of threat to the CFR's grand area, and with the virtual end of any plausible threat to open markets and raw materials, any plausible threat to traditional core national interests seemed to have ended. While the calculated presidential interest continued to include security concerns and protection of American business interests abroad, there is also a whole host of normative interests that might or might not have been pursued: promotion of democracy, protection of human rights, peacekeeping, ending ethnic, nationalist, and separatist conflicts, and so forth.[31] The question was (and to some extent remains), how many of these "noble" but nonessential goals are going to be considered to be in the national interest, with the *real* question being how many soldiers' lives and how much money are these interests worth? The answer was anything but clear and was still contested over ten years after the end of the Cold War, as of the 2000 presidential campaign, where one of the few issues the candidates significantly disagreed on was the proper role of the United States and its soldiers in terms of peacekeeping and nation building.

Considerable thought and discussion has gone into what the American national interest should contain in the postwar world. Political scientist and journalist James Chace suggests that core interests will likely remain the same, namely, "the stability of Europe, the balance of power in East Asia and the Western Pacific, and the security—economic and social—of North America."[32] Beyond these core values, Chace also suggests that, to the extent that the West depends on Middle Eastern oil (a considerable extent), it is in the U.S. national interest to see that a free flow of oil at reasonable prices remains available to the outside world, which clearly requires stability in the Persian Gulf region.

The Commission on America's National Interests (a commission sponsored by Harvard's Belfer Center for Science and International Affairs, The Nixon Center, the RAND Corporation, and the Hauser Foundation—a fine example of the elite foreign policy planning network) published a report in 2000 that detailed the following five "vital" U.S. national interests:

> (1) to prevent, deter, and reduce the threat of nuclear, biological, and chemical weapons attacks on the United States or its military forces abroad; (2) to ensure US allies' survival and their active cooperation with the US in shaping an international system in which we can thrive; (3) to prevent the emergence of hostile major powers or failed states on US borders; (4) to ensure the viability and stability of major global systems (trade, financial markets, supplies of energy, and the environment); and (5) to establish productive relations, consistent with American national interests, with nations that could become strategic adversaries, China and Russia.[33]

The Turn of the Century/The Contemporary Era

The vague drift in the national interest brought on by the end of the black and white world of the Cold War, lacking in plausible and concerning threats to the national interest, was brought to a sharp halt by the attacks of September 11, 2001. While the above list of national interests developed by The Commission on America's National Interests makes clear that scholars and planners believed in the possibility of real threats, the attack on the Pentagon and the destruction of the World Trade Center highlighted the reality of those threats in a previously inconceivable way. Protection of the American homeland and combating terror at its sources increased in salience by several orders of magnitude. This radical change in the climate and context within which national interests are constructed contains a clear mandate for action in foreign policy that has not been available since the heyday of the Red Menace. Foreign policy aimed at nation building and other humanitarian goals have taken on new prominence, as the public and policy makers alike seem to have recognized that reducing the number of people in the world who are inclined to hate the United States for one reason or another is just as important in the war on terrorism as the elimination of known terrorists.

In the post-9/11 climate, claims in the legitimation national interest that centered around combating or preventing terrorism resonated well with the public national interest. This situation could have resulted in a reasonably strong concordance among the three national interests, but does not necessarily have to. The calculated presidential national interest, particularly with regard to the administration's selection of allies and opponents in the war on terror, continues to follow a different construction process than either the public national interest or the legitimation national interest and is particularly worthy of attention. Now, several years removed from 9/11 and with the United States embroiled in operations in Iraq and Afghanistan with ambiguous final outcomes, the public national interest is perhaps less inclined to be accepting of claims connecting policies to terrorism.

USE MADE OF NATIONAL INTEREST DURING EACH INTERVENTION CASE

In this section, I discuss the way in which the national interest was invoked in each of the four U.S. military interventions in Central America since World War II. Where possible, I discuss what real interests were at stake and entered the calculated presidential national interest (the "real" motive for policy as evinced in decision-maker memoirs or exposés), what was claimed (the legitimation national interest), and how it related to the public national interest.

Dominican Republic

As Krasnser notes,

> Between 1960 and 1965 the United States brought the full range of its foreign policy instruments to bear against the Dominican Republic. American actions included diplomatic protests, economic pressure, covert assassination attempts, and overt military intervention. In the Dominican Republic there were substantial American investments including ownership of much of the sugar industry. However, the Dominican case illustrates far more clearly than the Cuban the primacy of general political objectives in American foreign policy. It also illustrates, as did American actions in Guatemala, the potential for misperception that afflicted American policy-makers. One indication of

their pursuit of an ideological foreign policy was a tendency to exaggerate the danger of communist penetration.[34]

Details of the events leading up to the U.S. intervention in the Dominican Republic can be found in the first section of the case narrative in Chapter 2. As Krasner observes, and all of the evidence I found confirms, the main motive for the intervention was fear of a communist take-over. Not that such a take-over was particularly likely, but that fact was somewhat less than obvious at the time, and these events did take place during the height of the Cold War, and the Caribbean basin is solidly within the grand area and clearly within the United States' hemispheric "sphere of influence." While the Dominican Republic itself could scarcely be argued to be a threat, the spread of communism was opposed by all three of the American national interests. Curiously, "prevention of communism," while eminent in the internal discussions of decision makers, was not invoked in the claims justifying the intervention.[35] Instead, the need to protect American lives and a desire to save Dominican lives and restore order and peace were all that was claimed, and the only claimed vital interest was defense of American citizens, which interest, arguably, was protected as soon as the evacuation phase of the operation was completed, well before most of the over 10,000 U.S. soldiers had landed on the island.

While both the protection of American lives and the need to prevent communism were salient to decision makers, there are other identifiable interests in Dominican affairs that may have played a role in presidential national interest calculations. First, the United States had a considerable history of involvement in Dominican affairs, including that the Dominican Republic was the Latin American "showcase for democracy" after the Trujillo assassination a few years earlier. Given all the attention the United States had focused on the island and the wonderful claims made about the Dominican system of governance, a successful communist revolution would have been really embarrassing. U.S. involvement was not just government involvement, but included considerable business involvement, particularly in sugar production, which is the other interest involved. Several scholars note the considerable involvement of U.S. sugar interests in the Dominican Republic and suggest that these interests might well have had an influence on U.S. government involvement.[36] Scholars Fred Goff and Michael Locker go so far as to assert that "[a] considerable number of individuals with financial, legal, and social connections to the East Coast sugar complex were well stationed throughout the upper echelons of the U.S. Government."[37] These individuals include presidential advisor Abe Fortas, who had direct connections to the sugar industry, and also direct access to the president.[38]

Consequently, the threat of communism, which is a threat to U.S. ability to do business in a country, and the threat of instability, which is also a threat to business interests, were joined by a plausible threat to American nationals in the Dominican Republic and were considered sufficient threats to motivate the military intervention. Since the intervention took place during American involvement in Vietnam, what little public discourse there was on the topic took place in that context. Government decision makers and analysts knew the intervention for what it was, an anticommunist intervention. The public suspected as much and would have been happy to accept that, but the administration made the error (by its own admission) of trying to legitimate the situation in a different way.[39] Surprisingly, a large part of the calculated presidential national interest (fear of communism) was very close to a core value of the public national interest. By making claims based on a legitimation national interest that was distant from both the calculated presidential national interest *and* the public national interest, President Johnson invited (and received) considerable criticism.

The short-term success of the operation made any contestation of whether it had been in the national interest moot. The intervention had occurred, order was restored, a friendly regime was put in place, and the soldiers had left. Public debate on the national interest was much more strongly focused on policy toward Vietnam, not on the Dominican intervention, which, in the eyes of most Americans, had become history almost before it had begun.

Grenada

> The Grenada Invasion, or, as it was termed by military planners, Operation Urgent Fury, has been viewed as falling within the general category of a Caribbean-style intervention. All the elements were present for the United States to follow an oft-used script for invading a neighboring nation: American citizens apparently in some danger, internal political unrest after the assassination of Prime Minister Maurice Bishop, an unpopular governing regime with ties to our adversaries, shipments of arms entering the country from Eastern Europe, and the construction of an airport by Cuban engineers that raised the suspicions of the Pentagon. Each one of these developments in Grenada linked up with established national security and national interest objectives that in the past had pushed the United States to either take military action or implement some form of destabilizing operation.[40]

In fact, Grenada posed no real threat to any identifiable American interests. In June 1982, Congressman Ron Dellums's testimony before the House Subcommittee on inter-American Affairs asserted, "Following extensive and comprehensive briefings, I came away with the absolute impression that nothing being done in Grenada constitutes a threat to the United States or her allies."[41] Given that no interests were at stake, threats to interests were marginal at best. However, there was some perception of threat on the part of the administration. It was impossible to confirm the absence of threat to the approximately 1,000 U.S. medical students on the island, with no way to absolutely guarantee their safety, and given the political consequences the Iran hostages had for the immediately previous Carter administration, protecting the American medical students was certainly on the minds of decision makers (see chapters 2 and 7 for further details). The psychological threat of another Cuba, even though the situation was in no way comparable and the geographic extent and population of Grenada are laughably small relative to Cuba, also cannot be discarded. With these factors playing into presidential calculations, the best way to describe the invasion is as opportunism, seizing a chance to be rid of a small left-leaning government that had annoyed (and nothing else) the administration, particularly President Reagan.

The intervention was claimed to be in the (legitimation) national interest on two grounds: first, to protect American medical students (an argument that, while touching on strongly held beliefs of the public national interests, does not explain the choice of occupation over evacuation), and second, a need to support U.S. obligations to allies in the Caribbean (referring to a request made by the OECS [Organisation of Eastern Caribbean States], an organization to which the United States is not a party) for U.S. assistance in restoring order to Grenada (an appeal that was in violation of the OECS's own charter). There was considerable opposition to the operation and its justification in Congress following the Grenada intervention in October 1983; However, as political scientist Samuel Kernell observes, the legitimation national interest ultimately succeeded in its appeal to the public national interest:

> Shortly after the U.S. invasion of Grenada in the fall of 1983 all opinion indicators pointed to a confused and ambivalent public. Politicians within both parties were uncertain what posture they should assume toward the President's action. Some Democratic spokespersons, including House Speaker O'Neill, began lobbing salvos at the White House, describing the invasion as "gunboat diplomacy." Democratic senator Daniel P. Moynihan publicly declared the invasion to be "an act of war," adding, "I don't know that you restore democracy at the point of a bayonet." One Democratic representative went so far as to announce a petition drive calling for the President's impeachment. For the most part, however, Democrats—including, prominently, those seeking their party's presidential nomination—and Republicans temporized.
>
> With the military operation concluded and public opinion appearing increasingly to echo the President's critics, President Reagan went on national television to account for his actions. The poll takers were poised; when they revealed the public's early, highly favorable response, the critics hushed up, and Reagan's previously silent partners became vocal. One Democratic senator remarked, "Most people, once they saw the polls come out, went underground." Within two weeks after his initial criticism, Senator Moynihan conceded, "The move is popular and therefore there's no disposition in the Senate to be opposed to it."[42]

Panama

American interests in Panama in 1989 are easily identified. First and most obviously is the Panama Canal. While lacking the strategic importance it held earlier in American history, keeping it in reliable hands was important for regional stability and trade. Other U.S. interests include the lives and well-being of the large number of U.S. servicemen and women and their families stationed in Panama at the time. Finally, U.S. direct investment in the country was (and is) significant.

The threat posed by the Noriega regime to these interests was marginal, but perceived to be growing. In constructing the presidential national interest a much more substantial role was played by the threat Noriega posed to the reputation and ego of

President George H.W. Bush. Efforts to remove Noriega had begun well before Bush took office, and Noriega's removal was important to Bush. His advisors recognized that removing Noriega without changing the political structure in Panama would likely lead to another Noriega-esque leader, so they advocated the destruction of the Panamanian Defense Force and its replacement along with efforts at democracy building in Panama.[43]

The claims stemming from the legitimation national interest relied on several factors: first, the timing of the intervention as a response to an escalation in tensions in Panama involving the death of a U.S. Navy lieutenant; second, on the fact that interests in Panama, which had long been considered important components of the national interest (even if, perhaps, their centrality in the national interest was due for reconsideration), were threatened; and third, because personally Noriega was so loathsome a character. These legitimation claims were generally accepted as being within the public national interest; the invasion was very popular domestically. Internationally, however, the intervention was condemned as naked aggression.

Haiti

> Despite UN authorization of a U.S. intervention, there was still strong reluctance on Capitol Hill and among the American public for such a venture. There were basically two schools of thought. The first held that the United States must act to support democracy in the hemisphere by restoring democracy in Haiti and, therefore, must restore Aristide to power. Those supporting this position included the CBC and members of the Florida congressional delegation, which feared a new wave of Haitian refugees. This group also included a significant number of congressional members who were fed up with having to deal with Haiti at all and who thought Congress had more important matters to attend to.
>
> The second school, principally led by conservative republicans, held that there were no vital U.S. interests at stake in Haiti and, therefore, the United States should not intervene. Many were skeptical about the wisdom of sending young Americans to Haiti, possibly to die, for a decidedly undemocratic, anti-American radical such as Aristide.[44]

There were several identifiable American interests in Haiti, none of which were likely to be considered particularly vital according to the public national interest. The main interest and prime motivator in presidential calculations for the intervention was Florida, particularly the flow of Haitian refugees and their impact on Florida's economy and on Florida's political impact on national politics (which, in election 2000, proved to be quite large). The second major set of interests had to do with the American values of promoting democracy and human rights the world over, especially in our neighbors. The final interest was Clinton campaign promises, which included a change in his predecessor's refugee policy and a commitment to Haitian President-in-exile Jean-Bertrand Aristide's return to power. "Strategic and economic interests did not drive the intervention. Lack of such interest induced the U.S. public, the Republicans and the Pentagon to oppose an intervention, and

Clinton aides also emphasized ideology and feasibility rather than necessity in their efforts to justify it."[45]

Given the unavailability of the Cold War metanarrative,[46] President Clinton could not claim threat of communism, or really threat of any kind. Instead the intervention was legitimated as international social work, and the extent to which it was or was not within the parameters of America's post–Cold War national interest was hotly debated. This extensive public debate on the national interest was, in part, a consequence of the long public run-up to the intervention. The intensity of the debate and the failure to ever achieve widespread public support stems from the failure of the claims of the legitimation national interest to appeal sufficiently to the values of the public national interest.

CONCLUSIONS

Having reviewed several existing conceptions of the national interest, I found them wanting in two major ways. First, most failed to recognize the socially constructed nature of the national interest, and second (and more important), none recognized that the concept is too complex to exist as a singular unified and calculated entity. Instead, I argue for a dynamic tripartite model of the national interest that acknowledges the importance of all three national interests: the calculated presidential national interest, the legitimation national interest, and the public national interest. By detailing the process through which the three national interests are constructed I hope I have demystified the origins of peoples' conceptions of the national interest and shed some light on the ongoing construction of, and changes to, these various conceptions.

In the historical discussion, I have shown how the general trend of the public national interest has changed over time and how the end of the Cold War made presidential pursuit of certain interests more difficult to justify. After the turn of the century and the attacks of 9/11, the return of real and easily legitimized threats to a set of more clearly core national interests will give presidents a much freer hand in appealing to the national interest and launching military adventures abroad.

In the case study section, I discussed the specific interests pursued in the calculated presidential national interest differ substantially from what is acceptable in the public national interest, but the claims presidents make (the legitimation national interest) have appealed to values within the public national interest and have resulted in successfully legitimized interventions. The legitimation troubles experienced by the Johnson administration in the Dominican Republic case stemmed from the rare situation in which the public national interest and the calculated presidential national interest were closer to each other than the claimed (legitimation) national interest. Legitimation troubles for Haiti occurred because the claimed legitimations were not close enough to the content of the public national interest to be compelling.

As a final note, I would like to observe that the national interest is fundamentally a "state's reasons for state's behavior" approach. If one naively accepts the concept (or the constructions) at face value, one might well fail to apprehend the complex integrated structural and social processes that go into determining the various national interests and state behavior. The tripartite national interest should provide a conceptually useful linkage between expressed decision-maker motives and more complex sociological explanations of governance. If an interest or institution affects the process by which the national interest is defined, it potentially influences state policy, without having direct influence on the specific policy decision-making process. The national interests observed in the case analyses are potentially consonant with versions of class or elite theory, but do not reflect well on pluralist explanations.

5

The Decision-Making Process: Who Participates, and How?

One fact is clear to anyone with experience in government: the springs of policy bubble up, they do not trickle down.

—*Dean Acheson*

INTRODUCTION

In this chapter, I explain both *who* participates in military intervention decisions and *how* they participate. I argue that participation is strongly conditioned by the primary characteristics of the intervention, along with the organization and institutions of U.S. government bureaucracy. These organizational and institutional influences exist within a larger framework of structured contingency, which also conditions participation, and contributes to an impression of capriciousness and unpredictability in the military intervention decision-making processes.

Figure 5.1 summarizes my central argument regarding military intervention decision making. The institutional structure of decision making and the characteristics of the situation itself determine the primary character of an intervention decision which in turn affects who participates in the process and how they participate to a remarkable extent. Both of these relationships take place within a larger context of structured contingency, based on government institutions and policy.

The Situation

Unsurprisingly, the details of the situation that motivates the military intervention affect the decisional process. The characteristics of the situation, including the history of U.S. relations with that country, the level of perceived threat to national interests involved in ongoing events in that country, geography, and so forth, can all contribute to the initial decisions (or nondecisions[1]) made in response to the situation. These initial decisions, conditioned by the situation, determine the primary characteristics of the intervention decision-making process.

Primary Character

There are certain characteristics of the decisional process that are in some sense primary and inhere more in the situation or in the initial perception of the situation

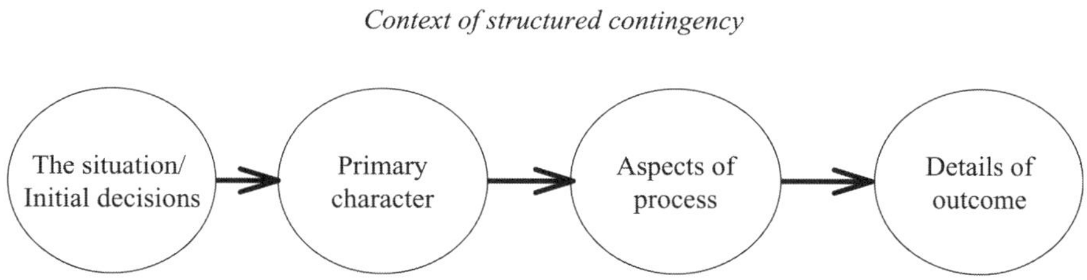

Figure 5.1 Decisions in Context

or are decided before decision making meaningfully begins. These primary characteristics have a significant effect on decision participation. Principal among these are crisis vs. premeditation, and secrecy vs. public knowledge. A case's location on these two dimensions shapes several important aspects of the process from the outset, most notably who participates in the decision and the character of that participation.

Crisis vs. Premeditation

A decision to stage a military intervention occurs in response to events found to be unacceptable occurring or existing in the target country. "Unacceptable," in this case, is only with reference to U.S. perceptions; just because something is viewed as unacceptable in the country in which it occurred does not make it so to the perceptions of the U.S. foreign policy making apparatus, and vice versa.

The unacceptable situation will have either come about imminently and surprisingly (crisis) or have been existent or building in the target country for some time (noncrisis, with the response, therefore, being premeditated). Here, crisis is a situation that is surprising *and* time pressing. To be time pressing, a situation must require immediate action by virtue of imminent unacceptable consequences, the threat of an imminent change in the situation that would make the situation even more unacceptable, or the threat of a resolution that returns the situation to below the threshold of minimally unacceptable, but is not the most favorable resolution in the eyes of U.S. policy makers (a missed opportunity). A U.S. foreign policy crisis, then, is a situation with possibly unacceptable consequences for U.S. interests or goals regarding which a decision for action (or inaction) must be reached within a short (a matter of days) time.[2]

The alternative means to arrive at a decision to address an unacceptable situation in another country by military intervention is through a process of premeditation. Curiously, the common alternative to "crisis" in the decision-making literature is "routine," which is a totally inadequate way to describe the process of premeditating military interventions. Premeditated intervention decisions are more complex than crisis decisions, as there is complexity inherent in a situation that is clearly unacceptable (requires a military intervention), but not so urgently unacceptable that it requires an *immediate* military intervention.[3] The question *When?* becomes gigantic.

In a crisis intervention, *When?* is as soon as possible. When premeditating, *When?* is far from obvious and is contingent on a great many factors.

Secret vs. Public vs. Full Public Arena

Whether an intervention is decided in secret or made public knowledge has a dramatic effect on the decisional process. In principle, this is not a simple dichotomy between secret and public, but is a full spectrum from maximum OPSEC (operational security) to a decision that is reached in full public view with input from within the public arena. In fact, the cases under consideration have been (and the nature of interventions in general seems to suggest the relationship generalizes) either secret or in the full public eye.

The level of secrecy is a *decision* taken by the decision makers. The default position is secrecy, because of the private nature of presidential decision making and because of possible advantages inherent in surprise and possible changes in behavior in the target country based on knowledge of an impending intervention. Electing to make an intervention decision public, then, results from one or more of several factors. First, if a U.S. intervention is anticipated, it is possible that behavior in the target country will change *favorably*. Publicly planning an intervention can be a powerful diplomatic tool, a classic form of "saber rattling." Second, if the troop mobilizations necessitated by the scope of the planned military operation are impossible to conceal, secrecy will be lost, so it might as well not be sought in the first place. Finally, if policy makers want preapproval for an intervention (either from Congress, the public, or an international body such as the United Nations), they must abandon secrecy. The decision to maintain or abandon secrecy is generally taken very early in the process and is driven strongly by the situation. Secrecy or the lack of secrecy has important effects on decision participants and on the decisional process in general, as elaborated below.

Bureaucracy and Process

Most of the activities that constitute the decisional process take place within the executive bureaucracy. Variation in bureaucratic participation exists, and much of that variation is conditioned by the primary character of the decisional process. Most of the actual details of process concern who does what, when, and the factors that constrain who does what, when. These details concern bureaucracy. In this section I discuss the formal organizational structure of the decision making, how the bureaucratic structure shapes the decisional process, and the impact of the primary characteristics of the decision on participation in the process.

Structure of the Decision-Making Process

> In the United States, the President is preeminently charged with making these final choices in foreign policy matters. The import of this fact for understanding strategies of influence, although self-evident, is often inadequately appreciated. In contrast with

domestic policy, where the President shares the authoritative selection of alternatives with many other officials (especially in Congress), in foreign affairs the President often is the sole authoritative decision-maker.[4]

Formally, the president, as the chief executive and commander in chief of the armed forces, is in charge of crisis management and is the final arbiter of intervention decisions. While there is some debate over the proper extent of the president's ability to move troops and effectively make war without a formal declaration of war from Congress, in practice, the skirmishes over these disagreements did not prevent any of the intervention cases studied here from taking place. Presidential Scholar Richard E. Neustadt lists several formal institutional changes that have affected presidential power over the past 50 years; other than the enactment of the 1973 War Powers Act (requiring the president to consult with Congress before deploying troops abroad) and the political skirmishes surrounding it, none of these changes has affected the president's position as "sole authoritative decision-maker" in these cases.[5]

This very "personalist" institutional arrangement, where decision making is structured in such a way that the president is the final authority, is somewhat rare in the world at large. In other democratic but parliamentary states, executive positions and authority are shared among a number of ministers, none of whom are directly appointed by the chief executive. This American personalist structure contributes to the role played by many of the facets of bureaucracy that contribute to decisional processes and is a theme that emerges repeatedly in what follows.

Organization

The whole of the decision-making bureaucracy plays diverse (and sometimes surprising) roles in the four interventions considered here. Variation in decision participants, the participation of top-level and lower-level decision participants, and the location of the decision (and the decision participants) are all influenced by the general character of the decisional process and have an impact on the outcome.

Noted scholar of American government Theodore J. Lowi separates crisis from noncrisis foreign policy decision making, as I do. Regarding noncrisis decision making, he notes,

> [I]t will not be so easy to analyze as the crisis dimensions because non-crisis decisions involve institutions. So far nothing has been said of institutions. Indeed, a fundamental feature of crisis decisions is that they involve institution leaders (holders of the top posts) *without their institutions.* Only when time allows does the entire apparatus of the foreign policy establishment come into play. And when men and their institutions are involved, the decision-making process is bound to differ from when only the men are involved. Thus the long sections on non-crisis decision-making which follows is basically an analysis of institutions.[6]

While I agree with Lowi that the central decision makers play an immediate and central role in crisis decision making, I disagree with his assertion that they do so *without their institutions.*[7] While the central decision makers may be spending all of their time in crisis management mode, constantly reviewing the situation and asking for frequent updates, who is providing those frequent updates? The obvious answer is the lower functionaries of their respective institutions (organizations). Now, perhaps in a crisis institutional standard operating procedures for who gets to decide what, and whom information must pass through before moving up the hierarchy, get ignored or truncated to some extent, and to some extent *perhaps not.*[8] Understanding crisis *and* noncrisis decisions requires the analysis of both organizations and institutions.

Consequences of Crisis vs. Premeditated Decision Making

Crisis decisions, by definition, are urgent and escalate up the decision hierarchy very quickly. Organizational heads and "key decision makers" get involved early in a crisis and tend to request information and continuous feedback throughout the short duration of the crisis.

Lowi offers what I consider to be the typical statement of the perception of most scholars of the consequences of crises:

> *Crisis decisions in foreign policy are made by an elite of formal, official office-holders.* Rarely is there time to go further. Apparently rarely also is there need to go further, except immediately after the decision through ceremonies of affirmation and perhaps long after the decision, through criticism and "electoral punishment." Thus, a corollary to this obvious, albeit often overlooked, first proposition is that the people who make decisions in times of crisis are largely those who were elected and appointed to make such decisions. That is to say, *in foreign affairs crises our government has operated pretty much as it was supposed to operate* [emphasis in original]. There is a normative corollary as well: Since our record of response to crisis is good, then the men in official positions have been acting and are able to act rationally.[9]

Lowi's statement (and the generally held positions on crisis management) makes too strong an assumption about the exclusivity of the decision makers in crisis and ignores some of the unavoidable process-based consequences of U.S. government structure (namely, the impact of bureaucracy, and contingency). While I agree that crisis draws the attention of core decision makers and truncates the process due to temporal urgency, one of the findings of this study is that even in crisis the character and performance of lower-level bureaucratic actors and the contingencies they act on and produce remain extremely important.

The principal differences between crisis and premeditation are, first, the temporal urgency that premeditation lacks, and second, the lack of a clear imperative to action (which, if it existed, would make the situation a crisis). The consequences of these differences vary. In premeditation, the lack of temporal urgency means that, unavoidably, people other than top decision makers will do much of the work and the planning; lower functionaries are allowed to do their jobs and are not bypassed by crisis. Planning will be complete, as there is no reason to rush. However, planning should be "better," as excuses based on inadequate preparation times (which might be accepted in a crisis) will not be acceptable. Expanding the decisional time frame also opens the process to participation by a wider range of players. Not only the top decision makers and the appropriate organizational functionaries, but congressional leaders and diplomats from other nations might take a role. Further, depending on the other policies being used to try to achieve the same goal and the extent to which intervention planning is being kept secret, there is the possibility of a fully engaged public discourse on the topic, radically impacting the decisional process.

The lack of crisis imperative creates a powerful tension in a premeditated intervention decision. Once plans are complete, rehearsed, and ready to go, the *When?* question remains. Plans might get stale, or secrecy might be violated. A legitimizable intervention requires the delivery of some kind of ultimatum to the country containing the unacceptable situation or some kind of change in the level of unacceptability of events there, serving as a "trigger" or "last straw" allowing the intervention to proceed behind crisis rhetoric. The wide range of social, psychological, and political factors that can influence decision makers during the process of a premeditated intervention creates an equally wide range of constraints and contingencies. Given that the formal structure of decision making changes very little from situation to situation, it is remarkable how much variation in process these primary characteristics create.

Secrecy also has consequences for participation. The higher the level of secrecy desired and maintained, the fewer people know about an intervention being planned, and the less they can participate or contribute. Secrecy prevents the participation of all excluded parties, be they critics or experts. Opening a decision up for full public scrutiny does the exact opposite, allowing participation by both critics and experts, along with participants from other branches of government, and from the general public. Full public knowledge increases the chances that all alternatives will be considered and that obvious flaws in plans will be spotted, but also increases the opportunity for dissent.

Contingency

Many aspects of the military intervention decision-making process take place in a context of structured contingency. This is an important part of my argument, as it pertains to *how* participants participate, and the consequences of that participation. Things occur during the decisional process that are or seem surprising, random, or unpredictable, and these things affect the outcome of that process. I wish to divide these contingent events into two types: "capricious" contingencies and "predictable yet unpredicted" contingencies. Capricious contingency denotes the truly random and the genuinely unforeseeable—such as the U.S. Ambassador to the Dominican Republic being in Georgia visiting his sick mother at the inception of the Dominican crisis.[10] Predictable yet unpredicted contingency, on the other hand, denotes events or decisions that seem random and could not reasonably have been foreseen by top decision makers, but *can* be easily explained after the fact with detailed information about the individual making the decision or predicating the event. I make this distinction so that my argument is not based on a claim of random or incomprehensible behavior (which, as a sociologist, I would find unappealing), but based instead on the acknowledgment that behavior that is consonant with a given lower-level bureaucrat's background and personality could be totally unexpected by higher-level decision participants (or historians) and thus seem (and, for all intents and purposes, *be*) contingent.[11]

Based on these predictable yet unpredicted contingencies, I argue that decisions made by participants below the "core" of top-level decision makers are important. I do not wish to suggest that lower-level functionaries are deciding the course U.S. military interventions will take, but rather that they are creating or constraining the range of choices and options available to the top-level decision makers in a contingent and often path-dependant fashion. This "structured contingency" stems from the way in which these decisional processes are organized, that is, the existing institutional structure of the various executive departments and the military. I also argue that the decisions made by the highest levels of decision makers are contingent and sometimes depend on factors that should not particularly inspire confidence in the U.S. policy-making process. Taken together, structured contingency in the bureaucracy and the personalist impact of the chief executive create a *context* of contingency in which military intervention decisions unfold. Following the presentation of the case studies, I elaborate the ways in which contingencies of several types affect the decisional process, and I give examples from the intervention cases. One of my most interesting findings is the way in which the contingent decisions, choices, or personality of participants at every level of the bureaucracy can impact the process.

Process Summary

While Chapter 2 recounts the processes resulting in these four military interventions in greater detail, here I briefly summarize the decisional processes of each one. I do this to prevent the reader from needing to continually refer back to that earlier chapter and to focus the narrative on certain key points.

Dominican Republic

In April 1965, Dominican rebels launched a coup that would topple the existing triumvirate government of the Dominican Republic and threaten to spark a civil war between rebel army units backed by citizen militias and antirebel army and air force troops loyal to a new junta. While U.S. attention to the situation was immediate, response was slow because of the assumptions first that the existing regime would survive the revolt and then that the alliance of antirebel military forces would certainly succeed against the rebels. When both of these assumptions turned out to be false, the United States, having made no serious effort for a diplomatic resolution and having offered minimal or tardy assistance to the groups in the conflict they supported, elected to ensure the outcome of the situation with a massive influx of American troops.

The decisional process for this intervention passed through at least three distinct phases. The first was an informational stage, in which the bureaucracy functioned as one would expect, passing information up the hierarchy so that everyone who needed to be was apprised of the situation. Participation was not completely "by the book" as most of the Dominican country team was not in the Dominican Republic at the inception of the crisis, so the ranking the U.S. Embassy official ended up being a Department of State charge d'affaires, an adjunct in the Embassy. The second phase was a dichotomous phase in which the "in-country" staff in the Embassy began to appreciate the severity of the crisis and realize that the outcome was very much in doubt, while in Washington the impression was still that the situation would resolve itself satisfactorily. In the third and final phase awareness of the crisis was universal, U.S. policy goals for the situation were finally clearly formulated, and, while it might have been considerably easier to realize those goals earlier in the crisis, military intervention became the only certain way to achieve those goals.

The process leading to the 1965 intervention in the Dominican Republic was unambiguously a crisis. The Johnson administration was caught flat-footed, with about half of the key Embassy staff out of the Dominican Republic at the time of the crisis. There was a surprise insurrection, the existing Dominican regime turned out to be surprisingly weak, and U.S. policy makers had no prior intentions or particular desire to intervene.

Events in the Dominican Republic were not immediately considered a crisis, because there was very little initial perception of threat. Even after events occurred that clearly constituted a crisis in the perception of those in the Dominican Republic (and to historians), that perception was not shared in Washington. During the middle of the first phase of the crisis, President Johnson announced that he would leave Washington for a long weekend at his ranch, clearly something he would not do if he perceived the situation to be a crisis or if vital interests might be at stake (perceptions in Washington did change, and LBJ did not make it to the ranch that weekend). According to the presidential daily diary, Johnson was involved very little until quite late in the process, when he was called on to consider a military intervention. By that time, the troops were already in the area, and quite a few steps toward intervention had already been taken. Once the crisis was acknowledged and the uncertainty of the outcome in the Dominican Republic became apparent in Washington, the president gave the situation his fullest attention. The perceived danger to American citizens and the threat of "another Cuba" during the Cold War gave the crisis utmost gravity.

> In fact, by the time he made his Sunday TV report his office log showed he had held 86 conferences with Bundy, 31 with McNamara, 15 with Rusk, and 52 larger meetings, with three or more officials present, during the first nine days of the Dominican crisis. Characteristically, he had also been on the phone 225 times to discuss the situation.[12]

Grenada

On Sunday, October 25, 1983, U.S. forces invaded Grenada, putting an end, once and for all, to the popular revolutionary government begun in 1979. The situation that became the Grenada crisis started on October 12, with a falling-out between ministers of Grenada's PRG (People's Revolutionary Government), leading to the resignation of the deputy prime minister. Over the next several days, the disagreement and factionalism increased. Things came to a head on October 19, when, after being released from house arrest by a citizen crowd, Grenadan Prime Minister Maurice Bishop and several resigned PRG ministers were publicly executed by Grenadan military forces.

The Department of State had been monitoring the situation since October 13, but did not consider it a crisis until the Bishop assassination on October 19. Constantine C. Menges, recently arrived in the office of the National Security Advisor, had taken an interest on October 14 and had mobilized some planners on both the military and the diplomatic side in case the situation changed and action became possible and preferable. Once the situation deteriorated on October 19, these protoplans rapidly gained steam, with Menges remaining an advocate. On Grenada, martial law was declared, followed shortly by the declaration of a new government. By October 24, things on the island had returned to a semblance of normalcy, with curfews lifted, and an estimated 70 percent of the population returned to work. On October 23, President Reagan had signed the final orders, and on October 25, ostensibly to protect the lives of approximately 1,000 U.S. medical students on the island, U.S. forces invaded.

The Grenada intervention consisted primarily of two stages. In a precrisis stage, information moved through the bureaucracy, the situation was monitored, and plans were prepared in case an opportunity to be rid of the leftist government of Grenada presented itself. This was followed by a crisis phase in which the planning was completed, the possibilities and their justifications discussed, and the decision to intervene taken.

The extent to which Grenada in 1983 was a crisis is slightly more ambiguous than the Dominican Republic. Some might argue that the decisional process began considerably earlier than Grenadan Prime Minister Maurice Bishop's arrest in October 1983, perhaps when Reagan began posturing against the tiny nation in March 1983,[13] or earlier still, during the U.S. Navy's Ocean Venture '81 Operation Amber and the Amberdines in 1981. Several facts lead me to discard this notion. First is the difference between premeditation and contingency planning. The U.S. government maintains a wide range of contingency plans. Second, while Reagan was certainly glad to be rid of the leftist PRG, the decision was contingent. The decision makers considered other responses or a total lack of response. Third, the situation was time pressing. The Grenada government was toppled, people were assassinated, there was chaos and uncertainty. Had American hostages been taken, it would have been too late; had the situation calmed and a new regime emerged and legitimized itself, the window of opportunity to stage an intervention would have closed. Finally, the poor preparedness of the troops executing the invasion in terms of intelligence about the island suggests strongly against premeditation. None of the troops involved in Operation Amber and the Amberdines participated in the 1983 landing. Most of the troops involved were diverted from reinforcements to the marine contingent in Lebanon. Most telling is the fact that the map lockers on the ships used to carry the invasion force did not contain maps of Grenada. Maps had to be faxed and reproduced, and many soldiers were forced to rely on tourist maps procured after landing. Poor map quality led to several near disasters and the bombing of a mental hospital during the intervention.[14] The decision to intervene in Grenada might easily be considered *opportunism,* but it was not premeditated.

Panama

While U.S. relations with Panamanian dictator Manuel Noriega had soured through the 1980s to the point where a considerable amount of diplomatic activity sought his retirement and a U.S. federal court indicted him on drug charges, it was not until President George H.W. Bush took office in 1989 that the military option for his removal seriously came onto the decisional plate. Throughout 1989, tensions increased and, behind the scenes, preparations were made for military intervention. Finally, in December 1989 a series of events at a Panama City roadblock (including the shooting of a U.S. soldier and the detention and harassment of a naval officer and his wife) served as sufficient provocation to launch the intervention, which began on December 22.

This rather lengthy decisional process passed through several stages. First was the atomized stage, during the early Reagan presidency, when some government agencies wanted Noriega to retire and others did not. This was followed by an "agreement of ends if not means" phase, where all agencies had Noriega's departure as a goal, but different agencies pursued different tactics in an uncoordinated fashion; in this phase, there was not sufficient consensus to consider a military solution. In the next phase, which began with Bush's inauguration, there was agreement on ends and means. Concurrent with this phase was the planning and preparation phase, lasting more than six months and taking place almost entirely within the military hierarchy. Finally, the decisional process entered a "ready to go" phase, where intervention plans were prepared and rehearsed, there was agreement that Noriega needed to go, that the military option was best, and all that was required was a sufficient trigger or catalyst to actually launch the intervention.

While several scholars discuss Panama as a crisis, I doubt any of them would deny that it was premeditated.[15] The many months of specific planning, the replacement of the commander of U.S. troops in Panama with an "action" general, and the memoirs of decision participants make the premeditation very clear.[16]

Haiti

The Haitian "crisis," as it is referred to in the literature on the topic (though clearly not a crisis by the definition in use here), began with the September 29, 1991, coup overthrowing democratically elected Haitian President Jean-Bertrand Aristide, almost three full years prior to the U.S. military intervention on September 19, 1994.[17] This three-year period constituted the decision space for the intervention. The process spanned two presidential administrations and, unlike any of the other cases discussed here, was publicly considered, discussed, and announced prior to the intervention's execution.

The decisional process passed through several distinct phases. The first phase was the "path of least resistance" phase, in which the Bush administration decided not to recognize the new Haitian junta and to support the return of Aristide to Haiti through the imposition of sanctions on Haiti. This phase included summary repatriation of Haitians fleeing the country when the flood of refugees became a burden on the U.S. Immigration and Naturalization Service's ability to process their applications and a burden on south Florida, where most of them landed. Despite promises to the contrary, this phase continued into the Clinton administration, where there were, initially, almost no changes in policy. The decisional process entered its second major phase when massive public pressure brought to bear by Aristide, the Congressional Black Caucus, and a number of their allies forced the Clinton administration to reconsider policy. In this second phase, the administration changed the refugee policy, increased sanctions (several times), and made more intense diplomatic efforts to force a resolution of the situation. The failure of the seemingly successful Governors Island Accord, which would have returned Aristide to power, ushered in the third stage of the decisional process, which included active planning for a military intervention and more aggressive posturing against the Haitian rulers by U.S. representatives. This third stage included obvious public preparations of intervention forces to make the U.S. commitment clear to Haitian leaders. The fourth and final phase of the decisional process was very short, lasting only a few days. Just before launching an invasion to restore Aristide, President Clinton allowed an 11th-hour diplomatic mission, headed by former President Jimmy Carter, to make a final attempt at a negotiated return for Aristide. The success of this mission resulted in a permissive entry intervention, rather than the opposed invasion that had been the intended contingency right up until that final diplomatic effort.

Haiti, again, discursively labeled "crisis" in many arenas, was clearly premeditated (perhaps in certain circles "crisis" is synonymous with "persistently annoying to the president and demanding of his attention"). Unlike Panama, the Haiti intervention was clearly one that the decision makers were none too keen on. In decision-maker memoirs and accounts of the decision to invade Panama, decision makers evinced frustration at the failure of other means to achieve Noriega's removal and a desire to go in and get rid of him. Conversely, in the case of Haiti, decision makers were frustrated at the failure of other means to restore the constitutional president of Haiti and were more frustrated at the exhaustion of all potentially effective means other than the unattractive last resort of military intervention.

ANALYSIS

Having introduced the central propositions of the chapter and provided a summary of the general characteristics of the decisional processes of the cases themselves, I now turn to analysis. In the sections that follow I frame and discuss the arguments of the chapter with evidence and examples from the case studies. I discuss the impact of primary characteristics, the role of the bureaucracy, and the role of contingency, in turn.

Case Characters

As I have argued, the level of secrecy of an intervention decision interacts with the crisis or premeditatedness of the intervention to provide its general character. If put in a simple grid (see Figure 5.2), a case can be quickly schematized by its location on the dimensions of these two primary characteristics.

Figure 5.2 situates the four cases at hand on a grid formed by the intersection of secret vs. public and crisis vs. premeditated. The axes are meant to represent the possibility of continuous variation from completely secret to totally public on the vertical axis and completely urgent crisis to totally premeditated on the horizontal axis; thus the cases do not fall perfectly in the center of the grid defined by dichotomizing the two dimensions.

Reading left to right around the grid of Figure 5.2 leads first to the 1983 Grenada intervention. This is the classic secret crisis military intervention: There was political instability in a country clearly within the U.S. sphere of influence, the situation was uncertain, and, arguably, American lives were in danger. Acting quickly (as the crisis nature of the situation demanded) and in secret (to prevent threat to the very lives they intended to save, and for the tactical advantage inherent in surprise), decision makers sent in U.S. forces. The efforts made to keep the intervention (or even its consideration) secret were considerable. Decision makers met in odd rooms (rather than designated crisis planning areas) at odd times, often arriving through different entrances to disguise the gravity of their conversations; in order to protect OPSEC the president and the secretary of state went on their planned trip to play golf, even while troops were steaming toward Grenada.[18]

This type of intervention decision follows the process-based limits inherent in crisis (as discussed above) and also has the characteristics of secrecy: namely, a limited sphere of persons are included, so potentially valuable expertise or input may not be included, *but* the sphere of participants is limited, so that influence from parties possibly opposed to intervention is avoided. By keeping the process out of the public

	Crisis	Premeditated
Secret	**Grenada**	**Panama**
Public	**Dominican Republic**	**Haiti**

Figure 5.2 Intervention Characters

eye, secrecy completely deprives any potentially interested actors of the opportunity to participate.

Continuing around Figure 5.2 leads to the Panama invasion of 1989. Here is the classic secret premeditated intervention. Plans were laid months ahead of time, troops were trained in secret, and some were smuggled stealthily (on civilian aircraft and out of uniform) into the target country well in advance. Intentions were kept secret because of the immense tactical advantages of surprise, the necessity of taking the dictator, Manuel Noriega, unaware, and to protect Americans resident in Panama from anticipatory reprisals. Additionally, secrecy had its usual benefit of preventing criticism of policy from elsewhere within the polity, or from other countries (at least before the intervention). The central tensions of a premeditated secret intervention remain the imperatives of secrecy (if secrecy is violated, there is likely to be plenty of time for other interested actors to mobilize and attempt to participate in the decision), and the actual timing of the intervention, once all is in readiness.

The 1965 intervention in the Dominican Republic was "public crisis." It was common knowledge (printed in the *New York Times* on April 27, 1965) that the USS *Boxer,* with her Amphibious Ready Group, was in the area of the Dominican Republic and available to intervene should the president decide that it was necessary to do so. As the situation deteriorated, troops from the USS *Boxer* went in to help resolve the crisis. While there was no real attempt at secrecy, there was no attempt to engage a public policy debate on the matter. In this case (and, in general, I would argue), the crisis characteristic overwhelms the public nature of the intervention. There was simply insufficient time for partially informed publics to participate. The question remains to what extent that "insufficient time" was a product of the technology and pace of policy making in 1965. Current developments in communications technology and the increased speed of information flow might reduce the temporal limits to public participation in crises. Whether this possibility will change the character of public crisis decision making or simply force decision makers to make sure that all crisis decisions are made in secret remains to be seen.

Finally, the unacceptable situation in Haiti began with the September 29, 1991, coup overthrowing democratically elected Haitian President Jean-Bertrand Aristide, almost three full years prior to the publicly premeditated U.S. military intervention. The process spanned two presidential administrations, and, unlike any of the other cases, was extensively considered, discussed, and publicly announced prior to the intervention's execution. The lack of secrecy and the duration of the premeditation opened this decision process up to full public scrutiny and participation, which totally changed the character of the process relative to the other interventions.

Process and Bureaucracy

Having made the general character of each intervention case clear, I now turn to the decisional processes that took place within the context of each of those characters. The analysis in this section considers who the decision makers *are,* along with the character and quality of their participation. I find several discernible levels and types of participants, each with different sets of roles in the process and constraints on their decisions.

Players/Participants

Who are "the decision makers"? Who, or what levels in the bureaucracy, actually participates? Several studies have assumed that the relevant actors in foreign policy decision making (for the United States) are the officers of the White House and the Department of State.[19] A RAND Corporation study in the 1990s found that the identities of intervention decision participants is fairly stable (the president, various cabinet members, and a subset of top Pentagon officials), which is in keeping with the common sense expectation of a core group of decision makers.[20] My findings based on these cases are consonant with the notion of the "core decision makers" being the president and his immediate advisors—those who are responsible for the decisions made and will be held accountable for them. I also find, however, that, even in crisis situations, many consequential decisions were taken by persons clearly *not* in the group of central decision makers.

Top level

Who are the core or "top-level" decision makers? "President and main advisors" is *precise,* if not *specific.* As the aforementioned RAND study finds, it is a *rather* stable group, but the exact constellation will depend on circumstance and on the preferences of the sitting president.[21] Consider the impact on the structure of decision making that the institution of the American presidency has; the president, as the final authority in these cases, chooses (subject to congressional approval) who his cabinet members and department heads will be, who his informal advisors will be, and which of them he will consult with on any given issue. In all four of the cases considered the president, the secretary of state, the national security advisor (or equivalent), the secretary of defense, the chairman of the joint chiefs of staff, the director of the CIA, and the vice president were involved in the decisional processes. Additionally, there were always some "second tier" department officers involved. In all four cases, at least one deputy or under secretary from the Department of State and/or the Department of Defense was involved (usually a handful from the Department of State). Additionally, in each case there were a number of regional specialists, both from the Department of State and from inside the White House whose specific portfolio the intervention country fell into. Finally, there were the other important members of the president's staff, the chief of staff and his various friends and personal advisors.

Home

Where to draw the line between top-level and the rest of the organizational staff is somewhat difficult. I draw the line empirically: top-level decision makers regularly attended decisional (as separable from planning) meetings in the White House.

Everyone else was a "lower-level" participant, if they were a participant at all. These lower-level participants were numerous. An easier distinction to make is the difference between the "home" bureaucracy and the "in-country" bureaucracy. This is the simple and important difference between those in Washington, D.C., and those in the country in which the intervention took place.

If under secretaries of state and defense are second tier but still "top" decision makers, then some of the most important decision contributors are the "third-tier" and "fourth-tier" home bureaucrats[22]: such people as Constantine C. Menges, the recently arrived National Security Council Advisor who first initiated planning for the 1983 Grenada intervention and was instrumental in making it a viable possibility,[23] and Harry W. Shlaudeman, the Dominican Desk Man at the Department of State during the Dominican crisis of 1965, whose successfully completed duty it was to bring the developing crisis to the attention of the deputy secretary of state. While Shlaudeman was certainly below fourth tier and never got to go to any White House meetings during the crisis, Menges worked in the White House and was involved in numerous crisis planning and a variety of interdepartmental meetings. He was not in the proper "decisional loop" and his specific personal advice was not asked for by the president. Conventional construction of core decision makers would exclude Menges, though his role in the Grenada process was considerable (at least in his account of events).[24]

The relevant home bureaucracy includes everyone who was not a core decision maker but *was* involved in the process, either as a planner, a briefing writer, a background consultant, a knowledgable regional informant, or a member of a relevant chain of command or line of communication in the Department of State or the White House. These involvements *tend* to be from within the departments of the executive branch and the military (except in the notable case of Haiti, with its full public participation). The Department of State and the White House contribute the most participants, followed by Department of Defense, and also including the CIA (Central Intelligence Agency), and occasionally staff or chiefs from other cabinet posts.

In Country

The in-country bureaucracy includes process participants in the country of intervention and includes the relevant staff in countries near to the country invaded, where they play a role (such as the U.S. Ambassador to Barbados in 1983, since the United States had committed no ambassador to Grenada at that time). Depending on the situation, the in-country bureaucracy can make almost no contribution at all (as happened in the Grenada case), can be important sources of information for decision makers (the usual case), or can practically single handedly determine the course of U.S. policy (as was arguably the case in the 1965 Dominican Republic intervention).

The in-country bureaucracy includes the ambassador, as well as his support staff, if they participate (because of the ambassador's initial absence, a chargé d'affaires played a significant role in the Dominican crisis of 1965). In-country participants can also include CIA operatives and officers, various military liaison staff (or, in the case of Panama, entire armies), and the directors of various U.S.–sponsored humanitarian efforts. Conceivably anyone who works out of or reports to the U.S. Embassy can provide information, either through observation or through his or her contacts, that could impact the decisional process (or they could fail to do so, which could also impact the process).

Consensus/Dissensus

Since there are potential decision participants at several levels and in several possible locales, their collective ability and willingness to pursue singular policy goals can have a huge impact on how decision making proceeds and on the ultimate outcome. One of the features of American constitutional government is the balanced "separation of powers" or, as Neustadt more accurately describes it, "a government of separated institutions *sharing* powers."[25] A major factor in decisional processes is the extent of consensus or dissensus among the relevant organizations about policy goals and appropriate courses of action. While I have pointed out the president's very personalist impact on the structure of the decisional process, strong disagreements among those with whom the president has chosen to consult could (and should) give him pause. The president is accountable and responsible for the decisions reached, but he is also responsible for getting good advice and reaching decisions that serve the national interest. Lack of consensus can impede the implementation of policy, even if the president has made a decision (see "Contingency of Execution" in what follows) and can damage the legitimacy of a decision (see Chapter 7 on legitimacy).

Crisis and crisis response tend to increase consensus for several reasons. First, the usual secrecy and the short time to respond decreases the opportunity for groups or organizations outside of the core decision makers (such as congressional leaders) to participate. If you are not involved, your agreement becomes less important. Second is the oft noted "rally to the flag" effect,[26] where, in the name of patriotism and support for the home team, criticism and disagreement are quashed, at least for a while (and forever if things go well).

Even in crisis, interagency conflict can have an impact, as evinced by the concern expressed by top decision makers. In several of the decision-maker memoirs of Grenada decision participants, they recall concerns of resistance from the Pentagon, or military "foot dragging."[27] For that same case, NSC's Menges recalls his concern that the Department of State would not advocate intervention and his pleasure when Secretary of State George P. Shultz turned out to be an intervention booster.[28]

For non-crisis cases, consensus is even harder to assure, and can immensely complicate the decisional process. The premeditation of an invasion of Panama could not even begin until all the relevant U.S. agencies agreed that Noriega's ouster was a goal. In the Haiti process, the skirmishing between Congress and the White House over the legality of a Haitian invasion without congressional permission, and the conflict within the core group of decision makers over the wisdom of sending former President

Carter and his 11th-hour diplomatic mission (Deputy Secretary of State Strobe Talbott argued so strenuously against sending Carter to Haiti that "his eyes were bulging out of his head"[29]), are examples of how consequential dissensus can be.

Locus of Decisions

Formally all intervention decisions are taken in the White House. However, when one considers the fact that an intervention decisional process actually consists of numerous subdecisions in addition to the actual final decision to "go," the locus of decisions becomes less obvious.

At different stages in the decisional process, the general locus of decision is in different places. In a crisis, the locus of decision is first in country. What is happening? When does it constitute a crisis? How will it be reported? Which level of urgency will be used to report it? (National security cables are labeled by priority: CRITIC, FLASH, IMMEDIATE, PRIORITY, or ROUTINE). Once the informational cat is out of the bag, the locus of decision usually moves to the Washington desk officer in the Department of State who is first informed. That individual then decides, based on the information he/she has received and his/her own perception, when and how to pass the information up the hierarchy. In an obviously critical crisis, the locus of decision can rest here for a very short time before moving up.

Once the crisis reaches the organizational heads, the locus of major decision is clearly planted in the White House; however, while major and final decisions will be taken by the president and other core decision makers, there are still immediate situations in the crisis country that may require the in-country staff to make a snap decision; there are still immense information flows that are distilled by lower functionaries before passing on to the core decision makers. While these lower-level decisions may seem likely to be inconsequential, empirical reality indicates otherwise (see the later section on "Contingency").

In a premeditated intervention, defining the beginning of the decisional process can be difficult, so identifying the initial locus of decision can, too. The collection of information and reporting decisions that ultimately raise the salience of events in the target country for the president and his core decision makers are fairly nebulous and difficult to pin down for a premeditated intervention, but suggest a diffuse initial locus of decision depending on the baseline salience of the country and events in question. For example, if events are all over the news, then the top decision makers begin right away to decide for themselves how they might consider responding. If, on the other hand, events occur out of the public eye, then lower-level bureaucrats perform their assigned filtering function and pass information up the hierarchy that may or may not increase salience for higher-level decision makers.

When a clear beginning to a premeditated intervention decisional process is discernible, the locus of the decision is at the top. Salience to top-level decision makers is sufficiently high, and the president orders intervention plans or requests commencement of contingency planning. Then, while plans are being drawn up, the locus of decision passes into the military bureaucracy and into the hands of diplomats pursuing other policy options. Finally, before the premeditated intervention can be launched, decision making returns to the top, as the president must evaluate the plans that have been prepared for him and decide when and if to put them into use.

Military Bureaucracy

Because of this strange and special relationship between military plans and civilian decision makers, the military planning bureaucracy deserves some special attention. The military bureaucracy is in its own separate hierarchy and has procedures and institutional arrangements somewhat different from other government agencies.

"Joint doctrine calls for the development of 'deliberate plans' for use against specific, identified threats to U.S. national interests, and the construction of 'crisis action plans' when an unanticipated situation arises that may require employment of U.S. forces."[30]

Military contingency plans (the umbrella term for both deliberate plans and crisis action plans) are developed by joint planning groups, consisting mostly of colonels (or equivalent) and their staffs, reviewed by appropriate generals or admirals, from "joint" groups representing all of the major services (each planning group may not have members from all the service branches, but operations are considered joint, or "purple," nonetheless).

The important fact about these plans in terms of process is that they do not and cannot be finalized overnight. Deliberate plans can easily take upwards of six months to fully develop. While planning could be accelerated, it would be nearly impossible to fully develop a plan for a ground troops military intervention in the limited time frame of a crisis. When the military option comes onto the decisional table during a crisis, the plans are most likely existing contingency plans, either already designed to be specific to that country and situation or plans generic to a situation or region that have been at most partially modified. The lack of preexisting plans could be a serious impediment to intervention. The further the operation required deviates from existing and rehearsed plans, the more likely errors in execution will be, and the knowledge of this fact will lead to serious apprehension on the part of military decision makers, which should impact all core decision makers. If the military (secretary of defense and chairman of the joint chiefs of staff) indicates that a certain intervention is not possible, unlikely to be executed successfully, or likely to result in unacceptable American casualties, it is a "showstopper"; the decisional process is pretty much over, unless goals are brought in line with military capability or time is allowed for further military planning and preparation.

In all four cases considered here, there were either reasonably proximate existing plans or abundant time to develop new plans. Note also that in all cases the military forces potentially in opposition to the intervention were virtually negligible relative to U.S. military might, excepting Panama, where the PDF (Panamanian Defense Force) might have been considered "marginal" relative to U.S. forces. In that case, the invasion took place at night, maximizing surprise and technological differences between the forces (since U.S. forces had night-vision capability) and took place with truly overwhelming U.S. forces.

Planning

One of the constraints in a premeditated intervention is certainly the military planning. No excuses for poor performance are acceptable in an intervention that was planned well in advance, so plans need to be complete, tight, and their execution well rehearsed, all of which take time. Historical scholar John R. Ballard provides a detailed account of the steps the plans for the Haiti intervention went through, including the careful and quiet planning of a number of different Haiti interventions (both permissive and nonpermissive) that were being planned before the administration had formally decided to consider a military intervention.[31] The account of the decisional process for the Panama invasion by Bob Woodward details the various rounds of revisions made to existing plans after intervention premeditation began, the changes made in the military structure (the replacement of the commander of SOUTHCOM (Southern Command), the forces in Panama, and the assignment of additional troops to the area), and the extensive rehearsals that took place before plans were "ready to go" and the invasion could be launched when the core decision makers deemed the time right.[32]

Contingency

Contingencies of both kinds (capricious and predictable but not predicted) played important roles in the cases discussed here. While little can be done about the truly random events, decision makers and decision analysts stand to gain considerably through awareness of contingencies that stem for bureaucratic behavior in general, and the behavior of individual bureaucrats. This section discusses the various forms of contingency observed in the cases and some of their consequences.

Lower-Level Contingency

The lead quote of this chapter is former Secretary of State Dean Acheson's observation that "one fact is clear to anyone with experience in government: the springs of policy bubble up, they do not trickle down."[33] This is a clear acknowledgment that the actions and decisions made lower down in the hierarchy affect policy outcomes. Lower- and middle-level bureaucrats constantly confront a tension between doing what are ostensibly their jobs and the fact that their jobs are delegated from higher authorities and that those higher authorities will be held responsible if something goes horribly awry. The very decision of what constitutes a routine occurrence that a bureaucrat can handle himself or herself and what constitutes a crisis or potential crisis that requires either notification of, or consultation with, a superior is a potentially consequential and *contingent* decision. Bureaucrats often find themselves placed in positions where they get to make these decisions only if they have repeatedly demonstrated discretion and good judgment in the past, so it is usually the case that things move up the hierarchy in the way one would want them to, but it is not necessarily so. These decisions are not random (capricious contingent) but are made intentionally by (mostly) rational individuals with the information available to them and *in accordance with their own world views.* The fact that these bureaucrats are individuals with different sets of life experiences, backgrounds, social networks, and personalities makes the decisions they make seem to be contingent (and affect the decisional process as if they were) even if they are perfectly understandable given good information about that specific individual. Lower-level bureaucrats create or constrain contingency in several significant ways, each discussed in a major subsection, below. They include the general constraint of options inherent in normal operation, contingency of execution, and caprice or "cock-up."

General Constraint of Options Inherent in Normal Operation

Political scientists Ole Holsti makes this observation about the flow of information in an organization operating normally:

> Information normally enters the organization at middle levels or lower, and the need to reduce it to a manageable quantity as it flows upward may result in qualitative distortions arising both from motivated and unmotivated biases. Incoming information may be filtered through and fitted into existing images, preconceptions, preferences, expectations, and plans. Officials may screen out some data adverse to their own interests and magnify others that are favorable; information may also be distorted by a tendency to make it reflect, more closely than reality warrants, what superiors are believed to want to hear. Aside from these more or less deliberate distortions, the taller the organizational hierarchy, the greater the "uncertainty absorption" as information moves upward.[34]

Even when maximum care is taken to place decisional power at the top of the hierarchy, constraints develop in the course of normal operations. Planners and contingency preparation staff can be asked to consider only so many options. If asked to present a range of options, planners will choose a reasonable subset and develop them sufficiently for presentation. In many respects, this makes decision making possible. Decision makers cannot consider *every* possible response to a situation in any detail and make any progress. Once the number of options under consideration reaches a reasonable number, decision makers can seriously weigh and assess them and ultimately make a choice. While one would imagine that the top-level decision makers make those initial choices of options to consider, it is not always the case. Or, more likely, top decision makers make a broad selection of options, such as "intervention, with such-and-such primary objectives," and then lower-level planners will make the next several rounds of constraining decisions.

A case in point: for the premeditated intervention of Panama, President Bush decided he wanted to have the military option on the decisional plate. Several high-level military men, including Chairman of the Joint Chiefs of Staff (JCS) Colin Powell and new Commander of SOUTHCOM Maxwell Thurman, took an interest in planning. They employed a number of lower-level (relative to top-level decision makers; still colonels and majors) military planners in Panama and in the United States to revise existing plans, plans codenamed Blue Spoon. Serious revisions took place, and the final Blue Spoon plans were tighter plans, with better integrated communication codes, and a shorter lead time for deployment and preparation. The plans included a rescue for a captured CIA operative held in a Panamanian jail, a variety of snatch and capture options for Noriega, the target dictator, at most of the places he frequented, and a large number of coordinated strikes to eliminate the effectiveness of the PDF.[35] When the president broadly requested intervention plans, the generals narrowed the field some, and then detailed planners narrowed the range of choices of military operations quite a bit more.

When the harassment of a naval lieutenant and his wife at a Panama City roadblock occurred, which ultimately served as the trigger event for the U.S. invasion, General Thurman relayed to the president (via the chair of the JCS) the options he saw at that time: The first was to do nothing, just protest. The second was to execute some part of the Blue Spoon plans. The third, and his recommendation, was the full execution of Operation Blue Spoon.[36] In fact, because of the integrated nature of the plans and the "structured contingencies" already realized, the only real options facing the president were to do nothing or to intervene with the full plan.

Contingency of Execution

Another important role for lower-level decision participants is as the executors of decisions reached during the decisional process. Again, here I refer to process decisions other than "the decision"; once the decision to launch the intervention is reached, the decisional process stops. The process contains a host of subdecisions regarding information transition, information request, planning, choices of options, communication with other countries, and preparedness. All of these subdecisions that require some action to fulfill might be contingent in their execution.[37]

Some of this contingency has to do with competence or willingness on the part of the participants, some with politics. As Neustadt notes, "If the President's decisions are not put in writing and then guarded by his White House watchmen, his intentions may be warped or even lost."[38] For example, during the long decisional process for Haiti, Walter B. Slocombe, the Deputy Under Secretary of Defense for Policy, boasted at a party that by turning back the USS *Harlan County* (a ship loaded with lightly armed Canadian and American military engineers, sent to Haiti to do some construction and help professionalize the Haitian military after the Governors Island Accord, which would have, if adhered to, restored Aristide to the presidency), he had helped save the United States from a "small war." He said that "the Pentagon would not risk American soldiers' lives to put 'that psychopath' back in power."[39] The failure of the USS *Harlan County* mission is one example of contingency in execution; Slocombe's failure to subscribe to administration policy goals is another.

Some outcomes are contingent because they involve participants outside the nominal hierarchy of the U.S. government. During Haitian President Aristide's exile, a compromise plan popular among U.S. top decision makers put forward by Haitian

Prime Minister Robert Malval failed because Aristide would not compromise at all.[40] Indeed, neither the invasion of Panama nor Haiti would have needed to take place had diplomatic initiatives to remove Noriega or restore Aristide been successful.

Some contingencies do not stem from poor or faithless execution, or from the intransigency of persons outside of the decision-making hierarchy, but because they are genuinely, intrinsically contingent (capricious contingent). Another account provides an example in the 11th-hour Carter mission to Haiti, that arranged for the intervention to be permissive:

> Whether it was appreciated or not, the Carter mission to Haiti may have saved Clinton's presidency. It was clear from the Haitian military leaders' action that they had prepared to resist the U.S. Invasion. It was only through the breakthrough with Yannick Cedras that finally convinced General Cedras that stepping down was the right course of action. Had the United States fought their way into Haiti, there would in all likelihood have been U.S. casualties. And there was little doubt that Congress, having been denied an opportunity to vote on intervention, would have taken it out on the administration.[41]

The "breakthrough" with Cédras's wife was partially contingent on Carter's effective personal style and could conceivably have gone differently with a different diplomat, or even a few different conversational choices.

Caprice or Cock-up

Historical sociologist Michael Mann identifies a residual theory of the state, which he labels "foul-up" or cock-up theory.[42] This position, generalized to the cases at hand, suggests that many of the things that happen during decision processes are in keeping with no one's intentions; they are mistakes, or results of caprice, or simply random. Even when a decision made by a lower-level functionary makes sense given that individual's personal history and the information available to them, the ultimate outcome of that act may not be anything that he/she (or anyone else) intended.

For example, at the beginning of the Dominican Republic crisis of 1965, the ambassador was out of the country. Ambassador William Tapley Bennett, Jr. was not the only member of the U.S. Embassy "country team" who was out of the country: USAID (United States Agency for International Development) Mission Director Carter Ide, Public Safety Advisor Anthony Ruiz, and 11 of the 13 Military Assistance Advisory Group officers were also out of the Dominican Republic.[43] The ambassador's absence was actually in part because the Department of State took events in the Dominican Republic seriously; Bennett had been called to Washington for high-level consultations, an unforeseeable error in timing.

Also during the Dominican crisis, U.S. intervention might have been avoided had more and earlier support been given to the forces of the favored "junta to be." One of the factors impeding the progress of these "antirebels" was poor communications. Ambassador Bennett (after his return to the Dominican Republic) realized that the military outcome was very much in question and that improved communications would help. He requested walkie-talkie radios for the anti-rebel forces.[44] The Department of State's negative response to Bennett's initial request for radios illustrates the lag of appreciation of events between the U.S. Embassy in Santo Domingo and Washington. This failure to intervene more mildly earlier, coupled with several missed diplomatic opportunities, resulted in the massive military intervention.

"Ambassadorial Autonomy"

One the most remarkable findings of this book is the considerable role the in-country bureaucracy played in several of these interventions. While I expected to find participants below the level of the core decision makers making a contribution, and my examination of the in-country bureaucracy showed the constraint of options inherent in day-to-day operations and contingencies generated and realized by lower-level bureaucrats, I was still surprised by the nearly determinant role played by the Ambassador to the Dominican Republic during the crisis there in 1965. Not only was the U.S. Embassy virtually the only source of information, but also virtually the only resource for launching policy other than intervention (i.e., any attempts to diffuse or resolve the crisis diplomatically).

President Johnson notes in his memoir, "It has been argued with hindsight that Ambassador Bennett should have tried to negotiate a settlement on the afternoon of April 27. It was a decision the ambassador had to make on his own, since there was no time for consultation with Washington."[45] The list of decisions the ambassador "had" to make on his own or *chose* to make on his own goes on and on. Most noteworthy, and most exemplary of this kind of autonomy, is the actual decision to intervene. Once it became clear to him that the antirebel forces were not likely to prevail, Ambassador Bennett urged intervention in a CRITC cable.[46] Almost immediately after sending this cable, Bennett contacted the commander of the Caribbean Ready Group (aboard the USS *Boxer*) and requested helicopters to pick up American evacuees and to augment the marine guard at the Embassy by a platoon. Consequently, intervention marines were en route before the critical cable requesting intervention had even reached President Johnson's desk. The time lag is considerable and noteworthy. While the president could have rejected the ambassador's advice and recalled the marines, he did not. He indicated in a public statement that "on Wednesday afternoon, there was no longer any choice for the man who is your President."[47]

Abraham F. Lowenthal's detailed history of the Dominican intervention notes that,

> The landing of additional American forces on Dominican soil had already begun, in effect, by the time President Johnson himself could consider whether the United States should intervene (although the President presumably could still have restricted these troops to an evacuation-related role at the hotel or to protection of the embassy building.)[48]

In the Grenada case, the ambassador played almost no role, certainly not a catalytic or deterministic role as in the Dominican case. However, on closer reflection, the ambassador did make an important autonomous contribution. Why did the nearby U.S. Embassy in Barbados, whose portfolio included Grenada, play almost no role in the decisional process? Because the ambassador, Milan Bish, was a hard-line anticommunist and refused to deal with leftists at all, refusing to maintain even routine contacts with the island's government, and having forbidden his staff from visiting Grenada.[49] Bish had exercised his ambassadorial autonomy *before* the decisional process and in such a way that he could not positively contribute to the process once it had begun. This situation is reminiscent of Bachrach and Baratz's notion of nondecision making.[50]

Finally, the Carter mission, which, as mentioned in a previous section, led to a permissive rather than an opposed U.S. intervention in Haiti. President Clinton let Carter go on the condition that he limit his mission to simply discussing with the military leaders the mode of their departure, and Senator Sam Nunn, a critic of the intervention, and Colin Powell went along. Clinton approved the delegation's departure for Haiti with the provision that they leave by noon on the day after their arrival (so they would be clear well before the intervention was scheduled [secretly, even to the delegation] to begin later that day).[51] Carter had been instructed to leave the country by noon, deal or no deal, and had been instructed to work toward only a limited kind of goal. Carter accomplished the most important goals, but he trammeled the imposed limitations, which was surely frustrating to the president, relieved only by Carter's success. Carter requested and received a three-hour extension, but the deal was not ultimately closed until 8 P.M., five hours after the extended departure deadline, and well after intervention aircraft were in the air and their launch was known to the Haitians, who could have, had they been inclined to, seized the envoys for hostages.[52] Admittedly, this is not as striking an autonomy as that demonstrated by Bennett in 1965. Arguably, some ambassadorial autonomy is necessary, as a diplomat trying to negotiate a resolution needs some freedom within which to actually bargain. The question remains, in this case at least, was all of the freedom to negotiate freely given by the president, or was it simply taken by the diplomat?

Several factors contribute to the possibility of ambassadorial autonomy, most of which stem from the structure of the decision-making process. The first factor is the baseline salience of the intervention country. If the country is relatively unimportant or has been "quiet" for a long time, producing no serious signature on the foreign policy radar, then the number of persons knowledgeable about current events in that country is likely low. In this situation, it makes sense to follow the ambassador's lead, as he lives there and is presumed to know what is going on. Case in point, during the Dominican crisis of 1965, there was only the Dominican desk officer and former Ambassador Martin who constituted the genuinely knowledgeable "experts" in or available to the home bureaucracy.

The level of communications technology also creates space for ambassadorial autonomy. As noted, the level of information available and the time it took to travel up the hierarchy in 1965 was considerable. An acknowledgment of the necessity of ambassadorial autonomy where information is low and communication of information is limited is implicit in the fact that President Johnson sent his best home expert on the Dominican Republic, former Ambassador John Martin, along with Ambassador Bennett to the Dominican Republic to help deal with things on that end.

The final contributor to ambassadorial autonomy again rests with the way in which the president has chosen to structure the decision. The autonomy of the Carter mission was permitted by President Clinton. The autonomy of Ambassador Bennett was supported by President Johnson. Clinton could have ordered Carter out of Haiti at any time during his negotiations, and Johnson could have kept Bennett or Martin in Washington to improve his own understanding of the situation or given specific orders for decisions to be delayed for his (Johnson's) confirmation, but he did not.

Contingency at the Highest Levels

The fact that outcomes remain contingent at the highest levels is unsurprising. In this section I discuss things that generate contingency at the highest level *other* than the merits or costs or benefits of the policy in question. Most of this extra contingency stems from the personal proclivities of the president. Neustadt discusses numerous ways in which the power of individual presidents has varied, including the ways in which they organized their staff, the attention they were inclined to give to reputation building, and other aspects that varied as a function of their personalities.[53]

The president's general inclination to discuss policy with his advisors can dramatically affect the amount of discussion that goes into an intervention decision.[54] For example, according to the presidential daily diary, President Bush had very few, and almost no extra, conversations with his advisors between December 16 and 20, 1989, that could have been regarding Panama other than the two major meetings on the topic.[55] President Johnson, on the other hand, had, as mentioned in the section on salience, earlier, an absurd number of consultations, meetings, and phone conferences regarding the Dominican Republic during the first nine days of the crisis there. Some of this variation has to do with the differences of the two situations, but most of it is accounted for by the difference between the two men.

Presidential feelings also exist as an animus in the other decision makers in the administration. President Reagan had taken an immediate dislike to the Grenadan regime on taking office and had publicly postured against the tiny nation and the possible military uses of the airport they were building in a speech in early 1983. Constantine C. Menges referred specifically to Reagan's known dislike of that regime and to his own position as a "Reaganite" in the administration as important contributors to his initial encouragement of giving serious consideration and planning to intervention.[56]

President Bush's personal dislike of Noriega may have been catalytic in beginning the premeditation for the Panama invasion. Knowledge of that antipathy certainly made military planners and chiefs believe that military action was not just a possibility, but a likely possibility, and encouraged a level of preparation consonant with that likelihood. Adm. William J. Crowe told senior members of the joint staff after Bush's inauguration, "I don't know when it's going to happen, I don't know what's going to precipitate it, but I am convinced that we are going to have to go in with military force into Panama to resolve the situation, and we need to be ready to do it."[57]

Probably the most well-studied aspect of high -evel contingency is the impact of cabinet organization and ground rules. The most famous study of cabinet interaction is Irving L. Janis's "Groupthink" study. Janis himself summarizes,

> The central theme of my analysis can be summarized in this generalization, which I offer in the spirit of Parkinson's laws: The more amiability and esprit de corps among members of a policy-making in-group, the greater the danger that independent critical thinking will be replaced by groupthink, which is likely to result in irrational and dehumanizing actions directed against out-groups.[58]

Numerous other authors agree that the organization of advisory groups can impact problem solving and policy making.[59]

Of the numerous impacts the personalist presidency has on the structured contingencies of the decisional process, the cabinet is the most striking example. The president determines not only who all of the cabinet advisors will be, but how much he will consult with them, how the consultations will be organized, what weight he will give to their advice, and what level of disagreement he will tolerate or demand. Political scientist Steven B. Redd has confirmed with experimental evidence that the relative importance of advisors and the order in which they offer their advice can affect foreign policy decisional outcomes.[60]

The cases at hand offer a few examples. During the buildup to the Panama invasion in 1989, immediately prior to the attempted and failed "flaky" Panamanian coup attempt in October, the president met with his chief advisors to discuss the possibility of supporting the planned coup. In his memoir, Chairman of the Joint Chiefs Colin Powell recalls this about the meeting:

> This was my first opportunity to see the Bush team in action, and I was surprised that critical deliberations were taking place with no preparation or follow-up planned. The PRG system that Frank Carlucci and I had created had been dismantled by the new team. Brent Scowcroft, a sharp player, later diagnosed the problem and re-imposed order be reincarnating the PRG as a Deputies Committee, chaired by Bob Gates, his deputy. But all this was in the future. On this day, the Oval office debate was a free-swinging affair, and the freest swinger of all was the President's Chief of Staff, John Sununu. Sununu did not suffer fools gladly, or smart folks either, for that matter. He cut people off in midsentence and pursued his pet tangents, a behavior, I noticed which did not seem to bother the President. Bush listened, spoke little, and made sense when he did talk. . . .[61]

Another example stems for Constantine C. Menges's experiences in trying to be a decision participant during the 1983 Grenada crisis. At that time, the bureaucratic structure of the "restricted interagency group" left the bureaucrats at the Department of State with the responsibility (but not obligation) to include all relevant persons. In practice, this often led to the exclusion of those who were not likely to follow the Department of State line. Menges managed, through his personal connections, to stay apprised of the content of meetings he was not invited to and to continue to advocate intervention.[62]

These have been just a few examples of the way in which a president's personal proclivities can affect the structure of decision making and the decisions themselves. Other important presidential preferences that might influence the decisional process might include the value the president places on consensus and how much the president values (or takes into consideration) public opinion.

Salience/Presidential Attention

One factor that impacts intervention decision-making processes regardless of the general character of the intervention is the salience of the country to be invaded (or of the events in that country) to various concerned parties in the United States. The salience of events in an intervention country determines the level of attention the president will give the situation and the level of attention the public will give the situation. The general importance and salience of the country in question prior to the events leading to the intervention will determine the availability of prior information and the level of "institutional concern," as well as the number of U.S. informants, operatives, diplomats, and experts who will be available as sources of information.

Salience can be gauged by considering the following questions: Are vital national interests at stake? How vital? Are American citizens in danger? How many, and how much danger? Are U.S. business interests at stake? Since different people will answer these questions slightly differently (or ask slightly different questions in the first place), salience is not an absolute quality of an event, but varies from person to person based on their interests and their perception of the situation. I think there is a temptation to treat salience as epiphenomenal of "true significance," but I believe this would be a mistake. "Importance" in the policy process, however defined, is socially constructed. "Salience" conceptually retains a constant reminder of the fact that perspective and position are partially determinant of perceived importance. Thus, in the sense that I am using it here, salience is potentially contingent. For intervention decision making, the perception of the salience of events to the central decision makers is most important.

The president's perception of the salience of events strongly impacts the level of attention he gives it. If he perceives that the stakes are low, or that the stakes are moderate but things seem to be well in hand, the president will not devote too much time or attention to an issue; further, where the attention of the president goes, so goes the attention of other high-level decision makers, leaving events unimportant to the president to be acted on by lower-level functionaries in a routine fashion, with the nominal supervision of their organizational heads. If the president perceives salience to be high, he and the other core decision makers will spend a considerable amount of time and attention on the issue. More presidential attention means more action, more reports, more planning, and a greater intensity of decision- and policy-making activity, much of it focused in the highest level of decision making.

Conclusion

The institutional structure of decision making and the characteristics of the situation itself determine the primary character of an intervention decision which in turn affects who participates in the process and how they participate to a remarkable extent. Both of these relationships take place within a larger context of structured contingency, based on government institutions and policy. The two primary characteristics (crisis vs. premeditated, secret vs. public knowledge) condition the character and level of participation at all levels of the bureaucracy. The existing institutional structure of the U.S. government, the important role played by the personal proclivities of the president, and the often unexpected impact of personalism at the lower levels of the bureaucracy create numerous contingencies (or seeming contingencies) in the process.

One of the major themes running through this discussion has been the way in which intervention decision processes are affected by factors whose influence runs from the bottom up and also from the top down. This theme shows strongly in three ways. First is the way in which decisional processes contain a great deal of contingency at the lower levels, but as structured contingency bounded by the intuitional conditions and organizational rules in place. Second is the way the process is impacted from the top by the nature of the very personalist American executive, where the personal proclivities of a president have a huge impact on process, including, to some extent, the very "structure" of the structured contingency available at the lower levels. Third is the way in which decisions at the bottom influence decisions at the top by creating constraints in a path-dependent manner, and the way decisions at the top affect the participation of organizational actors at every level of the bureaucracy through executive order and executive preference.

The other major findings hinge on this tension between the personalist American presidency at the top and extremely consequential bureaucracy at the bottom (and middle). The president's perception of salience plays a significant role in structuring the decision-making process, including the extent of presidential attention. The locus of decision moves back and forth between the top and bottom (or middle) of the decision-making hierarchy depending on whether the decision is in an informational or planning stage, or in a major decision stage, sometimes overlapping. Ambassadors can exhibit a great deal of autonomy in a decisional process, depending on the characteristics of the situation, its perceived salience, and how much reign the president allows them.

Finally, the surprising variety of levels at which the behavior of individuals involved in these decisional processes created or constrained possible outcomes leads me to highlight the role of individuals, and to a partial explanation of intervention decisions through an appeal to the "not so great man" theory of history. Let me clarify: I am not arguing that any of these individuals wholly determined the outcome of the decision-making process by themselves, nor am I suggesting that their contribution to the process was made without benefit of their institutional position or surpassed what was likely given the level of structured contingency available in that specific process. Rather, I am suggesting that, in a process that should be dominated by adherence to bureaucratic procedures and the careful deliberations of the president and his advisors, individuals have had a surprising and disproportionate influence on these decisional processes.

6

The Legacy of Previous Military Interventions for Decision Making in Subsequent Interventions

Dead battles, like dead generals, hold the military mind in their dead grip and Germans, no less than other peoples, prepare for the last war.

—Barbara W. Tuchman, regarding August 1914

INTRODUCTION

There is an obvious kernel of truth to the old saying, "Generals always fight the last war." This chapter explores the extent to which this aphorism is true and explains why it is true, to the extent that it is. Further, it considers the possibility that generals are still fighting the war *before* the last war and tenders an explanation for why they are (to the extent that they are), and why they are *not,* if they are not.

There are important legacies existent in the context in which intervention decisions are made. These legacies go beyond simple historical analogies. These legacies are institutionalized in two different ways: first, through changes in formal rules or procedures, and second, in the "taken for granteds," "schemas," and accepted wisdom of policy makers and ordinary citizens alike.[1]

Each military intervention leaves institutional legacies that have a distinct impact on the immediately subsequent military intervention. Further, each intervention or foreign policy event may or may not leave more durable legacies that, once modified by subsequent policy events, form a "legacy chain" running through the institutional context for numerous subsequent decisions. This chapter includes a discussion of the mechanisms through which these legacies are formed, transmitted, and transformed.

After a discussion of the theoretical precursors and the details of the argument advanced here, the chapter proceeds with several propositions about the mechanisms through which legacies are realized and the theoretical consequences thereof. Following a discussion of methods and case selection, I provide evidence of specific legacy chains through a thematic discussion of some of the legacy chains of the post–Cold War era and a summary table of the trajectories of the major legacies and their sources.

While the focus of this book is "marines on the beach" interventions in Central America and the Caribbean, it is impossible to discuss the general context of these interventions, their legacies, and the legacies that affected them without making reference to other events in U.S. policy and the world. To effectively examine the legacy chains of which my four cases are a part, this chapter briefly examines a much wider range of U.S. military activities and policies. While this chapter discusses numerous major U.S. military interventions since World War II, the discussion is more elaborate and contains specific detailed evidence for the four central cases (the Dominican Republic, Grenada, Panama, and Haiti).

THE ARGUMENT

The fact that previous policy impacts pending policy is obvious. *How* is not. The legacy chains argument is predicated on the notion of path dependency and on political theorists Kenneth Finegold and Theda Skocpol's notion of policy legacies. They note,

> Past and present policies are connected in at least three different ways. First, past policies give rise to analogies that affect how public officials think about contemporary policy issues. Second, past policies suggest lessons that help us to understand the processes by which contemporary policies are formulated and implemented and by which the consequences of contemporary policies will be determined. Third, past policies impose limitations that reduce the range of policy choices available as responses to contemporary problems.[2]

All three of the issues they raise suggest important ways in which what has gone before affects what comes after. Central to their argument is the notion of path dependence: "what paths are available now depends on what paths were chosen before."[3] Virtually synonymously, political sociologist Robin Stryker defines path dependency as "the contingent, yet cumulative and constraining effects of past action on future possibilities."[4] Making the connection between path dependency and policy clear, sociologist John David Skrentny suggests that "past policies affect future policy choices by transforming or expanding state capacities and shaping administrative possibilities."[5] As political sociologist Ronald Aminzade points out, effective use of a path dependence argument requires the specification of mechanisms that sustain movement along the "path" of path dependency.[6] This article argues that path dependence is an important part of the explanation of legacy chains, with a contribution that goes well beyond the minimal path-dependent requirements of unidirectional time. The section on "Legacy Construction and Maintenance" specifies how.

Legacy Chains

While a previous policy can leave legacies in several different institutional spheres, it often leaves a single major legacy in a specific sphere. For example, one of the war in Vietnam's legacies was the 1973 War Powers Resolution, which changed the relationship between the president and Congress with regard to war making and deployment of troops. Subsequent military interventions were influenced by this institutionalized tension between the executive and legislature branches and have, in turn, left their own legacy (legal scholars might call it *precedent*) as a link in that chain. "Legacy chain" serves here to describe the legacies left by sequential policies in a specific institutional area or subset of institutions.

Legacy chains are legacies left in a specific institutional sphere by sequential policy events. Each policy event is constrained by the legacy of all prior links in the chain, but the legacies of earlier links are transformed slightly by the institutional impact of the next previous event. For example, U.S. involvement in Vietnam left a legacy in the sphere of press/military relations that affected the intervention in Grenada in 1983. The Vietnam legacy also affected the Panama invasion of 1989, but the legacy had been transformed slightly by the impact of the Grenada invasion on the institutions of press/military relations.[7]

Because of the different ways in which policy legacies are institutionalized, some legacies have unintended institutional consequences. The 1973 War Powers Resolution was intended to curtail presidential war-making powers and return authority to Congress. The joint resolution failed to force presidents to include congressional participation, but had the unintended consequence of forcing them to change the way they planned interventions (see the extended example in what follows).

The legacy chain argument moves beyond the policy legacy argument advanced by Finegold and Skocpol. Legacy chains reject simple policy legacies in favor of connected, complex legacies with multiple path-dependent steps. Figure 6.1 provides a diagrammatic abstraction of the difference. Policy at time 3 is not independently affected by legacies from policy at time 1 and legacies from policy at time 2, as is implied by Finegold and Skocpol's model, but by legacies from policy at time 1 as mediated by legacies of policy at time 2.

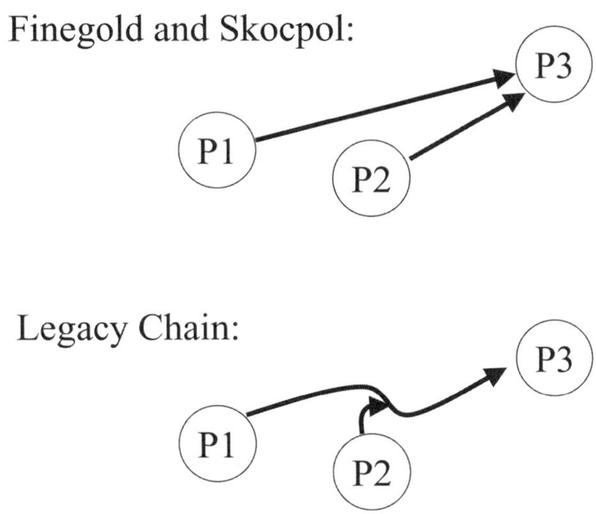

Figure 6.1 ***Simple*** **vs.** ***Complex*** **Legacies**

Analogies in Decision Making

In addition to Finegold and Skocpol's acknowledgment of "policy legacies" in policy formation more generally, there is a strand of research in political science that concerns itself with the role history plays in decision making, specifically the uses decision makers make of history. While not specifically discussing the way in which historical events constrain the decisions possible, they do discuss the "lessons" decision makers have learned from history, and the several ways historical analogies are used or enter into decision deliberations.[8]

There is a tension within this strand of research over the way in which "analogies" are used in decision making (a tension that may very well reflect an empirical tension). Some scholars argue that analogies are used solely for justification and advocacy of decisions arrived at by other means (and they argue that this is a poor use of history that is likely to lead to "poor" decisions), while other scholars assert that analogies can be and are used for analysis, which, if done properly, might improve decision making.[9]

Empirically, I found repeated use of analogies in military intervention decision making. I do not wish to enter the debate over whether analogies are used for analysis or solely for justification and advocacy. I perceive what I am proposing as being logically prior to the question of analysis or advocacy. I argue that the legacies that inform decision makers analogies have become a part of the institutional context and available organizational culture in such a way that they cannot be ignored. If policy makers then use analogies for analysis, advocacy, or both, so be it; the legacies have been institutionalized and their inclusion in decision deliberations is virtually unavoidable. Decision-maker choice to use them for analysis or for persuasion is not nearly as significant as their *nonchoice* to use them at all.

The Availability Heuristic

Within the analogies camp, Yuen Foong Khong discusses what she calls "The Availability Heuristic."[10] In this argument she notes the limited number of recent events that make up the analogy space available to any given decision maker. The main heuristic includes events during the decision maker's lifetime. She notes how different decision makers will make use of different analogies (and feel differentially persuaded by them) based on their age and personal recollection of the events from which analogies are drawn.

I think this is a very important observation. However, rather than focusing on specific individual decision makers' personal experiences of history (which I do believe are important), I believe that this heuristic is important to all individuals at all levels of the decision-making process. As I have shown in Chapter 5, lower-level bureaucrats play an important role in the decisional process. It follows, then, that their perceptions of important recent historical events can have an effect on the way they prosecute their roles in the decisional process. In fact, the legacies I discuss here might be productively conceived as products of a "collective availability heuristic" inasmuch as available and salient events play a role in the constitution of the institutional context and the relevant "culture," as elaborated below.

Institutions and Culture

Since I define institutions deeply and inclusively (see Institutions in Chapter 3), this particular argument requires the use of several subconcepts for specificity. Here, institutions are discussed in three ways: first, and most broadly, the institutional context; second, the formal institutional rules; third, the informal institutions, or schemas. By institutional context, I mean to include all of the institutional structure that bears on an intervention decision-making process; "the institutional context" is the entire situation of encouragements, constraints, rules, guidelines, understandings, relationships, and operating procedures that decision makers exist in and are bounded by as they make policy.

The changes in the institutional context that constitute policy legacies tend to be of two different types. The first type of institutional legacy is a formal change in rules, structure, organization, or procedure. The second type is the sort of broad taken-for-granted logics that *inform* decision making. This includes institutionalized preferences, perceptions, informal rules, and schemas. The most important difference between the two has to do with how the legacy comes about. Changes in taken-for-granted logics and schemas involve subtle shifts in assumptions based on demonstrated challenges to previously held assumptions or beliefs. These changes may or may not be undertaken consciously and reflexively, but they are certainly not something that is discussed and decided on; rather, they are a product of collective logic, sense, and unspoken consensus. Formal organizational institutional legacies, on the other hand, are the product of active decision making and are codified in rule or law. As the product of a decision-making process these are "intended" changes, and, if the language formalizing the change is not precisely aligned with the intention, or if the schemas that develop in the implementation of the change do not correspond with its intentions, unintended institutional consequences can result. The section below on the mechanisms of legacy construction discusses the processes by which these two types of institutional legacies might come about.

Logically prior to institutions is culture. Following sociologists Ann Swidler and William Sewell, this book defines culture as "what people know," forming the "tool kit" out of which schemas and institutions are selected.[11] While institutional scripts may define appropriate behavior in the vast majority of situations (a strong institutionalist position), taken for granted and shared cognitive frameworks (culture) create opportunities for new actions when institutional factors do not dictate or completely constrain action.

Legacy Construction and Maintenance

As Aminzade suggests, the final and most important part of an argument that relies on path dependence is "to identify mechanisms that sustain movement along the chosen path and prevent reversal or subsequent shifts to alternative possible branchings."[12] This requires, in the legacy chain context, consideration of both sides of the issue: first, things that prevent change and maintain existing paths; second, things that cause or allow change in the existing institutional context (specifically factors that allow the formal and informal institutional changes that I argue carry legacy chains).

The first aspect of this part of the argument is to solidify the assertion that factors in the institutional context (writ large) do, in fact, considerably constrain the range of possibilities considered by policy makers. This argument (and most path-dependence arguments in general) is probabilistic. That is to say, institutional factors that constrain are not necessarily perfectly determinant, but decrease the likelihood of the event constrained against depending on their institutional force. Likewise, institutions that promote certain policy outcomes do not determine outcomes, but encourage or increase the likelihood of those events to a greater or lesser extent.

The general phenomenon of institutional constraint is called "institutional inertia" and receives considerable attention in research conducted in the "new institutionalism."[13] Institutional inertia is the product of formal rules and procedures (how things must be done), informal understandings and practices (the accepted way things are done), and the limits of culture (the ways we can think of doing things).

Beyond the formal and informal rules for how policy is made are the limits imposed by what is and is not *conceivable* within the organizational culture or societal culture more broadly. Things that cannot be conceived cannot, by definition, be considered until such time that they enter the culture and become available. More noticeable as a constraint are things that are *inconceivable* (things that can be conceived but are beyond the pale in some way). Policy options often become or move toward the inconceivable after some "critical shift," a shock or failure of immense salience. For example, "plausible deniability" (the policy that held that U.S. forces and operatives could muck about in the internal affairs of other nations provided that U.S. involvement could be "plausibly" denied) became inconceivable after the fiasco at the Bay of Pigs in Cuba (thereafter operations would either be more genuinely covert or publicly overt).[14]

Inconceivability is in part a product of the institutional force known as "the legitimacy imperative."[15] Skrentny notes, "Formal organizations, including state bureaucracies, take for granted a 'legitimacy imperative.'"[16] In the organizational case of the highest level of U.S. state decision makers, particularly in the office of the president, legitimacy weighs in considerably in decision-maker calculations.[17] The operation of the legitimacy imperative is quite straightforward. Previously legitimate or successful policy approaches are easily proposed and repeated, while previously failed or delegitimated approaches are difficult to even get on the table. Shared cultural understandings (and the schema and other institutions based on them) provide many imperatives and constraints in policy making in this way, especially in heavily publicized policy at the highest level.

Following a similar logic, and almost the opposite of "not conceivable," are highly salient threats: things that are conceptually available, but more, are feared (perhaps unreasonably), and perhaps believed to be more likely than they really are.

Institutionalized fears of this kind increase the likelihood of certain types of policies or responses. A strong example would be the general American fear of hostage taking after the 1979 Iran hostage crisis, and the steps taken to avoid subsequent similar events.

To summarize, path dependence in military interventions is about what is formally and informally possible, and what is likely, preferred, and legitimate based on relevant cultural precepts. Change, then, presupposes either change in institutions or in the "relevant cultural precepts." Since culture provides the toolbox out of which institutions are constructed, it makes sense to begin a discussion of institutional change with cultural change.

If culture is what people know, cultural change can result from nothing more than new information. One of the main mechanisms of institutional change and legacy transmission is the information resulting from the experiences of a major event or military intervention. As the success, failure, or other consequences of an intervention become clear and enter general cultural understanding, institutions and schemas built on those understandings can and do change. It is difficult to predict exactly what cultural and institutional lessons will stem from a military intervention. Sewell notes that such things can be very varied; for example,

> The new prestige, wealth, and territory gained from the brilliant success of a cavalry charge may be attributed to the superior discipline and élan of the cavalry officers and thereby enhance the power of an aristocratic officer corps, or it may be attributed to the commanding general and thereby result in the increasing subordination of officers to a charismatic leader. . . Any array of resources is capable of being interpreted in varying ways and, therefore, of empowering different actors and teaching different schemas.[18]

Once these new schemas are in place, they have entered the institutional context and apply (probabilistic) path-dependent weight to subsequent policy choices. New information that contains a critical shift is most likely to leave a discernible legacy. Critical shifts produce information that is either surprising by virtue of introducing something previously inconceivable or demonstrating that a prior cultural "fact" is incorrect or is highly salient in some other way, such as being associated with either a brilliant success or horrific failure. The more dramatic these critical shifts are, the longer the cultural information they produce is likely to be included in the construction of institutions. As cultural information becomes old or "stale," institutions built in part based on that knowledge will be more vulnerable to change. The impact of this decay relationship for military interventions is clear. As the cultural information informing a legacy ages and loses salience, the institutions constituting the legacy become more vulnerable to change through new or more salient-seeming information.

Having covered cultural change, it makes sense to briefly touch on institutional change, one step closer to legacies. This chapter argues that legacies and legacy chains are constituted through institutional changes, either in formal law and procedure, or informally in taken-for-granteds, assumptions, schemas, and beliefs. The process through which formal rules and procedures are changed is a well-documented aspect of governance and is explained more or less well by the various theories of government decision making. However, the origins of the *motives* for formal institutional changes (why the procedure for change is pursued) and the way in which informal institutions change in response to events to form legacies are both similar and subtly complex. The way in which new cultural information is transformed into schemas and other informal institutional structures is variable and complex, and an excellent topic for further research. For now, I observe that change of this sort does take place. The empirical example that follows evidences institutional change and includes suppositions about underlying cultural change and their relationship. It is methodologically problematic to do much more, and thus beyond the scope of this book.

Theoretical Implications

Military intervention legacy chains have important theoretical implications for governance and decision making. The argument as advanced here is not a highest level or "grand" theory of the state, but rather a sort of "mid-level" theory based firmly in empirical observation. While my argument does not seek to supplant any of the classic theories of governance (pluralism, elite theory, and class theory; see Chapter 3), it does seek to add a corollary to all of them. The legacy chain argument suggests that, regardless of whose interests are being served by the state, states will do what they do in part as a product of the institutional legacies of what they have done before.

This view of governance does not adjudicate between any of the classic positions. Each of the classic positions might even be used to make an argument about how new cultural information is transformed into intuitions, or which institutions make the greatest probabilistic contribution to the observed path dependency. I am not arguing that policy is wholly determined by previous policy and policy outcomes, but rather that previous policy cannot be discounted in any effort to give a reasonable answer to the question of governance.

This chapter also contributes to the larger consideration the book gives to the "structure-agent" problem. As introduced in Chapter 3, here "state actor" is used to denote individual persons within the apparatus of that state rather than reified "states" as monolithic actors. The actions of these actors are constrained by institutions in a path-dependent way; state actors follow their institutionalized scripts when they are able and implement solutions out of their cultural toolbox when they are not.[19] These institutions, writ large, act as constraints on the range of possible and conceivable actions state actors can undertake. However, in the interstices between these constraints, actors have some freedom to choose between institutionally and culturally viable alternatives. These spaces between constraints widen in unusual situations, where institutional scripts are not available (arguably the case, to some extent, in many situations leading to military interventions), leaving the purposive actor more freedom still.[20] Further, these actors are aware of some of the institutional constraints under which they operate (usually new formal intuitions or recent and salient changes in cultural content) and may act in a reflexive way to attempt to influence the subsequent institutional context, attempts which may or may not succeed, and may or may not succeed in the way intended.

The Narrative Method

In order to demonstrate the proposed path-dependent legacy chain relationship between military interventions, this chapter relies on narrative historical methods.[21] Narrative methods are fundamentally comparative,[22] but also recognize the importance of time and temporal ordering to historical events, such that they "allow us to capture the unfolding of a social action over time in a manner sensitive to the order in which events occur."[23] This factor is critical, given that the military interventions and legacies under examination become very difficult to understand without reference to the sequentially developed context of other interventions and their legacies.

As sociologist Andrew Abbott notes, there are "two ways of seeing historical processes more generally. One focuses on stochastic realizations and aims to find causes; the other focuses on narratives and aims to find typical patterns."[24] While not initially causally focused, after demonstrating "typical patterns" of events within the changing context over time the narrative method does seek to offer a plausible explanation. In the first instance, narratives offer an account of events. Properly constructed narratives do more: "explicitly or implicitly, narratives not only tell us what happened but they also explain why it happened as it did and not otherwise."[25] Narrative explanations are compelling to the extent that the argument made and the narrative evidence provided is compelling. Narrative results are not falsifiable in the directly conventional sense, but can be falsified or superseded by a more compelling narrative explanation. For an excellent example of the fully effective use of the narrative method in historical sociology, see historical sociologist Michael Mann's work in both volumes of his *The Sources of Social Power.*[26]

Case Selection and Data

Choosing cases under the narrative method can follow the general logic of comparative historical analysis, but can follow other logics as well. This chapter expands beyond the four core cases of the book in a way that was a completely natural part of the research process. During initial historical investigations to select cases I was struck repeatedly by the connections between U.S. involvements (be they full "military interventions" or otherwise). My preliminary investigations revealed important legacy connections running through military interventions, "non-marines on the beach" involvements, and other historical events. With those connections in mind, I expanded beyond my four Caribbean cases through a process of inductive case selection. I first added the historical events that had led me to the notion of legacy chains in my preliminary investigations. Since the mechanism of legacy transmission hinges on salient events producing new cultural information that affects the institutional context, I then added as cases events that were salient to decision makers, as evidenced by their rhetoric and thinking during the recorded process of the military interventions and other events. Finally, since I propose a role for public awareness and perception of events in the creation and transmission of legacies, I examined foreign policy opinion polls throughout the time period looking for salient events. Table 6.1, later in the chapter, lists the interventions and other events considered.

Legacy Chain Examples

In the sections that follow, I detail three legacy chains that run through the period in question: (1) the legacies left for the relationship between the press and the government, (2) the policies that led to the 1973 War Powers Act and its legacy chain through other interventions, and (3) the legacy of multinational participation in military interventions, especially with regard to the United Nations.

Press

One of the most straightforward chains of legacies from post–World War II military interventions is the relationship between the press and the military. Military/press relations changed dramatically during U.S. involvement in Vietnam. This legacy affected, but was also transformed by, the subsequent (and sequential) U.S. military actions in Grenada, Panama, the Persian Gulf, and Somalia. Below I briefly detail the institutions of military/press relations at the time of each military involvement, what changed in that institutional sphere as a consequence of that involvement, and the effect that legacy had on the next intervention in the chain.

Vietnam

One of the most well-recognized "legacies" in the literature on the Vietnam War is the legacy of that conflict for the relationship between the military and the press. Prior to (and at the beginning of) U.S. involvement in Vietnam, the press relied heavily on the government and the military to keep it informed about military progress and to give it access to newsworthy events. It was taken for granted that the military would provide good information and the best access possible for press representatives without compromising operational objectives or reporter safety.

> What was distinctive about the interplay between the press and the government during the Vietnam years was not in the first instance the performance of the press, which was, by and large, not much better and not much worse than usual. What was distinctive was the performance of the government—and the impact that this had on the press and on its confidence in the reliability of what it was being told by the government.[27]

The information the government provided to the press was incomplete, becoming more and more disparate from reality as the war progressed. As the war drew on, the press became more and more skeptical of administration statements.[28] This skepticism led the press to more extensive investigations of its own and affected the tone of its coverage, encouraging skepticism in the American population at large. This led to "the so-called credibility gap."[29] "The press, at first a faithful medium for the administration's military message, broke stories of American atrocities, fragging in the military, and inflated body counts and labeled the daily Saigon briefings the 'Five O'clock Follies.'"[30]

As a consequence, institutional relations between the press and the military became strained. "For a whole generation of American military officers it fundamentally altered the way they look at the news media or the way they approach it."[31] This legacy affected not only military-press relations, but White House–press relations, too. In analyzing the legacies of press coverage of Vietnam, political scientist Michael X. Delli Carpini notes, "[T]here is now an institutionalized adversarial relationship with the White House that is much more likely to be set in motion than before the Vietnam era."[32]

Grenada

While the adversarial relationship between the White House and the press and the legacy of the credibility gap would play out for many years in domestic policy, the direct legacy of Vietnam era press relations between the military and the press would not be felt until the Grenada intervention in 1983. Grenada Task Force Commander Vice Adm. Joseph Metcalf requested that no press land with the intervention force to preserve mission secrecy and reporter safety.[33] The request was supported all the way up the chain of command, including the president. Reagan himself explained why: "Frankly, there was another reason I wanted secrecy. It was what I call the 'post-Vietnam syndrome,' the resistance of many in Congress to the use of military force abroad for any reason, because of our nation's experience in Vietnam."[34]

On Sunday, October 25, 1983, U.S. troops landed in force on Grenada. No reporters accompanied the invasion force, and none were allowed to land on the island by boat or air for several days. This press exclusion was a combination of two Vietnam legacies: first and most obviously, the legacy of the antagonism between press and military; second, and more subtly, the legacy of not "tying the hands of," or gainsaying, military commanders.

The Grenada operation was pretty much the low point for media-military relations. The reaction by the media was quick and vehement.[35] Keeping the press completely away from a major military operation was unprecedented. In response to the strong reaction from the press and from various prominent civil liberties advocates, the military began to consider a national emergency press pool that could be activated quickly for secret or fast-breaking military operations.[36] The "press pool" system received its first major test during the Panama invasion in 1989.

Panama

When the United States invaded Panama in December 1989, the press pool system was in place, and numerous press pool reporters were in Panama shortly after the invasion started. The formal institution of the press pool system was clearly the direct legacy of the failure of the Grenada operation to include a mutually acceptable (that is, to the president, the military, the press, and the public) level of press participation. However, the informally institutionalized tension between press and military that was a part of the Vietnam legacy had not disappeared. This is a good example of the two types of institutional forms that policy legacies take. On the one hand, there was still mistrust for the press institutionalized in the taken-for-granteds of military officers. On the other hand, there was the formal procedural legacy of the press pool system, intentionally institutionalized in an attempt to restore balance to press-military relations. As the balance of the Panama example demonstrates, these two types of legacies can interact with, and affect, each other.

The press pool system, as implemented in Panama, had some problems: "The press pool was late, didn't get to the scene, to the actual combat as it should have. It was held in an air base in Panama and actually watched part of the invasion on CNN while being treated to a dissertation on the history of the Panama Canal Zone by an American diplomat."[37] So, while the fighting took place, recalcitrant military officers, still "press shy," failed to give press pool reporters even the limited access the press pool system required. The response by the press community was again extremely uncomplimentary. The Department of Defense promised to do better.[38]

Press coverage, though limited, did nothing to improve relations between the press and the government. Colin Powell recalls in his memoirs his anger at witnessing news coverage shortly after the invasion that showed a smiling President Bush, pleased with the success of the operation, unaware that he was on a split screen with video feed of the first wave of flag draped coffins of U.S. soldiers killed in action being off-loaded at an air base.[39] While the feelings of policy makers toward the press had mellowed since Vietnam, some of their concerns remained, and with cause. Still, the response to the exclusion of press from Grenada and the shortcomings of the press pool system vis-à-vis the requirements of the first amendment led them to acknowledge that the press was a "necessary evil" that they would have to learn to live with and deal with more effectively.[40]

First Gulf War

The military maintained the revised press pool system during the first Gulf War. Press controls included limited access to the theater in Saudi Arabia and reporting restrictions on what could not be reported.[41] During the Gulf War, approximately 1,600 journalists and media support crew were in Saudi Arabia. Around 400 were assigned to the units fighting during the ground war. For the 1,200 journalists who were not at the fighting, however, the press pools were viewed as an unnecessary restriction, hampering their coverage of the war. They complained, leading to yet another review of the press pool system.[42]

Somalia

Somalia was the first chance for the media to turn the tables. Media and press representatives were already in Somalia long before U.S. forces arrived. The press filmed the first soldiers coming up the beach (in a way that would have been quite dangerous had there been any opposition to the landing). Members of the press knew their way around the city of Mogadishu, while the soldiers did not, and were not particularly inclined to have rules imposed on them by the military, "the new kids in town." While the press pool system was not invoked here, perhaps the legacy of the Pentagon's perceived good faith efforts to make a fair and reasonable press pool system prevented the strange situation in Somalia from causing a further deterioration in press-military relations.

Haiti

During operations in Haiti in 1994, the press was also able to gain access prior to the military's arrival. Because the intervention ended up being a permissive humanitarian operation and because of relatively positive short-term outcomes, Haiti provided an opportunity for the press and the military to cooperate successfully and paved the way for improved future relations.

U.S. forces maintained greater control over press access in Haiti than they had in Somalia, and some reporters traveled with military units in a fashion presaging the full "embedded press" system adopted during Operation Iraqi Freedom (OIF). The Haiti experience was relatively more successful than Somalia given that both the press and the military had to work together to establish a set of ground rules. Members of the press willingly complied with most of the military's operational security concerns and were given sufficient latitude to write their stories as they saw fit.[43] As sociologist Anne Holohan notes, the reporters "recorded what was happening on the ground: what the military were doing, how the local population viewed them, the discrepancy between the articulated aims of the White House and what the troops were being told to do or not to do on the ground."[44]

Bosnia and Kosovo

Soon after operations in Haiti, U.S. operations in the former Yugoslavia were accompanied by more press-military cooperation. This included another iteration of a protoembedded press system. In Bosnia the term "embedded press" was first used to describe a style of press procedures similar to those used in Vietnam, although far more formal and planned. The process of "embedding" referred to a reporter being assigned to a unit, deploying with it, and living with it throughout a lengthy period of operations.

Afghanistan

The recent U.S. engagement in Afghanistan represented a noticeable decrease in press access compared to similar operations in the past. This was a U.S. military intervention (as defined here) waged against nonstate actors (al Qaeda) and the regime that harbored them (Taliban). The restrictive press policy adopted in Afghanistan was partly due to the nature of the operation: the engagement in Afghanistan was difficult for the press to cover simply because most of the ground elements of the campaign were Special Operations Forces, which move rapidly and covertly over often very rugged terrain and make regular use of classified equipment or techniques, preventing reporters from covering their activities.

Although reporters faced great restrictions on access in Afghanistan, they did not make serious protests of the kind seen in previous operations. This may have been due in part to the press's interest in and concern for the events of 9/11 and other domestic issues. Awareness of the difficulties associated with covering air operations and Special Forces Operations may also have contributed.

Iraq

As I describe in greater detail elsewhere, U.S. operations in Iraq saw the broad and successful use of a system of press military relations called embedding.[45] Under this system, reporters agreed to a number of ground rules but then traveled with combat units for extended periods. While embedded, reporters saw what troops saw and experienced what they experienced. Press personnel were able to report as they saw fit with very few restrictions and without censorship.

Embedded press was heralded as a success at the time, and a 2004 RAND Corporation study I co-authored found that it is the best system to date for organizing press military relations when considering the interests of the press, the military, and the public.[46] As operations in Iraq have dragged on, commentators in journalism have become more critical of embedding. The legacy of success remains. Because of widespread positive experiences with embedding across publics, press, military, and decision makers, embedded press will likely be the system of press-military relations adopted during the next major U.S. military operation.[47]

The trend described by the legacy chain of military-media relations coming out of Vietnam follows an easily idealized pattern of response. This idealized progression is elaborated in Figure 6.2. Typically, a policy or event will occur that changes culture at some level, which dramatically increases the tension/relevance of that sphere within the institutional context and leaves a legacy. In this case, that event was the friction between the press and the military during the closing years of U.S. involvement in Vietnam. Following on the heels of this increased tension is a backlash, a peak of heightened awareness dramatically affecting the immediately subsequent policy event, in this case, the Grenada intervention. Note that even though the Grenada intervention was in the next decade after the close of the Vietnam War, it was, sequentially, the next major U.S. military intervention. Following the backlash, the tension of the legacy issue declines relative to its highest point, but can take quite a while to drift back toward its initial position, if it ever indeed arrives there. Consider the increased press participation in both Panama and the Gulf War, without completely eliminating the tension between press and military that was brought into sharp focus by Vietnam. Not until the press had the opportunity to "turn the tables" in Somalia and the further trust-building opportunities afforded by operations in Haiti did press-military relations find what appears to be a new equilibrium.

War Powers

Constitutionally, the president is the commander in chief of the armed forces, but, in the spirit of separation of powers, Congress controls the purse strings and is the only body authorized to make a declaration of war. Some of these dispersed powers were more or less combined in the executive branch during the course of American history, not with formal constitutional changes, but through precedent and

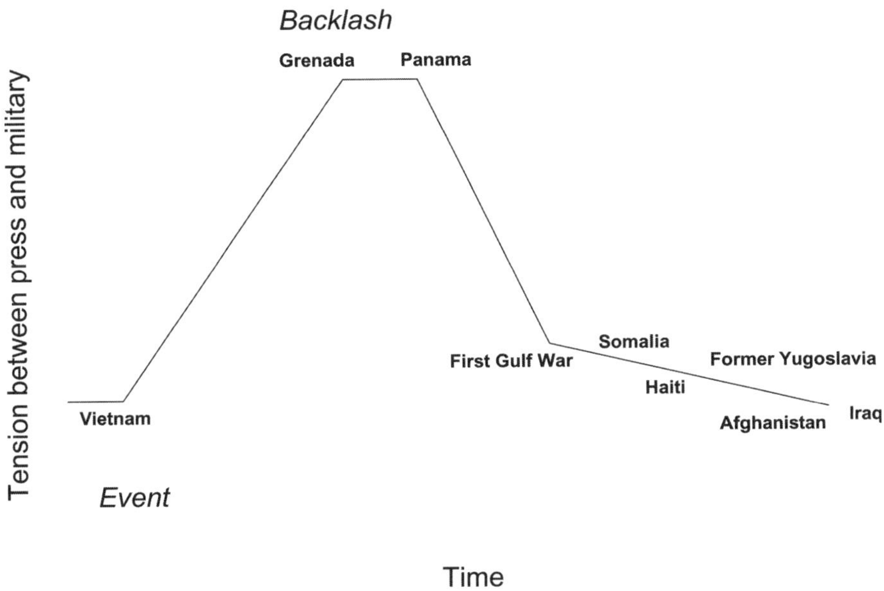

Figure 6.2 Press Legacy Idealized

convention. Control over war making is a perennial issue in the various contests between the branches of government over separation of powers. During the Cold War, having a strong executive empowered to respond as necessary to Soviet threats seemed like a good idea to almost everyone. This agreement changed after the 1964 Gulf of Tonkin Resolution, which gave President Johnson basically a blank check to use "all necessary measures" to deal with "aggression" in Vietnam. It was used to prevent further congressional participation in the ultimately very unpopular war. One of the most significant legacies of Vietnam was this increased tension between the executive and the legislature branch over control over war making, which ultimately led to the 1973 War Powers Act. The War Powers Act established limits on how long troops can be deployed (60 days) before congressional approval is sought in an attempt to ensure constitutionally given legislative privileges without destroying the executive branch's flexibility to respond immediately to crises.[48]

The legacy of Vietnam embodied in the War Powers Act is not just a legacy of restoration of one of the checks and balances with regard to the use of military might, but a legacy of conflict over power between the executive branch and Congress. President Richard M. Nixon vetoed the War Powers Act in 1973, but Congress passed it over his veto.[49] Presidents since then have resisted acknowledging the need for congressional participation, relying instead either on the commander in chief clause in the Constitution or on decisions reached by the UN Security Council and NATO (North Atlantic Treaty Organization).[50] The legacy chain of conflict over the War Powers Act dates back to Vietnam, but steps forward through each subsequent deployment of forces abroad.

While it is unclear whether or not the War Powers Act has prevented a president from using force when he might otherwise have wanted to (cases of decisions NOT to intervene are much harder to identify and analyze), numerous military interventions have been undertaken without seeking congressional approval, with the intention of getting *post hoc* congressional approval once the troops were in place, or of getting the troops in and out again before the War Powers time limit was reached, thus denying Congress a role. The first example of this presidential strategy was in Grenada in 1983. Wanting to maintain secrecy and expecting to be able to complete the operation within the War Powers Act time limit, Reagan chose not to consult with Congress.[51] Secretary of State George P. Shultz quotes House Speaker Tip O'Neill as saying, "Mr. President, I have been informed but not consulted" and promptly leaving when Reagan informed him and other congressional leaders of the impending invasion.[52] By following the letter if not the spirit of the Act, the Grenada invasion weakened the apparent force of the War Powers Act. Many in Congress were opposed to the invasion and intended to be intensely critical of the operation. Only the operation's success and the overwhelmingly positive response from the American public silenced this criticism.[53]

Following a form similar to the Grenada invasion (in that it was prepared in secret by the executive branch and not presented for congressional approval) was the Panama invasion of 1989. Arguably, this intervention without congressional participation weakened the spirit of the War Powers Act, being yet another massive use of U.S. forces. Congress did authorize the use and deployment of forces in 1991 for the Gulf War, but only after the UN Security Council had passed a resolution allowing the use of force. Because of the high level of public support for the pending operation and its public nature, Congress was able to authorize the use of force prior to the invasion (without ever actually having been asked to do so), thus avoiding a possible further weakening of the War Powers Act, and supporting the president and U.S. diplomatic efforts to resolve the situation by confirming the credibility of the American military threat.

The tension over War Powers returned to heightened sensitivity during preparations for the Haiti intervention of 1994. Unlike in Grenada and Panama, plans were not made in secret, so congressional leaders could not be completely excluded simply through keeping them ignorant. Most in Congress were opposed to U.S. intervention in Haiti except under certain very specific circumstances, and Congress passed a number of resolutions demanding a chance to participate in the decisional process.[54] President Clinton refused to acknowledge a need for congressional approval. There was some debate within the White House on the topic. "Secretary of State Christopher framed the argument against seeking a resolution in terms of presidential power, saying that if Clinton insisted on going to Congress, he would be constraining his successors."[55] The president ultimately ordered the intervention without congressional approval, maintaining the precedent.

The recent war in Iraq was preceded by a joint resolution in the House of Representatives and the Senate authorizing the use of force (resolved on October 10, 2002). While the George W. Bush administration sought the October resolution, it did not seek a declaration of war or any further congressional authorization prior to commencing hostilities in March 2003 and survived a token lawsuit (dismissed in February 2003) brought by several House Democrats and three anonymous soldiers who challenged the president's power to attack Iraq without a formal congressional declaration of war. The administration did comply with the formal reporting requirements of the War Powers Resolution, formally notifying Congress of the commencement of operations in a five-paragraph letter within 24 hours of the commencement of hostilities, and by making regular reports (at least every 60 days) thereafter.[56]

This sequence of events, including obtaining congressional support for a war without requesting or receiving a formal declaration of war, maintained the apparent stalemate on presidential war powers in favor of the power of the presidency while respecting the formal requirements of the War Powers Resolution, the lasting legacy of the links earlier in the chain.

While all of the military interventions in the War Powers legacy chain seem to backpedal on the congressional attempt to assert more authority over war making, the War Powers Resolution's impact on the institutions of policy making remain. While presidents have maintained the power to begin military conflict without congressional permission, they have made their military decisions constrained by the 60-day time limit, after which they will, by law, be required to make a full accounting to Congress and gain its permission. This is the most important legacy: post–War Powers Resolution military interventions are designed to be either short (so the 60-day mandatory reporting period ends with a *fait accompli*) or popular (so that public and congressional opinion are sufficient to approve of the operation).

Figure 6.3 presents another idealized graph of the progression of the legacies of the conflict over war powers. Note that, similar to the press-military relations chain, there was a catalyst event, perceived abuse of powers offered in the Gulf of Tonkin Resolution, and a backlash, the passage of the War Powers Resolution. Note again the unintended consequences of that backlash; in the press relations case, excluding the press was too forceful a response and trampled on First Amendment issues, forcing a compromise. In this case, the intended formal institutional consequences failed. Congress was not consulted meaningfully during subsequent military intervention decisions. However, because the legacy was institutionalized in law, even though the law did not accomplish what it intended to, it remained legally binding. Its unintended consequence was to force a strategic shift in the schemas of executive planning of military interventions to avoid entanglements with the 60-day reporting limit. So, presidential war-making powers were curtailed, but only to the extent that interventions would have to be either over or popular) within 60 days.

The War Powers Resolution is a clear example of a "formal" institutional legacy, with the legacy solution being codified in law. It is also a perfect example of unintended institutional consequences; while the War Powers Resolution was meant to return war-making powers to Congress, as implemented, it just forced a change in presidential intervention planning strategies. This kind of unintended institutional consequence, while central to the legacy chain argument advanced here, is missed by simple models of policy legacies.

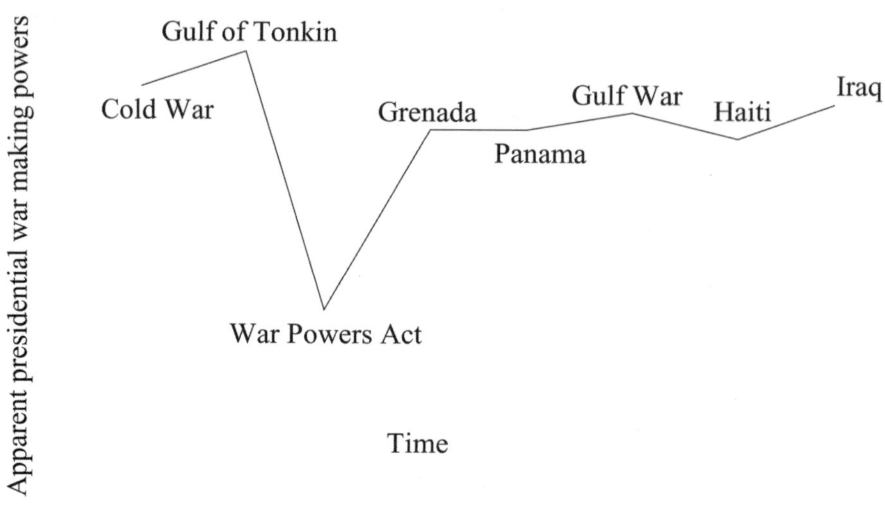

Figure 6.3 War Powers Legacy Chain

Legitimacy through the United Nations or Multinational Forces

While various U.S. military interventions have either strengthened or weakened the United Nations, collectively, U.S. interventions since World War II have left a legacy of encouragement for UN sanctioned or multinational interventions over unilateral action. Joint ventures all but ensure the acceptance of the international community (if they are truly multinational endeavors) and make blame sharing or exit much easier in the face of failure. Further, negative domestic and international opinion of several unilateral U.S. interventions (for example, Vietnam and Panama) have served as negative reinforcement in favor of the legacy chain encouraging international cooperation and approval of military activities.

The UN–sponsored U.S. "police action" in Korea began in 1950. U.S. involvement occurred in a Cold War context, to be sure, but was legitimized and carried out as a defense against aggression, supported by a UN Security Council resolution (obtained while the Russian delegate was boycotting the council). The June 26, 1950, resolution in the UN Security Council condemning "North Korean unprovoked aggression" and authorizing the United States and a multinational force to defend against it was the first use of this kind of legitimizing strategy, and it was very effective and prevented much international or domestic complaint.[57] This sits in stark contrast to Vietnam, where the United States ended up alone and divided against itself.

The legacy continued with the Dominican Republic intervention, that, while it began with a unilateral U.S. intervention, added a multinational troop component brought about through the OAS (Organization of American States) that constituted the first "joint" military intervention in the hemisphere and set a precedent for future such joint activities.[58]

U.S. participation in a UN–sponsored peacekeeping force in Lebanon led to the bombing of the U.S. Marine barracks there in 1983. This tragic event seems as if it could have "broken" the multinational force legacy chain. After this experience, the American public and American policy makers were much more careful committing troops to joint ventures that might result in American casualties. However, while the U.S. experience in Lebanon served as a slight discouragement to participating in peacekeeping activities, it did nothing to threaten the legitimizing force of multinational participation in and approval for military interventions.

The U.S. invasion of Grenada was nominally undertaken at the behest of the OECS (Organisation of East Caribbean States), in violation of the OECS charter. The "jointness" of this venture was so nominal and so tenuous, however, that it failed to prevent a storm of international criticism of the operation (no Caribbean troops participated in the landing, but several hundred OECS troops helped keep peace on the island during the transition to a new government).

International criticism of the Grenada invasion pales, however, in comparison to protest abroad following the totally unilateral invasion of Panama in 1989. Panama was the last unilateral and not UN-approved military intervention in U.S. history to date. Sequential U.S. military operations in the Persian Gulf, Somalia, Haiti, and former Yugoslavia have all been joint ventures or have been sanctioned by UN Security Council resolutions. Operations in Iraq did *not* win the support of the United Nations, despite considerable efforts to do so. Instead, the United States went to war with a "coalition of the willing," but the operation was viewed internationally largely as if it were a unilateral undertaking. Overall international legitimacy accorded to OIF is more ambiguous. Before claimed justifications for the invasion, including the presence of weapons of mass destruction and ties to the perpetrators of the 9/11 attacks, were demonstrated to be false, international perceptions of legitimacy were mixed but predominantly supportive. Now perceptions of legitimacy remain mixed, but perhaps less supportive on balance.

Figure 6.4 displays the idealization of the legitimacy through a multinational forces legacy chain.[59] This legacy chain does not graph as nicely in two dimensions as the other two, as the fluctuating vertical axis, international legitimacy, is not as easy to index as tension between press and military, and between president and Congress. The main point of this figure, and the fundamental legacy of these interventions, is to point out that the more genuinely or plausibly multinational an intervention is, the more legitimacy it is accorded internationally.[60]

OTHER LEGACIES

In addition to the lengthy legacy chains discussed above, each of the major military interventions or deployments the United States has undertaken since World War II (and some quasi-interventions) has left an impression on the institutional context. These legacies often do not extend beyond the immediately subsequent

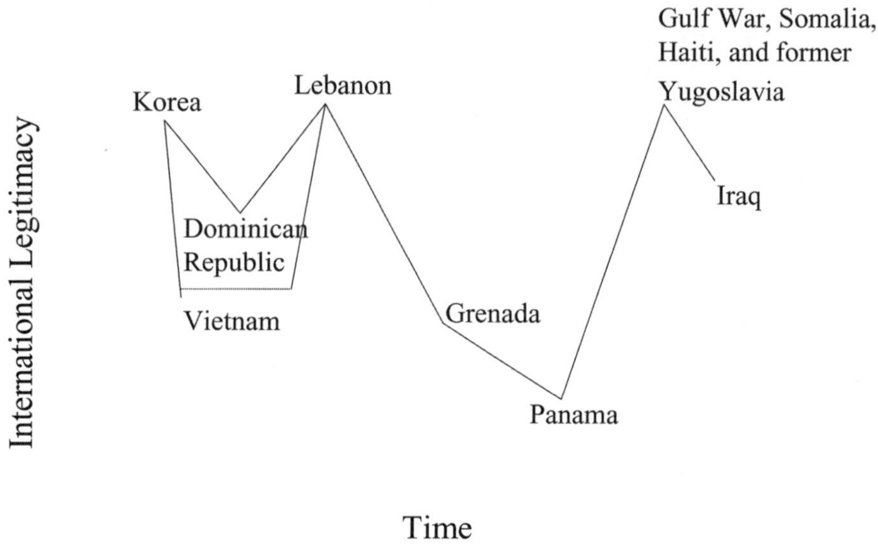

Figure 6.4 Multinational Force Legacy Chain

intervention. However, almost without exception, each intervention leaves an enormous legacy for the intervention that immediately follows it. This constitutes what I consider to be the most important legacy chain of all, the chain of U.S. military interventions. Each intervention has a strong direct connection to the intervention immediately preceding it and the one immediately following it. While this fact alone may seem unremarkable, the strength of these single-step legacies is often surprising.

While limits of space and focus constrain me to consideration of post–World War II military intervention legacies, the starting context for postwar interventions includes the legacies of previous policy and action, some of which can (and needs to be) disentangled from the balance of history. In this section, I begin with a discussion of the general legacy of pre–World War II U.S. policy toward Central America and the general contextual character of the Cold War. After touching briefly on those topics, I discuss each of the events in my collection of military interventions and military policies and the legacies they left along with the effect of legacies left to them.

Foreign policy making is not wholly divorced from domestic policy, and military interventions are just one aspect of foreign policy. In this chapter I discuss only the relationships and legacies between military interventions, leaving out the impact on the institutional context from other policy spheres. While I do not discuss them, I am very much aware of the lasting impact of certain "watershed" events in American history, such as the Watergate scandal and the end of the Cold War. These events have powerful legacies all their own and have received attention elsewhere.[61]

In Table 6.1, I present a summary of the legacies leading into and coming out of (exiting) each of the major legacy chain events and interventions since World War II

Table 6.1 Major Legacies from the Cold War to the Present Era

Event	Legacies Leading In	Legacies Exiting
Pre–World War II Central American Policy		Monroe Doctrine, 1823
		Roosevelt Corollary to the Monroe Doctrine, 1905
		Good Neighbor Policy (first tested 1933)
The Cold War in General		Truman Doctrine, 1947
		Extreme opposition to communism
		"Plausible deniability"
		Black and white bipolar world
		Domino theory (Eisenhower, 1954)
		Unquestioning support for Cold War objectives
1950—Korea	Domino theory	Successful defense against communism in SE Asia
		Successful legitimation through UN authorization
		"Froze" the Cold War
1954—Guatemala	Plausible deniability	Blow to plausible deniability
	Cold War bipolar mind-set	Legacy of success provided recipe for Bay of Pigs
1959—Cuban Revolution		Bolstered Cold War paranoia
		Imperative of avoiding "another Cuba"
1961—The Bay of Pigs	Success in Guatemala	Stout blow to plausible deniability
	Organizational inertia	Begins "sufficient force" legacy
1964—Vietnam	Cold War	Loss of confidence (end of exceptionalism, hesitancy to use military)
	"Loss of China"	Public distrust (credibility gap, war protest)
	Domino theory	Imperative to combat the two above (War Powers Resolution, necessity of an "exit strategy," imperative to win next time)
	Korean success	Extended Cold War legitimacy

1965—Dominican Republic	Cold War/ another Cuba	Helped silence/discredit early Vietnam protest
	Good Neighbor Policy	End of Good Neighbor Policy
	Sufficient force legacy	First "multinational" force
1979—Tehran hostage crisis		Fear of hostages
		Failed rescue reinforces "sufficient force" legacy toward "overwhelming force"
1982—Lebanon	"Successful" peacekeeping there in 1958	Unacceptability of peacekeeper casualties
		End of troops sent to "establish a presence"; no deployment without clear goals
1983—Grenada	Vietnam—attempt to combat hesitancy and loss of confidence	War Powers link
	Overwhelming force legacy	Press relations link
	Hostage legacy	"Near miss"—imperative to "win cleanly next time"
	Press relations	
	Another Cuba	
1989—Panama	Need to win cleanly	End of Cold War imperatives and legitimations
	Overwhelming force	Press relations link
	Legitimate trigger (no Gulf of Tonkin)	War Powers link
	Press relations	International outcry reinforced multinational participation or UN approval
1991—Gulf War	Post–Cold War	Multinational legitimacy
	Multinational legitimacy	War Powers link

	Overwhelming force/must win	Press relations link
	Exit strategy	Confirmed unacceptability of peacekeeper casualties
1992—Somalia	UN/ Multinational legitimacy	Constrained role of peacekeepers—peacekeepers must not cross the "Mogadishu line"
	General military hesitancy	International charity is not worth American lives
	Clear goals and exit strategy	
	Press relations	
1994—Haiti	International charity is not worth American lives	War Powers link
	War powers	Maintained "no deployment without clear goals"
	Exit strategy	
Former Yugoslavia	Hesitancy to use force	Too soon to tell
	International charity is not worth American lives	
2001—9/11 Attacks		Extensive legitimacy to act against "terrorist threats"; too soon to tell
Afghanistan and Iraq	9/11 as justification for previously inconceivable action	Too soon to tell

Sources: Philip Agee, *Inside the Company: CIA Diary* (Baltimore: Penguin Books, 1975); John R. Ballard, *Upholding Democracy: The United States Military Campaign in Haiti, 1994–1997* (London: Praeger, 1998); Benjamin R. Barber, "The Importance of Remembering: The Vietnam Legacy's Challenge to American Democracy," in *The Legacy: The Vietnam War in the American Imagination,* ed. D. Michael Shafer (Boston: Beacon Press, 1990); Richard J. Barnet, *Intervention and Revolution: America's Confrontation with Insurgent Movements around the World* (New York: World Publishing Co., 1968); William Blum, *Killing Hope: U.S. Military and CIA Interventions Since World War II* (Monroe, ME: Common Courage Press, 1995); Mark Bowden, *Black Hawk Down: A Story of Modern War* (New York: Atlantic Monthly Press, 1999); Mozilla N. Brown, "The U.S. Invasion of Grenada during the Reagan Administration: A Re-Evaluation," Naval Academy Foreign Affairs Conference: Keeping the Peace (1999); Alistair Buchan, "The Indochina War and the Changing Pattern of World Politics," in *The Legacy of Vietnam: The War, American Society and the Future of American Foreign Policy,* ed. Anthony Lake (New York: Council on Foreign Relations, 1976); Reynold A. Burrowes, *Revolution and Rescue in Grenada: An Account of the U.S. Caribbean Invasion* (New York: Greenwood Press, 1988); Christopher

Dandeker and James Gow, "The Future of Peace Support Operations: Strategic Peacekeeping and Success," *Armed Forces & Society* 23, no. 3 (Spring 1997): 327–348; Michael X. Delli Carpini, "Vietnam and the Press," in *The Legacy: The Vietnam War in the American Imagination,* ed. D. Michael Shafer (Boston: Beacon Press, 1990); Rowland Evans and Robert Novak, *Lyndon B. Johnson: The Exercise of Power* (New York: The New American Library, 1966); Georges A. Fauriol and Andrew S. Faiola "Chapter 11—Prelude to Intervention," in *Haitian Frustrations: Dilemmas for U.S. Policy: A Report of the CSIS Americas Program,* ed. Georges A. Fauriol (Washington, DC. Center for Strategic & International Studies, 1995); Louis Fisher, "Without Restraint: Presidential Military Initiatives from Korea to Bosnia" in *The Domestic Sources of American Foreign Policy: Insights and Evidence,* ed. Eugene R. Wittkopf and James M. McCormick (New York: Rowman & Littlefield, 1999); Lloyd Gardner, "America's War in Vietnam: The End of Exceptionalism?" in *The Legacy: The Vietnam War in the American Imagination,* ed. D. Michael Shafer (Boston: Beacon Press, 1990); Philip Geyelin, "Vietnam and the Press: Limited War and an Open Society," in *The Legacy of Vietnam: The War, American Society and the Future of American Foreign Policy,* ed. Anthony Lake (New York: Council on Foreign Relations, 1976); Fred Goff and Michael Locker, "The Violence of Domination: U.S. Power and the Dominican Republic," in *Latin American Radicalism: A Documentary Report on Left and Nationalist Movements,* ed. Irving Louis Horowitz, Josue Castro, and John Gerassi (New York: Random House, 1969); Peter Grose, *Continuing the Inquiry: The Council on Foreign Relations from 1921 to 1996* (New York: Council on Foreign Relations, 1996), 6; Thomas H. Henriksen, *Clinton's Foreign Policy in Somalia, Bosnia, Haiti, and North Korea* (Stanford: Hoover Institution, 1996); Trumbull Higgins, *The Perfect Failure: Kennedy, Eisenhower, and the CIA at the Bay of Pigs* (New York: W.W. Norton & Co., 1987); Warren Hinckle and William W. Turner, *The Fish Is Red: The Story of the Secret War Against Castro* (New York: Harper and Row, 1981); Irving L. Janis, *Victims of Groupthink: A Psychological Study of Foreign-Policy Decisions and Fiascoes* (Boston: Houghton Mifflin, 1967); Walter H. Kansteiner, "Chapter 7—U.S. Policy in Africa in the 1990s," in *Conference Report, U.S. and Russian Policymaking with Respect to the Use of Force,* ed. Jeremy R. Azrael and Emil A. Payin, RAND Report No. CF-129-CRES (Santa Monica, CA: RAND, 1996); John H. Kelly, "Chapter 6—Lebanon: 1982–1984," in *Conference Report, U.S. and Russian Policymaking with Respect to the Use of Force,* ed. Jeremy R. Azrael and Emil A. Payin RAND Report No. CF-129-CRES (Santa Monica, CA: RAND, 1996); Stephan, Krasner, *Defending the National Interest* (Princeton, NJ: Princeton University Press, 1978); Irving Kristol, "Consensus and Dissent in U.S. Foreign Policy," in *The Legacy of Vietnam: The War, American Society and the Future of American Foreign Policy,* ed. Anthony Lake (New York: Council on Foreign Relations, 1976); Michael J. Kryzanek, "The Grenada Invasion: Approaches to Understanding," in *United States Policy in Latin America: A Decade of Crisis and Challenge,* ed. John D. Martz (Lincoln: University of Nebraska Press, 1995); Deborah Welch Larson, *Origins of Containment: A Psychological Explanation* (Princeton, NJ: Princeton University Press, 1985); Eric V. Larson, *Casualties and Consensus* (Santa Monica, CA: RAND, 1996); Abraham F. Lowenthal, *The Dominican Intervention* (Cambridge, MA: Harvard, 1972); Richard L. Millett, "Chapter 9—Panama and Haiti," in *Conference Report, U.S. and Russian Policymaking with Respect to the Use of Force,* ed. Jeremy R. Azrael and Emil A. Payin, RAND Report NO. CF-129-CRES (Santa Monica, CA: RAND, 1996); Richard E. Neustadt and Ernest R. May, *Thinking in Time: The Uses of History for Decision-Makers* (New York: The Free Press, 1986); Robert Pastor, "Chapter 8—The Caribbean Basin," in *Conference Report, U.S. and Russian Policymaking with Respect to the Use of Force,* ed. Jeremy R. Azrael and Emil A. Payin, RAND Report No. CF-129-CRES (Santa Monica, CA: RAND, 1996); Colin L. Powell and Joseph E. Persico, *My American Journey* (New York: Random House, 1995); John Prados, *Presidents' Secret Wars: CIA and Pentagon Covert Operations from World War II through the Persian Gulf* (Chicago: Elephant, 1986); Ronald Reagan and Robert Lindsey, *An American Life* (New York: Simon and Schuster, 1990); Charles Roberts, *LBJ's Inner Circle* (New York: Delacorte Press, 1965); John P. Roche, "The Impact of Dissent on Foreign Policy: Past and Future," in *The Legacy of Vietnam: The War, American Society and the Future of American Foreign Policy,* ed. Anthony Lake (New York: Council on Foreign Relations, 1976); George P. Shultz, *Turmoil and Triumph: My Years as Secretary of State* (New York: Charles Scribner's Sons, 1993); Gary Sick, *All Fall Down: America's Tragic Encounter with Iran* (New York: Penguin, 1986); Gaddis Smith, "Haiti: From

Intervention to Intervasion," *Current History* 94, no. 589 (February 1995): 54; James Thomson Jr., "How Could Vietnam Happen? An Autopsy," in *The Domestic Sources of American Foreign Policy: Insights and Evidence,* ed. Eugene R. Wittkopf and James M. McCormick (New York: Rowman & Littlefield, 1999); Barbara Tischler, "Promise and Paradox: The 1960s and American Optimism," in *The Legacy: The Vietnam War in the American Imagination,* ed. D. Michael Shafer (Boston: Beacon Press, 1990); Caspar Weinberger, *Fighting for Peace: Seven Critical Years in the Pentagon* (New York: Warner Books, 1990); Bob Woodward, *The Commanders* (New York: Simon & Schuster, 1991), 85; Warren Zimmermann, "Chapter 11—Yugoslavia: 1989–1996," in *Conference Report, U.S. and Russian Policymaking with Respect to the Use of Force,* ed. Jeremy R. Azrael and Emil A. Payin, RAND Report No. CF-129-CRES (Santa Monica, CA: RAND, 1996).

to which my inductive case selection led me. Table 6.1 presupposes more historical knowledge on the part of the reader than is generally fair; however, the space to rectify that shortcoming is unavailable. I have tried to make the legacy labels as accessible as possible to allow the reader to follow the different and varied chains through Table 6.1 and present the results of considerable historical research in as condensed a space as possible.

Note that many of the events and interventions have considerable durations. This makes some events that were sequential appear not to be so. For example, the 1965 intervention in the Dominican Republic took place entirely during the U.S. involvement in Vietnam. Further, while U.S. peacekeeping in Lebanon began in 1982, the "critical shift" of the Beirut Marine barracks bombing occurred concurrently with the planning for the Grenada intervention in October 1983 (in fact, the decision to invade Grenada had been taken before the barracks bombing). Because of these temporal overlaps, the "immediately prior" intervention for Grenada is Vietnam, with the immediately prior salient nonintervention event being the Iran hostage crisis. The trajectories of the legacies affecting Grenada become much clearer with this information.

Pre–World War II Central America Policy

Standout context-defining events in the history of U.S.–Caribbean relations are the 1823 Monroe Doctrine, declaring Central America to be in the United States' "sphere of influence," the 1905 Roosevelt Corollary to the Monroe Doctrine declaring the United States to be the policeman of the Caribbean, and the extensive string of U.S. military interventions and occupations in the region resulting from these positions. President Franklin D. Roosevelt's Good Neighbor Policy (first put to the test in 1933) was intended to remove some of the blight from previous U.S. involvement in the region.

Roosevelt's policy had three components.[62] First, he pledged nonintervention in the internal affairs of Central America. Second, the policy encouraged freer trade through reciprocal trade agreements. The third element of the Good Neighbor Policy was a systematic effort by the United States to consult with its Latin neighbors through regular inter-American conferences.

The Good Neighbor Policy changed the context of U.S.–Caribbean relations while it was adhered to. It is difficult to get a precise count, but the policy was maintained several times in the face of possible U.S. military interventions in the region. With the dawn of the Cold War, the Good Neighbor Policy took a backseat; still, it had some influence. The postwar policy of plausible deniability (whereby U.S. involvement was considered sufficiently covert if it could be plausibly denied, rather than kept genuinely secret), which hallmarked the U.S.–sponsored invasion of Guatemala in 1954 and the fiasco at the Bay of Pigs in Cuba in 1961 (among others), was in part the product of Cold War anticommunist intervention, the "rules of the game" of Cold War sphere of influence relations between the United States and the U.S.S.R., and an attempt at lip service to Good Neighborliness.

Though the goodwill benefits of the Good Neighbor policy mostly died in the era of plausible deniability (while the American public might have been fooled about American participation, the citizens of Caribbean and Central American nations were not), the policy played a role in the decisional process of the first post–World War II military intervention in the Caribbean, the Dominican Republic in 1965. While the legacy of nonintervention ultimately lost out to the imperatives of the Cold War, Presidential Scholar Charles Roberts notes that "[p]residential advisors, while recognizing the need for more troops to stop the fighting, pointed out that any massive infusion of military manpower would be considered an abandonment of FDR's Good Neighbor Policy" during the decision to intervene in the Dominican Republic.[63] In fact, the failure to participate more modestly early in the Dominican crisis stemmed from a desire not to get too involved in Dominican affairs.[64]

The Cold War

While the origins of the Cold War are certainly very complex,[65] for my purposes here, it is sufficient to consider the Truman Doctrine of 1947 to be the beginning of the Cold War. In justifying his views President Harry Truman declared,

> I believe that it must be the policy of the United States to support free peoples who are resisting attempted subjugation by armed minorities or by outside pressure. I believe that we must assist free peoples to work out their own destinies in their own way. I believe that our help should be primarily through economic and financial aid which is essential to economic stability and orderly political processes.[66]

Along with this proclamation, Truman initiated an emergency request for $400 million to aid Greece and Turkey, threatened with communism.

Another major contributor to Cold War contextual qualities was the introduction of the "domino theory" by President Dwight D. Eisenhower in 1954.[67] The notion was, if Indochina fell to communism, then, like a domino, it would knock over a line of neighboring states in Southeast Asia. Eisenhower's domino theory left a powerful legacy, "cited again and again by his successors to justify American policy and applied even after the end of American involvement in Vietnam to developing situations in Central America."[68]

The Cold War had several qualities that color all of the interventions that took place during it. First, it was rabidly opposed to communism. "Opposition to communism more closely resembled a millennial goal, a religious quest, than a logical or a rational strategy."[69] Cold War America was so anticommunist that opposition to communism was allowed to run roughshod over traditional American values such as self-determination and democracy.[70] Second, the Cold War perspective was completely bipolar: not just the reality of superpower vs. superpower confrontation, but a complete dissolution of shades of gray into black and white; if you were not anticommunist, you might as well be a communist. Third and finally, until the later half of U.S. involvement in Vietnam, there was incredible and unquestioning support for Cold War efforts from the public and from every branch and agency of the government in the United States. Almost everyone genuinely believed that the fate of the world was at stake in the Cold War and that the president deserved maximum support for whatever ways in which he chose to attempt to ensure a positive outcome.

Korea

The UN sponsored U.S. police action in Korea began in 1950. U.S. involvement occurred in a Cold War context, to be sure, but was legitimized and carried out as a defense against aggression, supported by a UN Security Council resolution (obtained while the Russian delegate was boycotting the Council).

> How is it that the Korean War escaped the protests which surrounded the war in Vietnam? Everything we've come to love and cherish about Vietnam had its forerunner in Korea: the support of a corrupt tyranny, the atrocities, the napalm, the mass slaughter of civilians, the cities and villages laid to waste, the calculated management of the news, the sabotaging of peace talks. But the American people were convinced that the war in Korea was an unambiguous case of one country invading another without provocation. A case of the bad guys attacking the good guys who were being saved by the even better guys; none of the historical, political, and moral uncertainty that was the dilemma of Vietnam. The Korean War was seen to have begun in a specific manner: North Korea attacked South Korea in the early morning of 25 June 1950; while Vietnam. . . no one seemed to know how it all began, or why.
>
> And there was little in the way of accusations about American "imperialism" in Korea. The United States, after all, was fighting as part of a United Nations Army. What was there to protest about? And of course there was McCarthyism, so prevalent in the early 1950s, which further served to inhibit protest.[71]

Korea does not weigh in with any particularly heavy legacies, at least compared with its geographical and temporal neighbor, Vietnam. Four legacies of Korea are noteworthy: first, as a successful defense of a Southeast Asian country against communist aggression, it made U.S. involvement in Vietnam look like less of a horrible idea. Second, it played a role in the legacy chain leading to the War Powers Resolution; there was never a formal declaration of war, and U.S. involvement was justified as a police action under the auspices of the United Nations and was never brought before the U.S. Congress. Third, Korea also serves as a link in the legacy chain of successful uses of UN resolution as a legitimizing strategy to cover fundamentally unilateral interventions from storms of international and domestic protest (see Chapter 7 on legitimacy). Fourth, the level of participation of U.S. forces and Communist Chinese forces in the ground war that was, ultimately, a stalemate, effectively "froze" the Cold War by making clear to all the players the impossibility of effectively "winning" through the use of conventional forces. This final legacy contributed to the unwillingness on the part of policy makers to escalate troop strengths in Vietnam to the remarkably high levels that would have been necessary to "win."

Guatemala

In 1954 a small army of mercenaries and Guatemalan expatriates, with the help of the CIA, toppled the democratically elected Jacobo Árbenz government.[72] While no U.S. ground troops were involved, U.S. pilots flew sorties in outdated and disguised U.S. aircraft. The CIA role included not only the planning and funding of the operation, but a massive disinformation campaign that ultimately led to Árbenz's surrender and capitulation, even though the small invasion force had done little more than cross the border and occupy a few small towns.[73]

Before, during, and after the invasion, officials from several Central American countries accused the United States of plotting and coordinating the invasion, all of which accusations were denied by U.S. officials. After the invasion 11 different OAS countries protested the U.S. "aggression" and "intervention."[74] Widespread knowledge of U.S. participation throughout Central America was a blow to "plausible deniability," but not a sufficiently stout blow, because the American press accepted the government's denial of participation, leaving the American public ignorant of American complicity.

This blow to plausible deniability is one of the legacies of the CIA-run invasion of Guatemala, but not the most important one. While the Guatemala plan was "successful" from the CIA's point of view, that success hinged on the success of the disinformation campaign and the questionable loyalty of the Guatemalan military much more than on the invasion force.[75] The high degree of contingency in the outcome of the operation was forgotten in the wake of success, leaving only the impression of CIA potency. The main legacy of Guatemala was the recipe for the Bay of Pigs. This legacy led U.S. policy makers and the CIA to believe that the "formula" used in Guatemala had been a good formula (rather than just lucky) and that it applied equally well to the Cuban case, which was not so.[76]

The Cuban Revolution

In January 1959, Cuba's rightist dictator, Fulgencio Batista, fell before the forces of Fidel Castro. This transition to what would ultimately become a communist government for the island nation had an impact all out of proportion to the event for subsequent U.S. policy in the Caribbean.

> Cuba's status as a Soviet satellite '90 miles from our shores' revived and intensified traditional concern in Washington over a strategic threat to the United States through the Caribbean. The region was perceived as the fourth front of the cold war (the other three were Europe, Asia, and the Arctic). Thus, for nearly three decades after Castro came to power, the driving theme of American interventions in the Caribbean and Central America was the prevention of 'another Cuba' and the containment of Castro's influence whether expressed through his successful defiance of the United States or support for leftist movements.[77]

The legacy of "avoiding another Cuba" played a significant role in the decisional processes of both the Dominican intervention of 1965 and the Grenadan intervention of 1983 and was presumably important in determining the character of American participation and nonmilitary interventions in other countries in the region. The content of another Cuba as a legacy was not just the vindication for Cold War paranoia afforded by the establishment of a communist state very close to the United States. Rather, the way in which Castro came to power also contributed to the legacy of fear of another Cuba. The Eisenhower administration had misjudged Fidel Castro, who had masqueraded in the cloak of a reforming democrat and pledged free elections. "When Castro dropped his cloak and emerged as a puppet of Moscow, it was too late."[78] This contributed to the Cold War bipolar mind-set and made anyone in the Caribbean who was not an anticommunist into a possible communist, on Castro's example.

The Bay of Pigs

The failed invasion of Cuba at the Bay of Pigs by U.S.–supported Cuban exiles in 1961 is one of the most famous (and well-studied) fiascos of American foreign policy.[79] It was the product of several important legacies, and, because of its catastrophic failure, it left several as well. The plan used for the Bay of Pigs operation was drawn straight from the "successful" formula used in Guatemala six years earlier.[80] Unfortunately for U.S. policy makers, they were not the only ones to have learned from the legacy of Guatemala. Fidel Castro had watched what had occurred there and had taken steps to render his government considerably less vulnerable, the most important step being that he replaced the military with his own guerrilla army.[81]

The Bay of Pigs was a leftover policy in progress of the previous presidential administration. "Unfortunately, his untried successor thought with good reason that the already protean Cuban project had been fully staffed and approved by everyone concerned in the previous administration. Now Kennedy had either to run with his Cuban hot potato or drop it as quickly and quietly as possible."[82] Left with plans in place and troops in training, but unwilling to buck the machinery in motion and cancel the operation or overcome lukewarm enthusiasm and violate plausible deniability to furnish sufficient military support, Kennedy and his decision makers were in a trap from whicht they failed to escape.

The fiasco left two important legacies. The first was another stout blow to plausible deniability. While the administration had tried to maintain that minimum level of secrecy, it failed, even before the operation began.[83] With the catastrophic failure, U.S. participation became undeniable, and terribly embarrassing.[84] Subsequent U.S. interventions would either be publicly acknowledged or much more genuinely covert.[85]

The second legacy is more subtle and would need to be joined by additional experiences before finally having an institutional impact. Overlooking the host of mistaken assumptions made about the operation and its chances for success, had it been an out and out invasion, fully supported by U.S. air and sea power, and with a larger commitment of ground troops, the invasion would likely have gotten further than it did. When added with U.S. experiences in Vietnam later that decade, this would build into the "sufficient force" legacy, which contributed to the decision to use utterly and certainly overwhelming force in several later cases.[86]

Vietnam

American involvement in Vietnam was a huge watershed of legacies. No war has done as much to shape the post–World War II U.S. military context, except perhaps World War II's legacy of the Cold War itself. U.S. involvement in Vietnam spanned from the French defeat at Dien Bien Phu in 1954, through an ever-widening spiral of additional troops and expanded rules of engagement that never seemed to be quite enough, to the 1973 withdrawal of American military forces. Several legacies led into Vietnam, mostly what historian James Thomson, Jr. calls "the legacy of the 1950s," namely, the Cold War, the so-called "loss of China," the war in Korea, and the domino theory.[87] While the reasons for U.S. involvement in Vietnam are amply detailed elsewhere, here I focus on the legacies of Vietnam.

In my mind at least, the numerous legacies of Vietnam can be broken down into three broad categories: the loss of confidence, public distrust, and a set of new imperatives to combat the first two. Diplomatic historian Lloyd Gardner credits Vietnam with "the end of exceptionalism" in the American self-image.[88] Despite our superpower status, our commitment to fight communism, our willingness to pay with lives of young American men to keep that domino from falling, we lost. Several scholars agree that Vietnam caused a significant loss of confidence in America.[89] One of the specific legacies of this loss of confidence was a desire to return to isolationism.

> Essentially, in historical terms, this was a reversion to the conditioned reflexes of pre–World War II isolationism. These people were vigorous patriots, they despised the overt anti-Americanism of some of the antiwar militants, but they simply could not understand why half a million Americans were inconclusively fighting somewhere at the other end of the world.[90]

Tied in with this isolationism was an extreme hesitancy to use the military, lest protest tear the nation apart again, coupled with a hesitancy on the part of the military, which felt it had been horribly ill-used in Vietnam, having been asked to accomplish impossible and vague goals with one hand tied behind its back.[91]

The next major group of legacies stems from the public skepticism that developed during the war and its consequences. Gone was Cold War–driven consensus; left was an angry and divided public, distrustful of its own government, aware of the so-called credibility gap between what the government knew and what it said.[92] Vietnam forever changed the relationship between state and press, making the latter much less likely to trust and rely on the former, and dramatically increasing the tension between the two.[93]

Vietnam created the modern format for antiwar protest and made it part of the regular democratic response (evolved out of the nonviolent protest strategies of the civil rights movement of the same era). Vietnam effectively ended conscription in the United States, leading to the development of a large, professional, all-volunteer standing army.[94]

The final set of legacies stems from imperatives in response to legacies of loss of confidence and of public skepticism. Having been deprived of a role by its own passage of the 1964 Gulf of Tonkin Resolution, Congress took a major step to try to reign in executive war-making powers with the passage of the War Powers Resolution in 1973.[95] "One of the lessons for policymakers from the Vietnam War is that a military commitment by the United States must have the support of its people."[96] In order to ensure public support, a number of imperatives came into being. First was the idea of "exit strategies." If the conditions for their exit were provided before troops were deployed, fear of a "quagmire" and general ambiguity would be reduced.[97] Finally, the general loss of confidence dictated an imperative to win the next one, and the one after that. In order to ensure victory and instill confidence, overwhelming (not just sufficient) force would be required.

The Dominican Republic

The 1965 U.S. intervention in the Dominican Republic to end civil strife and ensure the victory of a rightist military junta over a possibly left-leaning coalition of other military units and armed civilians was a formula Cold War Caribbean intervention: Strife erupted, the vague possibility of communism threatened, and the U.S. intervened to prevent it.

"The aim of preventing a 'second Cuba' shaped American policy toward the Dominican Republic at every stage after Trujillo's death in May 1961."[98] Rafael L. Trujillo was the former dictator of the Dominican Republic, whose regime had been similar to Batista's repressive rightist government in Cuba.

> "'Batista is to Castro as Trujillo is to ______' was the implicit assumption, and Washington wanted to ensure that it could help fill in the blank," is the way one analysis formulated the problem. "As a result, the United States began to cast about for a way to get rid of Trujillo and at the same time ensure a responsible successor." Ironically, it was to Trujillo's Dominican Republic that Batista had fled.[99]

While the United Stateshad successfully negotiated a transition from Trujillo's regime to a democratic one upon the dictator's death, another coup was not long to follow. Since it was a rightist coup, it was allowed to stand. When that government toppled in 1965, U.S. decision makers maintained their distance, respecting "The Good Neighbor Policy" as long as it looked like yet another anticommunist coalition of military officers would prevail. When the outcome came into question, however, fear of another Cuba, Castro's legacy, ruled the day. Historian Abraham F. Lowenthal's study of the Dominican Republic intervention reveals that fear of another Cuba was very much present in the decisional discourse, being repeatedly mentioned by decision participants. Particularly telling was the written request for U.S. intervention submitted by antirebel Col. Pedro Bartolomé Benoit "to prevent another Cuba."[100]

In addition to the general Cold War legacy, and the legacy of Cuba, the Bay of Pigs and the ongoing war in Vietnam had a legacy for the Dominican intervention as well: send sufficient force to get the job done.[101] Former CIA operative Philip Agee who was stationed elsewhere in the Caribbean at the time of the Dominican intervention captures the point somewhat humorously: "'Fifty-eight trained communists' is our new station password and the answer is 'Ten thousand marines.'"[102]

The Dominican intervention left several legacies for future interventions. First, it temporarily served to discredit Vietnam protestors who had become even more vocal at the advent of Dominican involvement, by being a successful and short-term intervention.[103] Second, it strengthened the power of the Cold War context to include a virtually unlimited claim of legitimacy for armed intervention in civil strife[104] and the absolute end of the Good Neighbor Policy.[105] Finally, the Dominican intervention created the "joint venture" as a legitimizing strategy in the Caribbean.[106] After the initial landing of U.S. Marines, the United States sought support from other hemispheric nations for the intervention, ultimately getting the OAS to approve the creation of an "Inter-American Peace Force," nominally under the command of a Brazilian general.[107]

Iran Hostage Crisis

On November 4, 1979, Iranian militants stormed the U.S. Embassy in Tehran and took approximately 70 Americans captive. This terrorist act triggered the most profound crisis of the Carter presidency and began a personal ordeal for Carter and the American public that lasted 444 days.[108] The Iran hostage crisis was not a case of military intervention (though it did involve a failed helicopter raid/rescue) and did not involve communists, so it had very few legacies leading in to it. Due to its lengthy duration, the failed rescue, and the public displeasure at Americans being held as hostages, it left several important legacies.

First was the legacy of U.S. hostages. The strong public reaction, the duration the hostages were held, and the slow progress of diplomatic efforts to free the hostages (which were ultimately successful) cost President Carter any chance at reelection.[109] The political costs were high enough that subsequent administrations took note and would make every effort to avoid paying the same cost by avoiding any situation in which Americans might be taken hostage.

Second was the legacy of that failed rescue. On April 24, 1980, the United States attempted a rescue mission. After three of eight helicopters were damaged in a sandstorm, the operation was aborted; eight persons were killed during the evacuation.[110] Many believed the mission failed because too few helicopters were sent.[111] This served to reinforce the "overwhelming force" legacy of Vietnam and would appear as a consideration in the decisional process of several subsequent interventions.

Lebanon

American military intervention in Lebanon in the 1980s was influenced by the historical precedent (and legacy) of 1958 when the United States landed marines in Beirut. In 1958, using the leverage provided by 14,000 troops put ashore, U.S. policy makers calmed civil disturbances, chose the next president of Lebanon, and quickly withdrew the force without significant incident or casualties.[112] The Lebanon of 1982 was a much different situation, and one that did not lend itself to resolution so easily. With an active Israeli invasion of Lebanon under way, a besieged set of Palestinian fighters, a Syrian expeditionary force within their borders, and dozens of armed Lebanese factions who had been embroiled in combat for the previous seven years, Lebanon was a perilous land for well-meaning strangers.[113] There was no quick political plan or definable military objective that would significantly improve the situation. U.S. policy makers considered a military presence as a visible means of expressing concern for Lebanon. There was hope that a peacekeeping force would stabilize the situation, but there was no clear idea exactly how. Secretary of Defense Caspar Weinberger noted, "[T]his MNF [Multi-National Force] would not have any mission that could be defined."[114]

As should have been the obvious outcome at the time, the mission failed. As U.S. forces got more and more involved, their neutrality as peacekeepers was considered to be compromised by several of the numerous opposed factions in the country, resulting in more and more direct attacks on the marines, culminating in the bombing of the marine barracks in October 1983 (during the Grenada crisis), with 241 marines killed. Policy makers shortly found an excuse to redeploy the troops on ships offshore, and shortly after that, Lebanon was left to its own devices.

There are two clear legacies of the Lebanon involvement. The first is the unacceptability of pointlessly dead soldiers. While U.S. public opinion has been shown to be very resilient to American casualties when perceived national interest is high,[115] domestic public opinion has almost no tolerance for casualties where vital interest are not perceived to be at stake, and soldiers dying in their barracks is a waste, and was seen as such. Subsequently, security at military installations, camps, and at U.S. embassies would be considerably improved.

The second major legacy of Lebanon is the institutionalization of military rejection of deployment without clear goals. Deploying troops simply to establish a U.S. "presence" would no longer be acceptable to the military high command.[116] Coupled with the hesitancy legacy of Vietnam, this left an American military establishment that did not wish to be used except under very careful, well-defined, and necessary situations; this was not cowardice, but rather a very sensible prudence, having twice paid the cost of imprudence.

Grenada

> The Grenada Invasion, or, as it was termed by military planners, Operation Urgent Fury, has been viewed as falling within the general category of a Caribbean-style intervention. All the elements were present for the United States to follow an oft-used script for invading a neighboring nation: American citizens apparently in some danger, internal political unrest after the assassination of Prime Minister Maurice Bishop, an unpopular governing regime with ties to our adversaries, shipments of arms entering the country from Eastern Europe, and the construction of an airport by Cuban engineers that raised the suspicions of the Pentagon. Each one of these developments in Grenada linked up with established national security and national interest objectives that in the past had pushed the United States to either take military action or implement some form of destabilizing operation.[117]

The Grenada invasion of 1983 was the first time that some of the heavier legacies mentioned here reared their heads and was one more link in several legacy chains that run through the period. In many ways, Grenada was a response to the many legacies of Vietnam. Then President Reagan actually asserted that one of the policy goals of the Grenada invasion was the defeat of the "post-Vietnam syndrome" which he identified as "the resistance of many in Congress to the use of military force abroad for any reason, because of our nation's experience in Vietnam."[118] Secretary of State George P. Shultz also makes specific reference to the Vietnam syndrome, this time to account for his fear of "foot dragging" on the part of the military during the decisional process, suggesting that the military was very hesitant to use force unless it was assured of the support and resources necessary to succeed.[119] Secretart of Defense Weinberger makes a specific reference to Vietnam in his memoir when discussing the forces needed for success in Grenada.[120] He asked the operational commander how many troops he thought he would require, and then he told him to double it. He credited the failed Iranian hostage rescue and Vietnam with creating a desire to have more than enough military might available.

In addition to the Vietnam legacies noted directly by decision makers (congressional hesitancy, military hesitancy, and the imperative of overwhelming force), another important Vietnam legacy weighed in: the legacy of antagonism between the press and the government, mentioned above in the section on the media legacy chain.

The other major legacy that the Grenada invasion was a response to was the Iran hostage crisis. All of the major decision-maker memoirs make specific reference to fear of the approximately 1,000 medical students on Grenada being used as hostages.[121] Both Shultz and Weinberger make specific reference to Iran and mention discussing it during the decisional process. A cynical view would suggest that the medical students were in no real danger and that the mention of possible hostages was just legitimating rhetoric; even so, the legitimating power of the analogy is an important part of the legacy.

Finally, the last legacy leading into the Grenada intervention was the chance to avoid another Cuba. The strife on Grenada was due to a left-leaning government being overthrown by an even more left-leaning faction of that government, and the chance to step in and toss out the communists and replace them with a pro-American democratic government was just too good an opportunity to pass up.[122]

Grenada was a link in several ongoing legacy chains. While actively trying to avoid passing on some of the legacies of Vietnam, as mentioned, Grenada was a backlash against the role of the press in Vietnam and was an important step in the "War Powers" chain. In addition to passing on several legacy chains and attempting to blunt some existing legacies, Grenada left a few small legacies of its own, mostly for the military. While the Grenada operation was a "success," there were several significant military failures and near disasters. Part of the invasion force was diverted from reinforcements to Lebanon, and the ships on which they were transported did not have Grenada maps in their map lockers. Some troops were forced to rely on faxed maps or on tourist maps obtained once on the island. This resulted in the calamitous bombing of a mental hospital instead of the nearby fort that was the intended target, and nearly led to several similar disasters.[123] Because troops from different services were involved and there was not sufficient time to review communications protocols, some of the forces on the island were unable to communicate with other friendly forces.[124] While most of the worst possibilities were avoided, they left enough of a "near miss" impression on the military to make avoiding a repetition a priority.

Panama

The 1989 U.S. invasion of Panama is the first post–Cold War U.S. military intervention and, as such, has a curious position vis-à-vis the various legacies of the preceding decades. While free of the general legacies of the Cold War, this was still a military intervention, and it took place within the context of the legacies of other military interventions. One of the major legacies leading into Panama was the need to clean the sullied reputation of the U.S. armed forces. Following the humiliation of Vietnam, the horror of the Lebanon marine barracks bombing, and the messy near misses of the Grenada operation, there was a strong imperative to "win cleanly" this time.[125]

Another legacy input from Vietnam was the ambiguity of the trigger event for Vietnam, the incident in the Gulf of Tonkin, which led to the Gulf of Tonkin resolution giving the president freedom to do as he wished in Vietnam. The incident in the Gulf of Tonkin had turned out to be a less than clear case of unprovoked aggression and ultimately became somewhat of an embarrassment. When trying to decide whether the December 1989 incidents at a Panama city roadblock were sufficient provocation for the planned massive military invasion, decision makers invoked this analogy as one they were trying to avoid.[126]

As mentioned above, Panama served as another link in the press relations legacy chain. Finally, in terms of legacies left, it seems that decision makers were right to worry about the sufficiency of the provocation for the military intervention. The grounds on which the intervention was justified were not accepted by the international community and led to a storm of criticism abroad. This negative example served to reinforce the legacy of successfully legitimized joint forces interventions, making unilateral interventions much less likely in the post–Cold War era.[127]

Gulf War

On August 2, 1990, Iraqi forces invaded Kuwait. This aggression had three relatively rare qualities that made it rather straightforward to respond. First, it involved a threat to oil resources, on which the entire developed world is in some way dependent. Second, it was a clear-cut case of invasion of one state by another, something that is surprisingly rare, and is seen as a threat by all states. Third, it was post–Cold War, so there would be no opposition to a military response along established superpower polemic lines.

Needless to say, the Iraqi invasion met with widespread international condemnation and demands for withdrawal from the United Nations. On January 15, 1991, the UN deadline for Iraqi withdrawal passed, and allied forces began to fly air sorties against Iraqi forces and ground emplacements; on February 24, the allied ground attack began. The cease-fire took effect on February 28.

Several legacies affected the Gulf War. First, having reaped the disapproval brought by unilateral intervention, President Bush's second major military operation had the full support of the United Nations, and the cooperation of several major allies. In fact, this was the first "multinational" military intervention (not just peacekeeping operation) since World War II to have involved forces other than U.S. forces in the initial phases of assault (in the various Caribbean multinational actions, non-U.S. forces arrived only after the fighting was done).

The Vietnam legacy of overwhelming force, having been confirmed as a successful strategy in the interventions in the Dominican Republic, Grenada, and Panama, was confirmed again with the successful removal of Iraqi forces from Kuwait. Taking additional pages from the various legacies discussed previously, U.S. forces had the support of the American public, along with clearly defined operational goals, sufficient forces to achieve them, and a well-defined exit strategy. The Gulf War also served as a link in the legacy chain of military press relations and in the War Powers chain, as mentioned above.

Somalia

On December 4, 1992, President George H. W. Bush agreed to send almost 30,000 U.S. troops to Somalia to protect the distribution of food and medical supplies.[128] President Clinton inherited the Somalia intervention from Bush. Bush mentioned a desire to not leave it for Clinton when making initial plans for the intervention as a lame duck.[129] During Clinton's tenure of the involvement, the situation in Somalia deteriorated, with squabbling warlords threatening the peace and capturing and refusing to distribute much of the humanitarian aid. U.S. commanders decided to take action against the warlords and launched several daring raids to capture warlords and their major lieutenants in order to get the humanitarian aid back on track. Many elements of the Somali population did not appreciate this intervention in their affairs, so on Oct. 3, 1993, one of these raids turned into "the Battle of Mogadishu." After an initially successful raid and capture operation, a support helicopter went down a few blocks from the raid site. Army Rangers and Delta Force commandos on the ground moved to the helicopter to secure and protect the surviving crew and ended up stranded overnight, embroiled in a huge firefight against hundreds of hostile Somali militia. Eventually they were rescued by an armored convoy, after killing several hundred Somali fighters and suffering 18 American fatalities.[130] What might have been considered a military victory in other eras was considered a "loss" because 18 American soldiers died during what was supposed to be a peaceful humanitarian intervention and ultimately led to U.S. withdrawal from Somalia.

Several legacies led into the Somalia intervention. First, it exists as a link in the chain of UN-supported multinational interventions. Several other nations contributed troops to the humanitarian relief effort. "In fact, Bush's official and public decision came immediately after the U.N. Security Council adopted Resolution 794 calling for the U.N. Unified Task Force (UNITAF) to 'use all necessary means to establish a secure environment for humanitarian relief in Somalia.'"[131]

The planners of the Somalia intervention still had to deal with remaining isolationist hesitancy to approve of the use of U.S. forces abroad and the imperatives to mitigate them. Both Bush and Clinton, for the activities they approved in Somalia, made sure there were clear operational goals and emphasized exit strategies.[132] Somalia also served as another link in the press legacy chain.

U.S. involvement in Somalia left several important legacies. While following in many ways a traditional model for peacekeeping, the Somalia intervention unwittingly set some new rules for humanitarian interventions in the post–Cold War world. The decision to go after the warlords and the subsequent hostilities and loss of life left an important legacy for what constitutes acceptable behavior for peacekeepers. "To use a term coined by General Sir Michael Rose, the British commander of the UN forces in Bosnia, operations of this kind, traditionalists argued, should not cross the 'Mogadishu line.'"[133]

Finally, Somalia confirmed the American public's low toleration for casualties during humanitarian or peacekeeping operations.[134] The unmistakable legacy was that it is fine with the public to send aid and troops to help ensure its equitable distribution as international charity, provided the troops are not in harm's way, but international charity is not worth American lives.

Haiti

The U.S. intervention in Haiti had to face the legacy of post–Cold War humanitarian interventions, particularly colored by the U.S. experience in Somalia and the general legacy of hesitancy to use U.S. troops abroad. During the long run-up to the 1994 intervention, the Clinton administration made repeated efforts to gain public support for an intervention, declaring the importance of supporting democracy, garnering UN support and approval for a mission, making the goals of a prospective operation clear, and leaving clear exit strategies.[135] Public and congressional support was thin, so the ultimate intervention was precarious; had the mission failed, or been seen as a failure due to "unacceptable" U.S. casualties (in this case unacceptable might have been just about any number larger than 0), congressional and public outrage would have been extreme.

> Whether it was appreciated or not, the Carter mission to Haiti may have saved Clinton's presidency. It was clear from the Haitian military leaders' actions that they had prepared to resist the U.S. Invasion. It was only through the breakthrough with Yannick Cedras that finally convinced General Cedras that stepping down was the right course of action. Had the United States fought their way into Haiti, there would in all likelihood have been U.S. casualties. And there was little doubt that Congress, having been denied an opportunity to vote on intervention, would have taken it out on the administration.[136]

Congressional permission was not sought, allowing Haiti to serve as another link in the War Powers legacy chain, and dealing another measured blow to the War Powers Resolution. Congress passed several different resolutions to try to prevent U.S. intervention in Haiti without first seeking congressional approval, but ultimately failed in that goal. Instead, relying on a UN Security Council resolution and the possibility of completing the operation within the War Powers time limit, Clinton went ahead with the operation despite strong congressional resistance.

The Haiti process contains an interesting example of an immediate legacy. A critical turning point in negotiations to return exiled Haiti President Jean-Bertrand Aristide to Haiti (what the intervention was all about) was the failure of the Governors Island Accord, which would have returned Aristide to power peacefully. While the Governors Island Accord might have failed anyway, it was catalyzed to failure during "the Harlan County incident," when an armed mob on the docks prevented the lightly armed army engineers and military police aboard the USS *Harlan County* from landing in Haiti's capital. The decision to have the USS *Harlan County* leave Haitian waters (thus scuttling the Governors Island Accord) was taken with events the previous week in Mogadishu (the Battle of Mogadishu) very much in mind.[137] "Fearing another Somalia where, the week before, nearly a score of Army Rangers had died in a firefight with a clan leader's followers, the Clinton White House withdrew the ship. The message was clear—the United States could be pushed around and humiliated by weak but determined thugs."[138]

Bosnia

Here (as elsewhere) chronological order is difficult, as U.S. attention to the trouble in Bosnia started in earnest before 1991. However, 1991 was the first time military force came onto the decisional table as a possibility, although there were not significant US forces in Bosnia until 1995.[139] The legacies that contributed to that outcome had their effect from the beginning of the process.

As might be guessed from the delay between the 1991 first consideration of use of force to the deployment almost four years later, U.S. policy makers were extremely hesitant to use force in the Balkans. Bosnia seems to make a nice summary of many of the important legacies that trailed through these post–World War II military interventions. As career diplomat and former Ambassador to Yugoslavia Warren Zimmermann explains,

> Why this aversion to force? It seemed to have had three sources, not all of them articulated. The first was Vietnam. The "lesson" drawn from Vietnam was that even a minimum injection of American forces could swell inexorably into a major commitment and produce a quagmire. The second objection to force was the view that had prevailed during the successful prosecution of the Gulf War: there should be no U.S. military intervention unless the objectives were clear, the means applied to it would bring certain victory, there was an "exit strategy" (the earlier the better), and American casualties were sure to be minimal. The third factor was unexpressed: the coming presidential election of November 1992, which by the summer of 1992 undoubtedly bulked large in administration thinking. Pervading all these reasons was an almost obsessive fear of American casualties—an important change from the Gulf War, when large numbers of U.S. casualties were expected.[140]

As Zimmerman observes, Bosnia contained several of the Vietnam legacies and showed policy makers' respect for low public tolerance of peacekeeper casualties, as had been demonstrated in Beirut and Mogadishu.

One of the other factors delaying U.S. deployment was the complexity of the situation and a lack of clarity about what the role of U.S. forces would be. Gen. Colin L. Powell complained that establishing a U.S. presence without a goal had cost the United States 241 lives in Lebanon; he offered this fact to a reporter as to why the United States should not be in Bosnia in a "limited" way.[141]

September 11 Attacks and Response

At this writing (2008), the hunt for Osama bin Laden and his al Qaeda network continues, and military operations in Afghanistan and Iraq are ongoing. The legacies of the attacks of September 11, 2001, may be considerable and far-reaching and are certainly difficult to enumerate while we are still involved in their aftermath. However, one initial legacy was a virtual "blank check" and nearly unlimited domestic (and similarly enthusiastic though more guarded international) support for virtually any policy aimed at combating terrorism and protecting Americans from this suddenly very salient threat. However, the ambiguity of the outcomes of operations in Afghanistan and Iraq and the at best tenuous connection between Iraq and 9/11 appears to have squandered much of this "legitimacy capital." Time will tell, but the legacy of 9/11 as viewed through the lens of Afghanistan and Iraq is not what many might have expected.

Legacy chains in operation prior to the attacks of 9/11, though modified by the attacks, play into the U.S. response to the attacks. The desire for multinational participation and legitimacy both at home and abroad remains. An attack of this kind, however, makes legitimation much easier (see Chapter 7 on legitimacy). The desire to not needlessly spend the lives of American soldiers remains, but the stakes are considered to be sufficiently high that some casualties can be expected, and be expected to be tolerated (at least for a while).

Some legacy chains are likely to have been radically altered by the attacks. For example, reluctance to spend money and lives for international charity, particularly "nation building" could be considerably diminished given the now demonstrated threat that "rogue states" and the elements allowed to operate within their borders pose to consensual American national interests. It will be interesting to see what further changes in legacy trajectories emerge as events continue to unfold.

CONCLUSIONS

I have discussed military interventions and foreign policy events relevant to military interventions since World War II in terms of the institutional context feeding into and out of each event or intervention. These changes in institutional context constitute the policy legacies from these interventions. Military intervention legacies have their strongest impact on the immediately subsequent intervention, but can also leave more durable impressions on the institutional context, which, after being modified by subsequent military interventions, constitute "legacy chains."

Having detailed three specific military intervention legacy chains since World War II and presented a broad sample from the remainder, I am now prepared to draw conclusions about the general functional form that legacy chains are likely to follow. The functional form taken by these legacy chains is best described by a "step function," with each intervention contributing a step to the legacy, and extremely salient interventions leaving extremely large steps, which may, in many respects, "overshadow" smaller adjacent steps (think Vietnam). Figure 6.5 illustrates this notion.

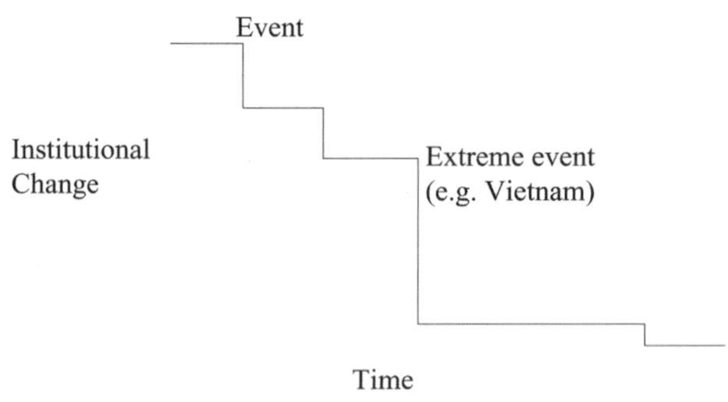

Figure 6.5 Legacy Chains as a Step Function

While I wish to argue that a step function best describes the general form, with punctuated institutional change in response to trigger events, I do believe that these institutions can change gradually over time as well. Specifically, the cultural relevance and thus institutional impact of an event will diminish slowly over time, particularly as it begins to hit the border for the collective "availability heuristic." However, the most significant changes to a previous legacy will occur with another "critical shift" or event, which will either reenforce, alter, or diminish the preexisting legacy as it is translated through the new event.

If the classic sociological question of governance is answered differently by the pluralists, the class theorists, and the elite theorists, then this position offers a corollary to any of those explanations. The legacy chain argument answers the question of governance with the following: "states do what they do largely as a product of what they have done before."

Note that this is different from the simplistic formulation "states do what they have done before." Further, it is more complex than "states try to repeat what has succeeded before, and avoid what has failed before." While states certainly do try to repeat successes and avoid repetition of failures, and those intentions are an important part of my policy legacy argument, policy making is meaningfully constrained by the (sometimes unintended) institutional legacies of previous policy.

Legacy chains have important implications for theories of the state and theories of decision making alike. While the legacy chain argument does not in itself constitute a theory of the state or of decision making, its theoretical and empirical strength demands alterations in existing theories to accommodate the important contextual constraints and imperatives made explicit here. In this way, this research supports the research agenda of the "new institutionalism," demanding that institutions and institutional change be considered in work in this area. Recognition of the intervention legacies and legacy chains identified is an important step toward understanding military intervention decisions. By acknowledging the role of the institutional context and the impact of previous policy on that context, both policy makers and policy analysts stand to have superior comprehension of some of the factors that constrain policy.

7

The Legitimacy of U.S. Military Interventions in Central America

If there was a mistake in the crisis, it was the way in which we presented our actions to the American people and the world.

—*Dean Rusk*

INTRODUCTION

Were these four military interventions *legitimate,* and it what sense? How and in what ways did the presidential administrations presiding over these military interventions attempt to justify them? How effective were those justifications, and why?

I argue that the particular structure of American presidential politics necessitates justification and that substantial differences between the genuine motives for interventions and what are normatively acceptable[1] justifications for interventions further complicate the process. There are different ways of legitimating interventions, and they are differentially effective depending on the circumstances. Presidents choose their justifications based on what they believe will be effective. Within that broad goal, the specific justifications chosen depend on three factors: the plausibility of a given justification, the difficulty of deploying that justification, and the perceived normative strength of the justification. While the specific elements contributing to this tripartite calculus vary from intervention to intervention depending on the details of the situation, a major shift in the likely characteristics of several different justification strategies came about with the end of the Cold War; this shift corresponds to a shift in the definitions of the national interest (see Chapter 4 for details).

In this chapter, I begin with definitions of legitimacy, legitimation, and justification, with a discussion of legitimacy for military interventions and the necessity of justification in American politics. Following this theoretical introduction, I discuss the nature of legitimation and detail the shifts in legitimizing that resulted from the end of the Cold War. I then list each of the major legitimation strategies used in my cases and explain the logic of the justification invoked, the normative foundation for that justification, and the likely position in the decisional process the justification might be deployed, for each. Throughout I have added notes, thoughts, and observations about the legitimation strategies available to the George W. Bush administration in its justifications of the policies of the war on terrorism in response to the attacks of September 11, 2001.

Definitions

While what I am concerned with here has much more to do with *legitimation* than with *legitimacy*, the two concepts are intertwined and require clarification and specification. Legitimacy is conceptually logically prior, so I begin with it.

Cognitive scientist Jonathan Waskan notes that "in the context of political theorizing, 'legitimacy' is roughly synonymous with 'justified' or 'acceptable.'"[2] He goes on to assert that "[i]f a people holds the belief that existing institutions are 'appropriate' or 'morally proper,' then these institutions are legitimate. That's all there is to it." Justified, acceptable, and appropriate will all serve as comfortable synonyms for legitimacy. In this construction, legitimacy is dependent on the views of "the people" and whether they accept the system of authority as justified, acceptable, and appropriate.[3] The work of sociologist Morris Zelditch, Jr. and his various collaborators[4] draws on notions of propriety and validity to distinguish an individual's judgment about the appropriateness of an act (propriety) from the apparent consensual view of the larger society (validity).[5] This work is important, both because it elaborates legitimacy as a fundamentally social process and explains how an individual who personally believes an act is wrong (lacks propriety) can nonetheless accept it as legitimate, because he or she perceives it as valid (accepted by the community).

I derive my notion of legitimation from Max Weber's discussion of "claims to legitimacy":

> What is important is the fact that in a given case the particular claim to legitimacy is to a significant degree and according to its type treated as "valid"; that this fact confirms the position of the persons claiming authority and that it helps to determine the choice of means of its exercise.[6]

As sociologist Joseph Bensman notes, "legitimacy is always *claimed* by a political, military, or religious leader or his staff. Weber, again, used the term *claim* [emphasis in original] in almost every discussion of legitimate domination."[7] So, if legitimacy is a product of *belief*, then legitimations are *claims* made by authorities to justify their decisions.

Justifications are a type of legitimation. Justifications are explanations of unexpected, untoward acts that accept responsibility for the act, deny wrongdoing, and explain why the action was taken.[8] Justifications serve as legitimations not only as claims to legitimacy, but as a necessary resolution of the tension engendered in any relationship when one party acts unexpectedly; by plausibly explaining the action, the actor can return to the "normal" state of the relationship.

Grounds for the Legitimacy of U.S. Military Interventions: The State, Foreign Policy, Military Interventions and the Presidency

In this section I discuss legitimacy in the general context of my theory of the state, foreign policy, and military interventions. I begin with a discussion of the legitimacy of the American government in general, then narrow the focus to a discussion of foreign policy, and finally focus in on military interventions specifically.

The classic argument is that legitimacy leads to consent. Where consent is virtually assured and system legitimacy is unassailable, then what does legitimacy mean? In general, the actions of the American state are accepted by its citizens as being in accord with right processes, having been done in accordance with constitutional principles and the specific laws governing governance. The system of authority is arranged in such a way (including representatives and a system of checks and balances) that each of the state's component apparatuses is accountable to some other part of the state. The general legitimacy of the state is never really an issue for the United States. The government is assumed to follow its own rules for functioning, and its own rules for correcting itself when errors in functioning occur. When a specific policy or decision is unpopular, citizens do not decry the legitimacy of the government, and complaints focus either on (1) a failure of the process that implemented a policy (and thus requires a corrective adjustment)[9] or (2) the specific decision or policy as being a poor one, in need of modification or removal through due political process. In both cases, the decision is accepted as both legitimate and binding, and citizen complaint remains (largely) within the context of the legal rational system.[10] Because this comfortable and resilient system is broadly and sufficiently embraced by enough of the American public, the U.S. government enjoys a high degree of legitimacy, and a strong default assumption of legitimacy for its individual policies. Supporting this argument is social psychologist Herbert C. Kelman's work that points out that legitimacy can be evaluated on at least two levels: the legitimacy of a claim or act itself, or the legitimacy of the claimant or actor.[11] If either is possessed of sufficient legitimacy, then the act is likely to be perceived as legitimate.

American foreign policy is a somewhat special subset of American policy making in general. State autonomy theorists find that state autonomy is most likely in the realm of foreign policy.[12] This is for several reasons. The first has to do with who participates in foreign policy. Historical sociologist Michael Mann identifies several potential participant groups for foreign policy and notes that the collection of possible participants is much smaller than for domestic policy.[13] Considering only American foreign policy, the number of likely participants is an even smaller subset of those identified by Mann. The foreign policy making apparatus, housed primarily in the executive branch, in the White House and the Department of State (with occasional congressional participation), is removed somewhat from domestic policy contests. Fewer groups participate, because fewer groups are interested. Some groups of interested citizens participate extensively on policy relevant to their specific geographic area of concern (for example, American Jews and policy toward Israel or Haitian expatriates and Haitian policy), but have no interests in other areas of foreign policy and thus do not participate. Most foreign policy issues are not salient to most citizens.

This normal low salience of foreign policy to general citizens changed, at least temporarily, with the attacks of September 11, 2001. But, while general concern within this certain issue area remains high, the general conclusions remain. While Americans feel threatened as a result of the attacks and want policy to protect them and eliminate threats abroad, citizens lack sufficient knowledge (and lack interest in acquiring sufficient knowledge) to participate in any way but at the level of broad encouragement for certain types of policies.

The second reason autonomy is likely in foreign policy is that while the laws and legal rational norms governing domestic policy are entirely domestic in nature, foreign policy is governed by internal rules and laws *and* external rules and laws. It is entirely possible (in fact, it is common) for an aspect of foreign policy to adhere to American norms, values, and rules while violating international norms or laws. The possibility of conflicting norms at the internal and international levels creates a complex "double standard" of rules for foreign policy makers to consider (for a further discussion, see the section "Internal vs. External Legitimacy").

These facts have an interesting dual implication for legitimacy. Because of limited participation by other groups in society and other parts of the state, the principal authority in foreign policy decision making is executive authority. While the general authority of the United States government is legal rational, the executive also inheres some traditional authority, not in the *person* of the president, but in the *position* of the presidency. So, while the legal rational norms governing presidential authority might conflict between the international and internal levels, the president can rely on the traditional authority of the presidency within the United States.

Finally, military interventions, as a further subset of foreign policy, have a slightly different character still. Military interventions are decided almost exclusively by the president and his close advisors (see Chapter 5 on process for details). As an aspect of foreign policy, most of the American population has no individual or expressed interests at stake in a military intervention situation,[14] but recognizes that interventions are potentially immensely consequential once they are begun and wants to understand why the intervention was undertaken by their government. While the "right process" for military interventions involves presidential judgment almost exclusively, it is insufficient to simply claim "the president took the decision" without saying *why* the president took the decision. While military interventions are likely to receive the same default assumption of legitimacy given general U.S. policy,[15] citizens are more likely to be curious about the reasons for the policy.

So, to summarize, the American state is generally considered to be highly legitimate, and its policies are accorded a high default level of legitimacy by the public. Foreign policy has fewer interested participants, but receives the same assumption of legitimacy, even though its legitimacy depends in part on potentially conflicting internal and external legal norms and on the traditional authority inherent in the position of the presidency. Military interventions are a special subset of foreign policy, in which an extremely limited group of persons makes extremely momentous military decisions. The legal rational and traditional norms governing this process are based primarily on presidential judgment, and, while grounds for intervention are assumed to be legitimate, citizens are curious what the judgment was based on, and this is where justification comes in.

The Necessity of Justification in American Politics

So, given the very resilient nature of the legitimacy of the American political system, and the straightforward traditional and legal rational legitimacy of the president making decisions to deploy troops in defense of the national interest, why do military interventions always include a justification or set of legitimation claims?

I would argue that it is not simply to make politics a "well-lubricated engine, with the least amount of friction and resistance" as political scientist Paul L. Rosen asserts, but rather because of the dependence of the president on public opinion for political power and because of the demands of the electoral cycle.[16] The popularity of the president is nowhere near as resilient as the legal rational and traditional authority of the institution of the American presidency, or the government as a whole. To effectively wield power, the president needs to keep public opinion high and maintain congressional support.[17] Maintenance of this support is the goal of legitimating claims about interventions.

The Difference between Motives and Claims

One of the most powerful observations of my empirical research is that in almost every case the true motive for intervention (as discussed and evidenced in decision-maker memoirs and exposeés) overlaps at most partially with the publicly *claimed* justifications for the intervention.

There is a tension between what is normatively acceptable and what is considered electorally pragmatic or in the national interest (see Chapter 4). The "real" motive for a military intervention (the calculated presidential national interest) may not fit well within the framework of normatively acceptable motives (the public national interest). For example, the 1994 Haitian intervention was largely driven by the political necessity of stemming the flow of Haitian refugees onto the Florida coast.[18] The claims and justifications for the Haitian intervention, however, focused much more on the restoration of the democratically elected but exiled Haitian President Jean-Bertrand Aristide. Now, this is not to say that Aristide's restoration was not part of the driving force for the intervention. Likewise, I am not suggesting that protecting the voters and the economy of Florida is not a worthwhile (and legitimate) goal for U.S. policy. Rather, I am arguing that "restoration of democracy" is normatively more attractive to the American public than "protection of votes in Florida" and that decision makers were aware of that normative evaluation and emphasized the former over the latter in their justification claims accordingly (the legitimation national interest).[19]

Having used Haiti as an example, I now provide similar information for the other three cases. Briefly, here are the ascertainable genuine motives for each intervention, followed by some of the claims made about each.

Dominican Republic

The intervention in the Dominican Republic was undertaken to prevent a communist take-over. During his deliberations, President Johnson repeatedly emphasized the unacceptability of "another Cuba in this Hemisphere."[20] The Department of State made policy goals clear to the Ambassador in the Dominican Republic: secure the International Safety Zone, cooperate with the Organization of American States (OAS) and the Papal Nuncio toward obtaining a cease-fire, and ensure that OAS action did not allow communists to take power.[21]

While the motive was clear and decision makers were very candid about that internally and in their orders, their public claims were not so clear. The justification offered for the intervention was that it was first to save the lives of Americans and other foreign nationals and, second, to restore order and save the lives of Dominicans. When asked about the presence of communists by congressional leaders during congressional notification of the impeding invasion, Adm. William Raborn (the CIA director) informed them that there were "7 or 8" possible communists in the rebel leadership and admitted that there was some concern of communism, but tried to pretend that it was not the primary motivation; thus began the slippery slope of legitimating what was fundamentally an anticommunist intervention as something else.[22] The decision not to admit that the intervention was basically anticommunist was actively taken by decision makers.[23]

Grenada

President Reagan offered three reasons for the invasion of Grenada: (1) to protect American lives, (2) to forestall further chaos, and (3) to assist in the restoration of law and order and governmental institutions.[24] While each of these may have been contributing factors to the genuine motive, an important and unclaimed part of the motive was an opportunity to be rid of a small, left-leaning government in the Caribbean with which the United States had very poor relations. The month after the invasion, Reagan claimed it as a great victory over communism, which cuts much closer to the real motivation (Reagan, as quoted in the *New York Times,* November 6, 1983: "Major gain not only in political but in strategic terms").[25] A final observation about the relation the public claims bore to the truth can be accurately gauged by the fact that three days after the invasion the deputy White House press secretary for foreign affairs resigned, citing "damage to his personal credibility."[26]

Panama

The question, then, becomes why after years of support for Noriega did the U.S. administration choose to implement economic sanctions and depose him. George Bush gave three reasons: (1) to restore democracy in Panama, (2) to protect American lives, and (3) to stop the use of Panama as a drug conduit and haven for money launderers. These three reasons, however, were not the real reasons for the decision to depose Noriega and invade Panama. "They were merely the legitimations."[27]

Christina Jacqueline Johns and P. Ward Johnson argue that the real motive for the invasion of Panama was to continue American control of the Panamal Canal and to remove Manuel Noriega.[28] While I found no discussion of the former in decisional process records, I found ample indication of the latter, for example, Colin L. Powell recollecting what was at issue in the meeting at which the decision was taken:

> The key issue remained whether we had sufficient provocation to act. We had reasons—Noriega's contempt for democracy, his drug trafficking and indictment, the death of an American Marine, the threat to our treaty rights to the canal with this unreliable figure ruling Panama. And, unspoken, there was George Bush's personal antipathy to Noriega, a third-rate dictator thumbing his nose at the United States. I shared that distaste.[29]

The publicly claimed motive for the operation was a response to the general situation in Panama along with the provocation of the death of a marine shot at a Panamanian roadblock and the harassment of a navy lieutenant and his wife at the same roadblock shortly thereafter. Accounts of these roadblock incidents in Bob Woodward's multiple interview study,[30] the various newspaper accounts, and memoirs indicate that this was the worst thing to have happened in Panama and was an inexcusable provocation.[31] Margaret Scranton offers a different account:

> These incidents were like hundreds that had occurred during the last two years; many of those were minor, but some had been just as serious, including several beatings and one rape. The events of the December 16–17 weekend, particularly Lt. Paz's death, were perceived differently. They were interpreted in Washington as part of an increasingly threatening pattern, and, significantly, in the context of the National Assembly's declaration and Noriega's statements.[32]

When I first discovered this nearly universal difference between claims and genuine motives, I assumed that this was evidence against the legitimacy (in some poorly defined and intuitive sense of the word) of these military interventions. If the main motive was not the claimed motive, then the main motive must be wrong, illegal, unacceptable: in short, *illegitimate* (or, in the terms presented earlier, "lacking propriety" in my judgment). Now, having fully analyzed these cases and thought a bit more about legitimacy and justification, I recognize an important tension between the two. In this chapter I define and discuss legitimation as a process. To be legitimate is to be successfully legitimated. While that is a very pragmatic and "real" definition in some sense, it leaves me with an uneasy feeling to ascribe legitimacy to events that involved deception and would likely not been deemed acceptable (not valid) by the public if full information had been made available. However, as psychologists Christian S. Crandall and Ryan K. Beasley argue, legitimacy is all about perception.[33] If the American polity perceives only the claim and the outcome, and perceives the claim and the outcome as legitimate, then the motive and the acceptability of that motive does not matter.

I reserve the term "ideal legitimacy" for the normative position that a policy would likely have been accorded had the public understood the true motive for the policy. This allows me to consider the Grenada intervention to be illegitimate, but successfully legitimated. Under this scheme, it is entirely possible for a military intervention to be successfully legitimated at the time, but to end up being something that is, in the eyes of history, illegitimate. A clear example is the U.S.–sponsored invasion of Guatemala in 1954. Arguably the ongoing operation in Iraq, partially legitimated based on unsubstantiated claims of the existence of weapons of mass destruction and on links between Iraq and 9/11, is another.

Normative Conflict (Counterclaims)

The belief that the president lied in his claims about the reasons and justifications for a military intervention would be a huge normative violation. As a consequence, decision makers take some care to make sure that their legitimating claims are at least plausible and that justifications offered are at least part of the true motive, even if not the largest part.

True or untrue, presidents are not making legitimating claims in a vacuum. Public discourse will potentially contain not only the administration's claims, but also counterclaims variously from the extremist media (either liberal or conservative), congressional leaders, skeptical analysts, domestic partisans of one of the stake-holding factions in the country invaded, commentators from other countries, or persons in the invaded country itself. The goal of these claims and counterclaims is to appeal to a specific norm or normative sphere and then focus public attention there, to the exclusion of norms to which the intervention is closer or farther from adherence. As Robert J. Robinson and Laura Kray note, "Most seemingly intractable social disputes are by their very nature subjective, and are characterized by attempts by the various sides to delegitimize the other while advancing the acceptability of their own views. It has long been known that this is a process much governed by the rules of social perception."[34]

These normative conflicts can be public and obvious, with claims and counterclaims appealing to different norms appearing side by side in the headlines, or they can be much more subtle. Claimants can chose to mobilize a norm that has previously not received much focus. An example of this selective use of norms comes from the political situation in Haiti during the early 1990s: while the human rights record of the regime that Haitian President Aristide replaced was deplorable, Americans opposed to Aristide chose to attack the (comparatively much better) human rights record of Aristide's short administration when Haiti and Haitian politics came into the limelight in the U.S. media.[35]

Ultimately, justification claims and counterclaims are waged as a public normative conflict to influence the hearts and minds of the American public. As political scientist Samuel Kernell offers in his account of the ambiguity following the Grenada intervention in October 1983:

> Shortly after the U.S. invasion of Grenada in the fall of 1983 all opinion indicators pointed to a confused and ambivalent public. Politicians within both parties were

uncertain what posture they should assume toward the President's action. Some Democratic spokespersons, including House Speaker O'Neill, began lobbing salvos at the White House, describing the invasion as "gunboat diplomacy." Democratic senator Daniel P. Moynihan publicly declared the invasion to be "an act of war," adding, "I don't know that you restore democracy at the point of a bayonet." One Democratic representative went so far as to announce a petition drive calling for the President's impeachment. For the most part, however, Democrats—including, prominently, those seeking their party's presidential nomination—and Republicans temporized.

With the military operation concluded and public opinion appearing increasingly to echo the President's critics, President Reagan went on national television to account for his actions. The poll takers were poised; when they revealed the public's early, highly favorable response, the critics hushed up, and Reagan's previously silent partners became vocal. One Democratic senator remarked, "Most people, once they saw the polls come out, went underground." Within two weeks after his initial criticism, Senator Moynihan conceded, "The move is popular and therefore there's no disposition in the Senate to be opposed to it.[36]

LEGITIMATION

Given that the U.S. government has a high degree of default legitimacy, it is unremarkable that all four of this book's core intervention cases were "legitimate" in the United States. Put another way, if our dependent variable is legitimacy, we observe minimal variance on it. Thinking in those terms, I propose another dependent variable: effectiveness of different legitimation strategies. To conceive it this way is to divorce legitimacy as active or passive consent (whether the populace *accepts* a military intervention), which is virtually unavoidable in the modern United States, from *public opinion* about an intervention, that slippery coin that is so important to the exercise of presidential power.[37]

In this section I discuss the nature of intervention legitimations themselves, the conflicts inherent in making justifications, and some of the general change trends in justifications offered since World War II. The end of the Cold War brought about a significant shift in the frequency with which certain military intervention legitimating strategies were used by U.S. decision makers. The shift from a bipolar Cold War world to a post–Cold War world with apparently fewer high-stakes events and crises heightened debate on the proper role of the United States in the world at large and shifted both the content of foreign policy and the claims used to legitimate it.

Internal vs. External Legitimacy

Legitimacy theorizing generally fits into two broad strands.[38] The first group holds that legitimacy is a product of conformance with *a priori* normative standards of acceptability (rules), while the second group maintains that legitimacy is embodied within the attitudes of a nation's citizens toward its government. While I have asserted that legitimacy is based on belief and is thus ultimately grounded in citizen attitudes (which are likely based on normative standards, albeit potentially inconsistent ones), I argue that both notions are useful in different contexts. Thus far, my discussion of legitimacy has focused on the *internal* citizens or subjects of a country, with no regard given to the legitimacy of policy in the *external* or international arena. While I have argued that legitimacy for the citizens of the United States is based on their composite beliefs about the legitimacy claimed by the government, citizens of other nations are much less likely to be swayed by appeals from traditional American authorities or charismatic American presidents, and international law and U.S. law are not always compatible. External/international legitimacy will be almost exclusively based on legal rational positions, much less influenced by U.S. administration normative claims, and much more open to counterclaims from the leaders in their own societies.

As a default starting position in international law, all military interventions are illegal and thus illegitimate. Very specific situations must exist before violating the sovereignty of another nation through invasion can be considered legal and make credible claims to legal rational legitimacy in international law. Such a situation was created by the attacks of September 11, 2001. Provided a reasonable connection to international terrorism is established, military action focuses on eliminating that terrorist threat, and the United States consults with and gains the cooperation of its traditional allies and the international community, U.S. policy makers expected to have a much freer hand in international approval of military interventions. Operations in Afghanistan qualified; operations in Iraq were more ambiguous.

This general default position of no legitimacy for military interventions is a very different starting position than the one I have discussed, regime legitimacy, as "the government" in a functioning democracy is assumed to be legitimate by its citizens until proven otherwise, and likewise the policy decisions of that government are assumed to be legitimate.

In the context of U.S. intervention decision making, different priorities are given and approaches taken to internal vs. external legitimacy. The section on specific "Legitimating Strategies" discusses the merits and implications for each strategy, both in terms of its contribution to internal and external legitimacy.

Legitimizing for External Legitimacy

In the realm of external legitimacy, claims are almost all legal rational appeals. Only very limited traditional normative arguments can be used internationally, appeals to traditional alliances, or to nations that share such norms as democratic values.

In general, administrations seem concerned primarily with internal legitimacy and second with external legitimacy. For example, after the 1983 U.S. invasion of Grenada,

> the invasion was almost universally condemned in Latin America, only the military dictatorships of Chile, Guatemala, and Uruguay expressing support. The United Nations voted its disapproval overwhelmingly. To this President Reagan responded:

"One hundred nations in the UN have not agreed with us on just about everything that's come before them where we're involved, and it didn't upset my breakfast at all."[39]

This favoring of internal over external legitimacy is due to several factors, including the odd nonenforceable and nonsovereign nature of the international system. As legal scholar Thomas M. Franck notes,

> The surprising thing about international law is that nations ever obey its strictures or carry out its mandates. This observation is made not to register optimism that the half-empty glass is also half full, but to draw attention to a pregnant phenomenon: that most states observe systematic rules much of the time in their relations with other states. That they should do so is much more interesting than, say, the fact that most citizens usually obey their nation's laws, because the international system is organized in a voluntarist fashion, supported by so little coercive authority. This un-enforced rule system can obligate states to profess, if not always manifest, a significant level of day-to-day compliance even, at times, when that is not in their short-term self-interest.[40]

As Franck goes on to observe there are certain benefits to adherence to international law, mostly being the benefits accorded members in good standing in the international community. Still, compared with the legal and political consequences of failing to adhere to U.S. law when conducting a military intervention, the relative nonconsequences of violating international law pale in comparison.

As mentioned, by and large, military interventions are violations of international law. Several different steps might be taken to make an intervention legal, or claimable and contestably legal. It is much easier to claim the moral high ground when a military intervention is at least *arguably* legal, even if the argument is not all that strong.

Legitimizing in the Cold War

The Cold War created strong legitimizing norms that were not based in the legal-rational sphere. Opposing the threat of communism very rapidly entered the American tradition and quickly became an overwhelming norm in foreign policy. Cold War presidents were afforded extra authority and legitimacy as "leaders of the free world" and the champions of the American public against the Red Menace. The imperatives of the Cold War rolled over other traditional values, such as nonintervention and self-determination.[41] Virtually any intervention could be considered and then legitimated through an appeal to the need to prevent communist expansion.

End of the Cold War

The end of the Cold War created a great deal of ambiguity in the U.S. role in the world generally, especially militarily. Gone was the monolithic menace of the Soviet Union, and the courageous fight for the survival of democracy explicit in Cold War rhetoric. Instead, Americans faced a "new world order" in which America was still number one, and American traditional norms and values were still important, just, perhaps, a little less urgent.

The lack of clear and obvious imperatives to action in the post–Cold War world is reflected in the general (and contradictory) foreign policy goals embraced by the American public. International relations scholars Charles W. Kegley, Jr. and Eugene R. Wittkopf report,

> They favor global activism but oppose sending economic and military aid to other nations. They yearn for peace through strength but are wary of international institutions.
>
> They fear nuclear weapons and their proliferation and support efforts to reach negotiated arms agreements with the nation's present and former adversaries. They oppose the use of force abroad; still, they back presidents when they chose force of arms and prefer military victory to limited war. They worry about the impact of free trade on their jobs, yet many are willing to open the United States to broader involvement in the world political economy.[42]

Since the collective public holds the beliefs that ultimately determine the legitimacy of military interventions, such obvious dichotomies of belief and contradictory desires can pose problems for justification strategies. However, the fact that these contradictory beliefs are not strongly held or based on any real interests makes them vulnerable to change in the face of a reasonable justification. This gives an administration a fair amount of play with regard to persuasion in its legitimation claims.

Changes in What Could Be Claimed

The most significant changes in post–Cold War legitimizing pertain to what could be claimed. One of the most important shifts was in what could legitimately be claimed as a crisis. Previously, presidents could draw on the "Cold War metanarrative" and discursively use unstable situations in many parts of the world as a stalking horse for the Soviet Union, and thus justify American involvement.[43] Once the Cold War ended, it became much more difficult to structure situations in other countries as "vital to the American national interest" than it had been during the Cold War. With the threat of world domination by communism removed, the internal affairs of small countries around the world returned, in many Americans' minds, to being "their" problem and not "ours." To discursively consider a situation to be a crisis, therefore, required an appeal to traditional norms other than prevention of communism. Lack of a single, massive, and almost universally accepted central legitimating principle would make this difficult; presidents have tried a number of different central legitimating principles, but none have been as successful as the crisis obvious in the threat of total annihilation implicit in the Cold War.

Lacking anything as powerful as the Cold War, presidents have tried to promote several different appeals to traditional norms to sufficiency for military intervention. On the eve of the end of the Cold War, the war on drugs was in full swing, and "narcoterrorism" and its prevention were claimed as part of the justification for the U.S. invasion of Panama in 1989.[44] While antidrug policy retains a focus on helping other countries slow their export of drugs, the war on drugs has not replaced the Cold War in any significant way.

More successful and durable claims have been made in the name of democracy and human rights, both important traditional American norms. For these claims presidents have found an important ally in the United Nations.[45] A UN resolution is a strong legal rational claim to international legitimacy, and external legitimacy can be used to claim internal legitimacy much more readily that the reverse. Even with the strength of the United Nations behind them, however, appeals to the norms of promoting democracy and saving lives in other countries have not been free from strong opposition counterclaims suggesting that, while these are noble goals, they are not worth the lives of American soldiers.[46]

Arguably, the attacks of 9/11 heralded the end of the "post–Cold War period" and created a new, "turn of the century" contemporary era. Where claims of narcoterrorism have failed, the war on terrorism brings with it considerable normative force. Throughout the Cold War, no attack nearing the magnitude of the 9/11 attacks was launched on American soil; while the new "enemy" is not as monolithic as the "Red Menace," it is perhaps more frightening and threatening in its own insidious way. The attacks of 9/11 have reopened the availability of several Cold War–style justification claims and may create more still.

SPECIFIC LEGITIMIZING STRATEGIES

In this section, I discuss various specific strategies that have been used to make legitimating claims. For each one, I discuss the general logic of the justification and the type of norm or norms appealed to, the general normative strength of the justification, and where it is most likely to occur in the decisional process. Before beginning this discussion of the specific strategies, I note some of the general character of legitimations, namely, their reflexive quality and the way they occur as part of the decision making-process, and discuss some further differences between internal and external justification.

Very Reflexive

Unsurprisingly, legitimation is very reflexive; leaders offer justifications strategically and thoughtfully, very much aware that they are trying to "sell" their decision to the public. Gen. Colin L. Powell candidly observed, "Once you've got all the forces moving and everything's being taken care of by the commanders, turn your attention to television because you can win the battle or lose the war if you don't handle the story right."[47] During the long run-up to the invasion of Panama, Secretary of State James Baker explained to a subordinate, "These things take time. We've got to wait for public opinion to build."[48] After the decision to intervene in Grenada, National Security Council Advisor Constantine C. Menges recalls a colleague musing, "[H]ow are we going to sell this to the public?"[49] As noted at the beginning of this chapter, Secretary of State Dean Rusk observed about the events surrounding the 1965 intervention in the Dominican Republic, "If there was a mistake in the crisis, it was the way in which we presented our actions to the American people and the world."[50]

Presidential leadership includes not only decision making, but "leading" public opinion through justifications. Kegley and Wittkopf quote President Theodore Roosevelt as quipping, "I did not 'divine' what the people were going to think. I simply made up my mind what they ought to think and then did my best to get them to think it."[51] Policy makers are reflexive about their legitimizing and about their chances for success. Although they are certain about their need for public support, policy makers are not always sure how to best get it. All of the various justifications discussed in what follows have been offered as claims about U.S. military interventions in Central America, but some have been more successful than others, and some have been more or less successful under certain circumstances.

Legitimation as Part of Process

In addition to being devised reflexively, justifications occupy space in the decisional process. Decision makers spend time considering how an intervention will be legitimized, and different justifications are considered at different phases in the decisional process. During the planning of the Haiti intervention, the Clinton team spent time in numerous meetings discussing ways to gain support from Congress and the public.[52] The general character of the process as crisis or premeditated and secret or public (see Chapter 4, on process) also impacts the justifications available.

In a premeditated intervention, greater time and care are likely to be given to formulating legitimations. In a public premeditated intervention decision process, justifications have to be offered well prior to the commencement of the operation, and a number of different justifications can be tentatively tested out to see which ones resonate with the public and other societal interests.

In crisis intervention decisional processes, on the other hand, legitimations have to be arrived at quickly; the amount of time between action and accounting for action is short. Some legitimations take too long to mobilize to be used in a crisis situation. Secret crisis interventions are legitimated wholly after the fact. The administration will have basically a single chance to account for its decision; it cannot "test-market" different justifications for the intervention and see which one works best. If not enough time during the decisional process is dedicated to legitimation planning, the administration can have trouble. Lowenthal notes that, after the troops were already in the Dominican Republic, a "new and complex phase of the Dominican crisis now began in Washington in which deciding what to say about events in Santo Domingo became almost as important as, and perhaps more controversial than, deciding what actions to take."[53]

LEGITIMATING STRATEGIES

Since internal legitimacy is fundamentally about domestic public belief, unsurprisingly, most internal justifications boil down to attempts to positively influence public opinion. "First, they must consider the value the public places in the venture, and they may try to use whatever persuasive skills they possess to enhance this value—that is, to sell the project to the public."[54]

Attempts to influence public opinion can include a wide range of activities, from a White House press conference announcing a change in strategy, to choosing the name of a military operation.[55] The best example of the latter was the last minute change from Operation Blue Spoon to Operation Just Cause as the operation name for the U.S. invasion of Panama.[56] Military press liaisons announced the implementation of Operation Just Cause shortly after it began, and the media reported the operation under that name, lending it considerable *prima facie* legitimacy.[57]

External legitimations, on the other hand, are targeted primarily at foreign governments rather than at domestic publics. The basic goal is the same, securing favorable opinion, but the range of potentially successful appeals is much smaller. Efforts at external legitimation will include legal rational grounds and will try to appeal to widely shared international norms such as human rights, peace, and security rather than naked U.S. interest.

In what follows I present the various justifications offered in my core cases. They are presented in order of likely normative force for internal legitimacy, from strongest to weakest. As mentioned, normative force is wholly contingent on plausibility; implausible claims based on strong norms do not generate successful justifications. For each legitimizing strategy, I explain the logic of the justification, the norms it is based on or appeals to, and where it is likely to be mobilized in the intervention process where that is not obvious.

Winning

Success is always legitimate. If an intervention achieves its goals and has a sufficiently low cost in American soldiers' lives to be considered an unqualified success, then it is going to be believed to be legitimate. Even if an intervention is not an unqualified success (as the Panama invasion appeared to be before Noriega was captured), compelling claims of success increase belief in legitimacy. Only when claims of success are ultimately proven to be untrue (as arguably happened in Vietnam) or premature (as with the infamous "mission accomplished" banner flown for President George W. Bush's May 2003 visit to the USS *Abraham Lincoln*)[58] is legitimacy threatened. In both the Haiti and Grenada operations, the justifications offered, respectively, by President Reagan and President Clinton might have left them exposed to intense criticism had they not been saved by the success of their operations.

Success can be mobilized as a justification only *after* a *successful* intervention. Success itself is often contingent on factors beyond a president's control (think Bay of Pigs). Adopting success as a justification can occur only late in the process, after the intervention has succeeded. This makes it much more useful in a secret intervention situation, where the president is not required to make a public accounting of the intervention prior to its execution. Finally, success gives no external legitimacy; if the international community objects to an intervention, it will object win or lose.

Declaration of Crisis

Important in American traditions are the core values of nationalism, and what is called the "rally to the flag" effect.[59] Pulling together to successfully resolve a crisis situation is a very popular sentiment. This creates a powerful rhetorical device for a president: "the crisis."[60] By declaring a situation to be a crisis, it is lent gravity, urgency, and legitimacy. While the events leading up to the interventions in both Panama and Haiti were premeditated and do not meet any rigorous systematic definition of crisis (see Chapter 5, the process chapter, for a more elaborate discussion), both were rhetorically labeled "crises" by the administrations that ultimately launched military interventions for their resolution. By labeling a situation a crisis, an administration can focus attention and receives, at least preliminarily, the benefit of the doubt. Of course, in order to be a crisis, some kind of vital interest must arguably be at stake. In the Panama crisis, the safety of American lives in Panama was claimed to be at stake. In the Haitian crisis, the crisis was claimed for democratic values and human rights, two values which, for many Americans, failed to pass the threshold requirements for "vital" American interests at that time. The normative strength of a claim of crisis depends on the perceived "vitality" of the threatened interests and the plausibility of the threat.

During the Cold War, many vital interests were perceived to be straightforward in a "black and white" way, and interventions could easily be tied to these interests. The possibility of total annihilation and the threat of losing a "domino" to communism were readily accepted as crises. While a claim of crisis usually lacks any force for external legitimacy, Cold War crises involving preventing the spread of communism created legitimacy in half of the bipolar Cold War world; U.S. allies accepted plausible threats[61] to the vital interests of the "free world" as sufficient international crises to lend their support. Of course, the Soviets and their allies decried all U.S. interventions as illegitimate, so much of the external legitimacy for Cold War interventions was split along the East-West divide.

Illegitimate Target Government

A subcategory of claims of crisis is attribution of crisis due to the illegitimacy of another state's government. When a government or regime can be successfully claimed to be illegitimate, the legitimacy of action against that government or regime is likely to be increased. In three of the four core cases discussed here, the government in the target country (the Revolutionary Military Council [RMC] in Grenada, Maximum Leader Manuel Noriega, and the collection of coup leaders led by Raoul Cédras in Haiti) were declared illegitimate governments, which allowed a threat to core American values to be claimed. This kind of appeal is an appeal to the norms of legitimacy and right process itself. Of course, at the time of each intervention, these target governments were by no means the only illegitimate governments in the world (in fact, at any given time, the United States considers several questionable or outright illegitimate governments to number among its allies), so illegitimacy of the target government is not a sufficient justification by itself and is, obviously, a claim that is selectively mobilized.

Governments can be declared illegitimate through appeals to a variety of norms. The RMC was a military junta, as were Cédras and his cronies.[62] While Noriega was the elected head of state of Panama, he had been charged with electoral fraud; interestingly enough, the actual legal claims made against Noriega were not that he was an illegitimate head of state, but rather that he was a wanted criminal, having been indicted for drug trafficking in a U.S. court.

Curiously, a claim of crisis due to illegitimate target government is the only kind of crisis justification that might generate external legitimacy (beyond Cold War bipolar crises). If the international community accepts that the target government is in violation of international norms and values, then claims of the necessity of forcefully dealing with that government are more likely to be legitimated (think Saddam Hussein or the Taliban).

Claim of Vital Interests

Public opinion can also be swayed through claims that appeal to traditional American values. These claims have exceptional normative force when they share a legal rational logic, for example, where the president is charged legally with responding to threats to the nation's vital interests and an American traditional value and a vital interest can be claimed to overlap.

While an appeal to generic "vital interests" is almost wholly dependent on the persuasiveness of the specific president, certain vital interests are normatively more compelling and thus are more likely to make successful claims. The protection of American lives, especially if made as a plausible claim, has great resonance with Americans. This is the primary source of claimed legitimacy for government policy in response to the attacks of 9/11. Appeals to related traditional values, such as rescuing American hostages or protecting Americans from being taken hostage, have also worked. Protection of Americans was part of the legitimatizing claims for all of the cases under consideration except for Haiti, Haiti being the only intervention for which the vital interests at stake were seriously questioned prior to the intervention. In the Dominican Republic, the vital interest was the protection of Americans and other foreign nationals; in Grenada it was the protection of American citizens, specifically the approximately 1,000 medical students on the island, and Panama was legitimated as a response to aggression against American citizens and to protect Americans from further threat.

As mentioned in the section above on crisis, certain American vital interests (namely, opposing the spread of communism) were also held to be NATO (North Atlantic Treaty Organization) vital interests and could thus be used to generate external legitimacy among allies during the Cold War. With the end of the Cold War, these same vital interests were radically devalued both at home and abroad. Both Americans and foreigners alike are now much more inclined to question the vitalness of any claimed vital interests, supposing instead that they might be selfish interests or, even if somewhat altruistic, less than vital.

A notable exception is the appeal to a need to protect American citizens. In general, defense of citizens abroad involves legal rational issues of sovereignty and citizenship, but also relies on norms of nationalism, solidarity, and protection of citizens. Though not legal by international standards, an intervention undertaken to protect American citizens could be accorded external legitimacy *if* it was done strictly as an evacuation, after which troops were withdrawn. In two of the four cases discussed here (the Dominican Republic and Grenada) the administration claimed a need to protect U.S. citizens, evacuated citizens to safety, and then left troops that pacified the respective islands in a way that was a flagrant violation of international laws of nonintervention. It is one thing to step in to protect your citizens when the indigenous government can no longer guarantee their safety; it is quite another to impose your will on the situation, and the international community makes its legitimacy beliefs based on that understanding. Had the Grenada and Dominican Republic interventions been just evacuations, they would likely have been met with considerably less international protest.

Exhaustion of Alternatives

Conforming with traditions of "right process" without actually being an appeal to law is the claim that "all other alternatives have been exhausted." Military intervention is always viewed as the policy of last resort in defense of vital interests. By focusing on all of the other efforts that have been made to realize policy and their lack of success along with the continued importance of the policy goals themselves, an administration can assert that it has been left with no alternative and must intervene. Not only does this strategy appeal to the "feel good" logic of seeking other means and exhausting alternatives, it shifts blame from the administration to the object of policy. For example, a president might assert, "If only the Haitian junta leaders had bowed to diplomatic pressure or the pressure of economic sanctions, they would not have forced us to the point were we have to intervene." Diplomatic pressure on the Haitian regime was considerable, and a number of different strategies, including various levels of sanctions, were tried.

> From May through August 1994, events quickly accelerated toward invasion. Clinton began to "carry out a series of diplomatic, public, and other steps that would allow him to assert that all other avenues had been exhausted," according to the September 25 *Washington Post.* In short, the United States needed to justify the invasion.[63]

For this strategy to work, substantial and credible efforts to realize policy by other means must have been undertaken. Further, the administration needs to effectively list the efforts, plausibly claim that they were potentially effective efforts given sufficient time to work, and show that the problem (or parties) that is the object of policy is genuinely intransigent. Because of the demands of actually trying other policies, this justification is available only to premeditated interventions.

UN Resolution or Invitation

Another justification that is commonly used involves seeking some form of external legitimacy and then waving that as a flag to increase internal legitimacy. The most common form this takes is either a UN resolution supporting action or an invitation from a regional multistate organization to participate in some kind of multinational intervention force. Once a UN resolution or foreign invitation is obtained, presidents can appeal to "our obligations to support the UN" or "the need to respond to the pleas of our international neighbors" to generate internal legitimacy and external legitimacy alike.

Three of the four interventions in Central America since World War II have involved some kind of appeal to external legitimacy that was then used as an internal justification. During the Dominican Republic intervention, almost as an afterthought, an appeal was made to the OAS to coordinate a peaceful resolution to the civil strife there.[64] Prior to the Grenada intervention in 1983, the Organization of Eastern Caribbean States (OECS) made an appeal to the United States to aid it in restoring order on Grenada. President Reagan made this invitation central to administration justification claims, referring in his public statements and memoirs to the imperative of responding positively to the pleas of our neighbors:

> We couldn't say no to those six small countries who had asked us for help. We'd have no credibility or standing in the Americas if we did. If it ever became known, which I knew it would, that we had turned them down, few of our friends around the world would trust us completely as an ally again.[65]

I have found no evidence to confirm it, but U.S. Ambassador to Barbados Milan Bish was in regular contact with several OECS representatives prior to the written invitation and may very well have encouraged that request to help legitimate the intervention that was already being planned at the time of the invitation.[66]

Prior to the 1994 U.S. intervention in Haiti, the Clinton administration had sought and received UN authorization and support for action in Haiti. The fact that the 1989 U.S. invasion of Panama had no sanction from an international body did not keep it from being wildly popular in the United States compared to the Haitian operation. Clearly, support of the UN or other international body does not always help sway public opinion.

In descending order of preferences, administrations would like UN sanction, multinational participation, and support from regional multinational organizations. A somewhat less reliable source of justification claims is an invitation to intervene.

UN Approval

The gold standard for external legitimacy is a UN resolution supporting a military intervention. Since the UN is the only body that purports to represent the whole world, a UN-sanctioned intervention is the epitome of international legality. Regarding international law, the international community prefers "national" sovereignty (rather than state sovereignty) in the current era.[67] This explains the willingness of the United Nations to support peacekeeping operations and to protect minority populations from the states within which they are contained. If an administration can get UN approval for an intervention, it will receive considerable external legitimacy. The only Central American military intervention to receive UN approval was the 1994 U.S. intervention in Haiti. On July 31, the UN Security Council passed Resolution 940, which gave the United States authority to carry out a military intervention in Haiti on the United Nations' behalf.[68] Presidential Scholars Edward R. Drachman and Alan Shank note that the Clinton administration worked hard to facilitate the adoption of this resolution.[69]

Regional Multinational Organization Approval

A cut below the United Natiosn in terms of the portion of the external environment it represents is the variety of regional multinational organizations. For the cases at hand, these include the OAS (which the United States is party to) and the OECS (to which the United States is not). These regional organizations have charters that very carefully lay out the circumstance under which they can use their militaries on each other. These bodies have been known to issue resolutions that violate their charters. For example, the OECS request for U.S. assistance in intervening in Grenada clearly violated its own charter; the charter calls for unanimous agreement of member states before intervening in a member state to restore order. Grenada is a member, and her representative was not present and thus clearly failed to vote to authorize the intervention.

Approval or support from a regional multinational organization can provide an administration with at least a contestable claim to external legitimacy. Clearly that claim will be stronger if it is unanimous and adheres to the laws embodied in its charter.

Multilateral

An intervention is much less likely to be viewed as selfish (clearly not a legitimate grounds for intervention) if it is undertaken in cooperation with other countries. If many countries, having goals that would differ if they were being selfish, share a goal and act to achieve it, it is more likely to be legitimate. Similarly, while one country might make a "rogue" intervention, it is less likely that numerous countries would violate international norms, again suggesting likely normative adherence and thus providing legitimacy.

If an administration can get allies to commit troops to an intervention, it can claim legitimacy through multinationality. This usually happens only as part of an agreement sanctioned by the United Nations or other regional body. None of the four cases discussed here began with multinational participation, though all but Panama added at least small international contingents after U.S. forces had secured the situation. These marginal levels of multinational participation (in Grenada it was basically a few hundred police/gendarmes from supporting Caribbean nations) were insufficient to tap into the potential normative force of multinational participation (think Gulf War levels of multinational participation for an example of useful levels for successful justification).

Ongoing operations in Afghanistan and Iraq began with and continue to have significant multinational military participation.

Invitation

If forces within a country invite military aid from another country, it is grounds for a claim of legitimacy. These grounds are weakened if the party issuing the invitation is not empowered by that country's laws to do so (often the case), or if the invitation issuer is not himself or herself the appropriate legitimate sovereign within that state. Still, any invitation, if properly presented to the American public, can serve as grounds for a claim of "look, they really do want us there!" With regard to external legitimacy, U.S. legitimators can benefit from any plausibly possible external legitimacy claim as the time frame for most interventions is much shorter than the time frame for international legal arbitration.

Invitations are often sought or requested in certain forms. During the Dominican Republic crisis, the antirebel Colonel Benoit submitted a written request (in English) for U.S. military support "to Prevent another Cuba," the text of which was cabled to Washington.[70] Department of State officials requested that he send another invitation making no mention of Cuba, but instead suggesting language referring to restoring order and saving lives, which he did. Prior to the Grenada intervention, "'sources close to Jamaican Prime Minister, Edward Seaga' asserted that the plea by the Caribbean nations 'was triggered by an offer from the United States'—'Issue an appeal and we'll respond' was the message conveyed by Washington."[71] With regard to the ongoing operation in Afghanistan, the Afghan Northern Alliance invited U.S. participation; while the normative force of other used justifications was more than adequate to legitimize the intervention, the claimed illegitimacy of the Taliban and the invitation of opposition forces within the country were available as supporting claims.

Claim of International Social Work

A relatively new strand in legitimizing has emerged with the end of the Cold War. The Cold War left the United States as the single superpower and with the sometimes resented role of world policeman. Political scientist John Mueller argues that presidents can make plausible and acceptable claims to stage military interventions as international social work, provided that the cost in lives of American soldiers is low (basically zero).[72] American citizens are inclined to be skeptical if a threat to vital American interests is claimed but that threat is not easily discernible (as happened in Haiti). However, if "good" things are done and American lives are not spent, the American public will ultimately accept (and thus legitimate) participation. While the majority of the public opposed sending troops to Haiti prior to the intervention, when the operation was a success and no troops were killed in the initial landings, grudging acceptance became available.

Regarding the justifications for the Haiti invasion, Clinton Administration Communications Director George Stephanopoulos notes,

> Actually, our polling showed that the American people were moved to altruism than naked self-interest. Since August, we'd been quietly testing various arguments for the invasion. Unlike foreign-policy elites who insisted the United States should deploy troops only when "vital" economic or military interests were at stake, the general public was more willing to use our power to protect innocent civilians from torture and terror. This was all relative, of course; risking even one American life was unpopular, but a humanitarian argument softened the opposition. How to use the evidence we had—graphic photos of maimed children and mothers with slashed faces—was dicey, and it revealed a subtle shift in the world of spin between the Reagan and Clinton administrations.[73]

International social work also has access to an appeal to external legitimacy. Humanitarian goals enjoy wide acceptance worldwide at the moment. Further, provided an administration is patient and waits for international and domestic opinion to build to support some kind of involvement from the international community, and then gets permission from the United Nations, external legitimacy is likely. This justification has historically worked best when coupled with others, such as UN approval or invitation, and almost requires the accompaniment of the next justification strategy, making low costs clear relative to the benefits.

Making Low Costs Clear (Relative to Rewards)

An important part of successfully claiming legitimacy for international social work involves claims of low costs relative to the rewards. Studies have shown that the American public is tolerant of relatively high levels of American casualties when the stakes are relatively high in terms of national interest, but correspondingly low when vital interests are not perceived to be at stake.[74] By appealing to this rational calculation of low costs relative to rewards, if the claims turn out to be true, the intervention is likely to be accepted. Note that this is somewhat risky strategy for an administration to mobilize prior to an intervention, as costs and rewards may be uncertain. Still, when attempting to legitimate international social work, indicating that costs are likely to be low is crucial. During the buildup to the Haiti intervention, the administration made clear that it believed opposition would be minimal and costs low: "Little Risk in Haiti—Military experts say there is minimum risk to American forces because the 7,000 members of the Haitian military and police forces are poorly trained and ill-equipped."[75] While claims that there was little risk of loss of American soldiers in Haiti were not sufficient to make the operation popular before the intervention (especially in the face of counterclaims that democracy in Haiti was not worth a single American life, a noncasualty rate the administration could not promise), but when the operation turned out to be successful and there were no American casualties during the initial phases of the operation, support for the intervention grew.

Seeking Congressional Approval (as Opposed to Permission)

Presidents have long been embroiled in the conflicts inherent in the U.S. Constitution regarding balance of powers and powers over war making (see the section "oWar Powers" in Chapter 6 for a full discussion). As a consequence, actually asking for (whether it was received or not) congressional permission prior to launching a military intervention would be seen as setting a precedent for a huge surrender of presidential prerogative. Because of this, presidents are unlikely to seek congressional permission as a legitimating strategy. However, presidents can (and do) seek the *approval* and favorable opinion of congressional representatives without ever formally submitting a proposal to Congress. Although legally presidents do not need congressional permission, consensus is an important American legitimating norm. By meeting with congressional leaders during the planning stages of a military intervention and through consultations and polls, presidents can ascertain whether they are likely to receive congressional protest or support when they announce the intervention. President Clinton went to great lengths to try to win congressional support during the long run-up to the Haiti intervention, but he never succeeded; only the success of the operation and the negligible American casualties prevented a fierce congressional backlash.

On the other hand, during the rather short planning phase for the Grenada operation, President Reagan had only one consultation with congressional leaders, and of that meeting, Speaker of the House Tip O'Neill said, "I have been informed, but not consulted."[76] Again, had Reagan's intervention not been publicly accepted as a success, he would likely have received intense congressional criticism after the intervention.[77]

Having congressional approval, if not permission, is an important part of avoiding counterclaims when it comes to legitimacy, as congressional leaders can be an important source of claims *against* legitimacy. Having congressional approval after the fact lends an intervention legitimacy; if one of the bodies to which the president is accountable believes in the legitimacy of an intervention, the American public is likely to do so as well. "Avoidance of Counterclaims" is discussed in a later section.

Rejection of Previous Policy with a Punitive Dismissal

When policy or opinion is not headed in the direction that an administration might like, one strategy is to force the public to make a new assessment. To force a reassessment, the administration needs to signal that there has been some kind of change in policy that is sufficiently different from what has gone before to require reconsideration. One of the signals that has been used is to announce policy change (or even failure) and to fire the official who was (nominally or otherwise) responsible for that policy.

The clearest example of this kind of punitive firing in the military interventions under discussion is the Clinton administration's removal of Special Assistant to the President on Haitian Affairs Lawrence Pezzullo during the long decisional process for the Haiti intervention.[78] The administration admitted that its Haiti policy had failed and terminated the architect of that failed policy. The administration's new policy was more popular, but ultimately not effective enough to avoid the necessity of military intervention to achieve policy goals.

The rational rules of bureaucracy require that someone unable to do his or her job be replaced with someone who can. While that may not be a fair assessment of what has happened, that is the basis on which the legitimating claim is made.

Avoidance of Counterclaims

A legitimating claim is much more likely to be accepted if no counterclaim, that is, another claimant making a different and contradictory claim, is made. Counterclaims can come from many quarters: they can come from Congress, from organized protest groups, from the skeptical media, or from groups in other countries. Administrations can avoid counterclaims in several different ways. First and most obviously, an intervention that adheres to as many norms in as many spheres as possible, and makes legitimating claims based only on those norms, is least vulnerable to counterclaims. Put simply, the closer claims are to motive, and the closer motive is to acceptable norms, the safer an intervention is from counterclaims.

The administration has a considerable advantage against counterclaims in general, and particularly in a surprise intervention case. If an intervention is not anticipated, the administration is not faced with well-prepared opposed experts making counterclaims. Instead, it has all the experts and the advantage of preparation. By the time concerned parties can marshal sufficient information and mobilize a counterclaim, it will likely be too late. This situation changes in a publicly discussed premeditated intervention, like Haiti, where there is plenty of time for all concerned groups to collect information and mobilize experts and claims.

In the realm of legitimizing an intervention that is vulnerable to counterclaims, an administration can make efforts to limit the threat from counterclaims. Strategies include the inclusion of groups (such as Congress) that are likely to make counterclaims in the decisional process, rejecting or discrediting counterclaims before they can be made, accepting some dissent and not focusing on it, ignoring counterclaims or counterclaimants, and attempting to discredit counterclaimants. Since all four of the cases here involved claims that differed from their motives, they were all potentially vulnerable to counterclaims, though only Haiti suffered for that vulnerability.

CONCLUSIONS

I began this chapter by asking *how* and *why* the presidential administrations that presided over the military interventions that constitute my core cases attempted to legitimate them. In order to answer that question, I have discussed the nature and necessity of justifications in American politics and discussed the logic and normative appeals of the specific legitimizing strategies used to legitimate Central American military interventions.

The American state is generally highly legitimate, and its policies are accorded a high default level of legitimacy by the public. Foreign policy has fewer interested participants, but receives the same assumption of legitimacy, even though its legitimacy depends in part on potentially conflicting internal and external legal norms and on the traditional authority inherent in the position of the presidency. Military interventions, as a special subset of foreign policy, are decided by an extremely limited group of persons. Because the legal rational and traditional norms governing the decisional process are based primarily on presidential judgment, while grounds for intervention are assumed to be legitimate, citizens are curious upon what the judgment was based. In order to maintain legitimacy and high levels of public support, presidents legitimate their military interventions.

Justifications during the Cold War and post–Cold War eras were generally based on slightly different normative appeals. With the end of the Cold War, the Cold War metanarrative of massive threat from communism ended, leaving no similarly strong normative replacement. The post–Cold War era contained a shift to more ambiguous situations, different roles for the United States in the world at large, and different justifications and legitimizing strategies. The attacks of 9/11 have ushered in a new era for the legitimacy of military interventions, perhaps very similar to the black and white world of the Cold War, only without the bipolarity. The presence of a skulking "evil" in the world, especially one that no order-loving participant in the international community could abide, leaves a great deal of residual legitimacy for any effort to root out that evil.

Justifications are reflexive, tactical, and part of the decision-making process. The closer motives are to claims, the more likely a justification is to be accepted as plausible. The more normatively palatable justification claims are, the stronger the support the public will offer the intervention.

8

Conclusion: Governance, Institutions, and Future U.S. Interventions

There is nothing more difficult to take in hand, more perilous to conduct, or more uncertain in its success, than to take the lead in the introduction of a new order of things.

—*Niccolò Machiavelli*

This book has focused on a variety of issues relating to military intervention decision making and related them to three core theoretical issues: the question of governance, the structure-agent problem, and the role of the institutional context. Each chapter has sought to provide some new insight into the general empirical issue of decision making while contributing to the larger theoretical inquiry. In this chapter, I review the significant themes that run through the entire project and the major theoretical conclusions of the entire enterprise. I also discuss the extent to which these conclusions and themes generalize to cases beyond those examined here. Finally, I discuss the implications of the attacks of September 11, 2001, for this research and the implications of this research for responses to those attacks.

RECURRING THEMES

Several significant themes have surfaced and resurfaced in the analysis from chapter to chapter. In addition to the specific topical conclusions of each chapter, these recurring threads deserve special attention here in the conclusion. Each theme influences either the analysis in one or more chapters or the outcome of that analysis. As such, each is discussed below in terms of its contribution to explaining the process of decision making for U.S. military interventions.

Process

One of the major recurring themes of this book is how so many different factors related to these decisions are the result of active or passive decision making, that is, part of the process. The national interest is defined through a social process; interventions are decided and planned through separate and complex processes; how the intervention is presented and legitimated to the public and to the world is both part of and the result of a *process*. Chapter 5 details the general and varied character of the military intervention decision-making process and thus takes a large step toward answering the question, "How does the United States decide to launch military interventions?" Several of the other chapters deal tangentially with process and focus more on how process affects outcome.

Characteristics of the Situation

Again and again throughout the chapters important differences in how military interventions were decided and factors that affected those decisions hinged on two sets of primary characteristics of the situation inspiring the intervention. Most consequential is whether an intervention is a response to a crisis or is a premeditated response to an ongoing but unacceptable situation. Crisis vs. premeditation played its most significant role in the discussion of process, dictating the time available for all the stages in the process (limited or abundant). In addition to the obvious implications for planning, preparation, and time to carefully consider a decision, this temporal constraint limits the potential for groups outside the government to mobilize influence. In a crisis, there is less time to contest the national interest, and no time to "test" different legitimation strategies.

Interacting with crisis vs. premeditation and playing an important process determining role is the decision to resolve the situation in secret or in the public eye. While the decision to make plans in public or secretly is actually a decision and is thus not inherent in the situation, it is a decision that stems from a whole collection of situation characteristics and is a huge "first step" decision that has a major impact on the subsequent process. Planning an intervention with public awareness opens up the possibility of public contestation, with important consequences for the construction of the public national interest and possible legitimation issues.

Taken together, crisis vs. premeditation and secret vs. public form a two-by-two table (see Figure 5.1) that largely structures the decision-making process. A large part of the answer to the question of why the U.S. decision-making process is the way it is has to do with these constraints inherent in the situation, coupled with the structural and institutional constraints also detailed throughout the book.

Institutions

Institutions of one form or another play a role in every single chapter and, I would argue, in every aspect of military intervention decision making. Many aspects of the process and the intent of U.S. military intervention decision making are heavily influenced or determined by institutions.

In Chapter 3 I accept Victor Nee and Paul Ingram's definition of institution, "An institution is a *web of interrelated norms* [emphasis in original]—formal and informal—governing social relationships."[1] These institutions take many important forms, including *organizations,* which are constituted by the various agencies, departments, and bureaus of the government, or the different corporations, foundations, and groups of the larger society, and *rules,* which include the laws governing the formation, structure, and support of organizations, as well as rules, norms, and assumptions about how work is done, what relationships and conditions are acceptable, and taken-for-granted understandings. These institutional rules are further divisible into *formal* institutional rules and *informal* institutional rules. Formal institutions are codified in law, rule, or procedure; informal institutions include everything else.

The formal and informal structure of the government, both in terms of the specific organizations and the institutionalized relationships and modes of interaction they share, heavily determines the way in which intervention decisions are taken. Some of why the United States decides to intervene using the process that it does has to do with formal institutional structures dictating that procedure. Another part has to do with informal institutional norms preventing any other way from being conceived of or previously failed but not formally prohibited options from being considered again. Both formal and informal institutions change over time, and the consequences of changing institutions are the focus of Chapter 6 on legacy chains, and also play a role in the definition of the national interest (Chapter 4) and the way in which interventions have been legitimated (Chapter 7).

Path Dependency

"A recurring lesson of policy history is path dependence: what paths are available now depends on what paths were chosen before."[2] The notion of path dependence is core to the legacy chain chapter (Chapter 6), but it also serves as a focal theme throughout the rest of the book. At every stage in the process, choices are made that constrain subsequent choices in a path-dependent manner. Given the ubiquity of the importance of process throughout, and the constant observation of path dependence within staged processes, path dependence is important in describing both the process and the aim of U.S. military intervention decision making.

The Public

A more subtle theme that runs through several of the chapters is the role of the American public in U.S. military interventions. The core theories of governance discussed here hypothesize virtually no role for the public (even the pluralists believe that the public either exercised its influence on the process at the electoral phase or needs time to mobilize around an interest) in a crisis intervention and at most a limited role in a public premeditated intervention (through the action of concerned interest groups). In terms of actual public *participation* in the decision-making process, my findings are very much congruent with this general expectation. Nonetheless, the public and the role played by the public are a major theme in two of the substantive chapters: Chapter 4 on the national interest and Chapter 7 on legitimation. The role of the public as the source of the public national interest and as the collective final arbiters of legitimacy creates a potentially powerful constraint on presidential action and is a frequent topic of presidential consideration. The way in which interventions are legitimated (and the way in which the legitimation national interest is constructed) is very much with regard to the public and its important (if passive, vis-à-vis the decision) role. Presidents can manipulate public opinion or avoid negative public opinion, but the fact that they must make their decisions with this in mind acts as a constraint.

The President

Orders of magnitude more important than the role of the public is the role of the president. In fact, my findings are that the public plays a role only though its ability to influence and constrain the president. The president, on the other hand, is the source of the presidential national interest, which is, ultimately, the national interest as will be pursued through military policy, as the president is the final and supreme decision-making authority for military policy. This is not to say that the president is alone and unconstrained in intervention decision making—far from it. The options available to the president are highly contingent on his advisors and on the lower-level bureaucracy. Still, relative to the formal organizational institutions of governance of other democratic but parliamentary states, the U.S. president is a uniquely "personalist" executive. So many presidential variables have proven to be so important in these cases (the salience to the president of the intervention country, presidential attention, the way in which the president has organized his cabinet and advisors, and so forth) that I must conclude that a president's personal proclivities have the largest single impact on how military intervention decisions are taken and what the outcome of the decisional processes will be. This is not to suggest that the president's proclivities are unique qualities of personality; presidential preferences are, of course, related to the president's background, political party, allies, personal leadership experiences, and advisors' advice, all of which are the product of complex social processes.

The End of the Cold War

The final major recurring theme of this research is the consequences arising from the end of the Cold War. The end of the Cold War provides the central empirical tension of the legitimation chapter (Chapter 7) and is also critical to other chapters on the theoretical level as it provides a major example of change in these critical institutions and processes.

The end of the Cold War created a vacuum in the focus of U.S. foreign policy. The loss of the powerful Cold War "metanarrative" included the loss of a powerful legitimating mythology. With the end of unitary policy goals based on a bipolar black and white (or, perhaps, red and white) world, shifts occurred in all three constructions of the national interest and in the ways in which military interventions were (and could be) legitimated, as discussed in Chapters 4 and 7, respectively.

Once the Cold War ended, the general U.S. government desire to enact "probusiness" foreign policy could no longer hide inside the larger narrative of Cold War anticommunism. However, even with the end of the "global threat" from communism, the United States continued to spend resources on probusiness authoritarian neighbor governments and failed to support more democratic if left-leaning opposition groups. This tension may explain some of the ambivalence within the government over the restoration of Haitian President in exile Jean-Bertrand Aristide, who was believed to advocate land reform and other redistributive policies opposed to conventional business interests.

GENERALIZING TO OTHER CASES

The case selection for this project was restricted in several important respects. First, these cases were sampled on the dependent variable. These findings are drawn from cases in which the United States intervened, without regard for cases in which an intervention was considered but then rejected. By failing to include elusive decisions *not* to intervene, I have abandoned the privilege of formally attempting to answer questions of the form "why here rather than there?" Second, while the cases addressed here represent the full universe of "marines on the beach" military interventions in Central America since World War II, their representation of all post–World War II military interventions is not as complete. Specifically, U.S. involvements in Southeast Asia, the Persian Gulf, Africa, and the former Yugoslavia are all absent. How well do the conclusions I have drawn about the military intervention decision-making process generalize outside of the Central American context? This section concerns itself with that very question.

Keeping in mind the relative homogeneity of the four Central American/Caribbean cases considered in this study, I want to shift the focus to other cases of U.S. intervention. All four of my core cases share regional similarities, including but not limited to being former objects of the Monroe Doctrine and being clearly within the U.S. Cold War "sphere of influence." With the possible exception of Panama, all four were not serious threats to vital strategic interests as defined within the various international relations perspectives (see Chapter 4) and were not viewed as being particularly important by the vast majority of Americans prior to the intervention (low baseline salience). Finally, the potential military opposition in three of the four cases was virtually negligible, and in Panama, only marginal, relative to the U.S. forces available. What changes in the decisional process when an intervention candidate arises in a country that is "more important"? What changes when potential military opposition is considerable?

Considered in the aggregate, low salience and low opposition make all of my intervention cases "small." A skeptic might argue that several of my core findings may not generalize beyond other cases that are similarly small. It would not be unreasonable to assert that in a larger, more important target country or crisis the role of lower-level functionaries, particularly in terms of ambassadorial autonomy, might be decreased; that the amount of genuine contingency in the process might be decreased by imperatives of magnitude; and that presidential autonomy and the variations resulting from presidential proclivities might be reduced. I acknowledge the likelihood of constraints of magnitude. Clearly, if a U.S. installation abroad is attacked by identifiable forces, there will be a retaliation, without contingency. However, the exact timing and nature of that retaliation will remain contingent, and the contingencies considered by the top decision makers will have been produced (possibly contingently) by lower-level planners. Magnitude will certainly decrease likely ambassadorial autonomy, as the number of experts on "important" countries and the number of information sources for events going on in them is exponentially larger than in small or unimportant countries. That said, if the ambassador has important personal connections in the crisis country, or is considered a top expert on events there, he or she may still have considerable influence through the presentation of his or her interpretation of what has transpired and his or her ability to impact ongoing events in the crisis country. While magnitude undoubtedly diminishes some of the effects and factors I have observed, I expect their consideration to remain important and anxiously anticipate further research in a similar vein, but on more "major" cases.

In the remainder of this section I discuss two major post–World War II U.S. military involvements, Vietnam and the first Gulf War (neither of which is small). I compare and contrast these two cases with the four core cases of this book in terms of their baseline and contextual differences and in the applicability of my conclusions and my general model of military intervention decision making.

Vietnam

From the perspective of this research, Vietnam should be considered as two different metaevents. The first is the decision to Americanize the conflict, taken during "the Long 1964,"[3] that roughly parallels an intervention decision-making process as described and discussed here. The second is the ongoing war in Vietnam, which has much less in common with the cases discussed here. Since the model of decision making implicit in this work is meant to apply only to intervention decision making, not subsequent military decision making or iterative processes in ongoing conflicts, in this section I discuss how my findings might generalize to the decision to Americanize the war in Vietnam, leaving the ongoing war in Vietnam to be considered as a case of something else (and by someone else).

On its face, Vietnam seems very different from my four cases in many ways; however, if one considers only the initial decision to Americanize the war during the long 1964, the differences remain significant, but can be enumerated. First, Vietnam was outside of the U.S. hemispheric sphere of influence and thus not included in the tradition of the Monroe Doctrine, and escapes other regional and contextual similarities. Southeast Asia is included in the "grand area" enumerated by the Council on Foreign Relations in the early postwar era (see Chapter 4), so it was considered to involve vital national interests, especially with the then-contemporary prevalence of the "domino theory" of world loss to communism. While this view and the ongoing U.S. involvement in Vietnam (dating back to 1954) led to relatively high salience among decision makers, the vast majority of American citizens cared little and knew less about Vietnam prior to the mid-1960s. In this regard, Vietnam parallels the cases discussed here; in the four Central American cases, the salience of events was much higher to decision makers than it was to the American public in general. To the decision makers, however, the baseline salience (the "stakes") in Southeast Asia were seen to be much higher than in any of the Central American cases.

One of the biggest and most significant differences is the magnitude of military threat faced. As conceived, Vietnam was not a simple "intervention" in which order or democracy would easily be restored and forces then withdrawn. The nature of the terrain, the size and armament of the opposing forces, the possibility of Chinese participation, and the "frozen" Cold War (in which the Chinese and the Americans realized they could not comfortably win a land war in direct opposition to each other) all combined to make the military action that was decided upon much different from the kinds of interventions discussed in this book.

After giving these two differences of magnitude (perceived stakes and significance of opposition) due attention, the decision to Americanize the war can be analyzed fairly reliably with the model and notions laid out in this book. To begin with, the primary characteristics that affect the decisional process, premeditated vs. crisis and secret vs. public, apply. The situation, though viewed as critical, was not a crisis as defined here. Decision makers had plenty of time to make their decision and to plan the addition of troops and their changing role before action was taken. The decision was taken in secret, and, while troops were not moved in secret, their expanded role was kept from the general public for some time. Historian Fredrik Logevall's study of the decision to Americanize the war in Vietnam reveals several aspects of the decision-making process that correspond perfectly with the findings regarding process of this work.[4] First, Logevall notes a considerable constraining role played by presidential advisors, particularly the secretary of state, and by the bureaucracy (the Department of State) in completely failing to prepare a diplomatic option. When decision-making time came, the president was presented only with an array of military options or withdrawal. Second, Logevall notes the immense relevance of the personal proclivities of the president to the decisional outcome, going so far as to argue counterfactually in his conclusion, that, had Kennedy not been assassinated, that the decision to Americanize the war would not have been taken.

Others have argued that the decision to Americanize the war or pursue some other escalation in the face of events was not a "*real* choice."[5] Presidential historian Robert Dallek places the point of no return in November 1963.[6] While no one should dispute (and the findings of this research certainly confirm) that the presidents involved certainly had the authority and opportunity to make different decisions, it is an open question whether other alternatives had been rendered "unthinkable" because of the pattern of perceived costs and the path-dependent choices already made. While the majority of path-dependent events observed during this research act as constraints on decisions *to* intervene, one can certainly imagine a slightly different flavor of *perceived* constraints on the decision not to intervene.

As mentioned in the legacy chains chapter (Chapter 6), Vietnam created numerous legacies, but was informed by a few as well. Most notable was the general legacy of the Cold War and its domino theory and the legacy of American success in Korea, which made war in Vietnam seem like less of a bad idea. Finally, Vietnam ultimately became a huge legitimation failure, because there was not just the usual discrepancy between motives and claims, but a discrepancy between *actions* and claims, that, when discovered, heavily damaged administration credibility.

Gulf War

While the situation did differ substantially from the Central American cases, like Vietnam's, the Gulf War's decisional process is unsurprising and easily understood within the context of this book's findings. The largest process-determining difference in the Gulf War case had to do with the size and effectiveness of Iraqi forces relative to available U.S. forces. According to Commanding General Norman Schwarzkopf, Iraqi forces were considerable in size, armament, and experience.[7] At the time of the Iraqi invasion of Kuwait, there were not sufficient U.S. forces in the region to even mount a credible defense of Saudi Arabia, let alone execute offensive operations to liberate Kuwait. "The 82nd airborne troops that were over there used to facetiously refer to themselves as 'Iraqi tank speed bumps', because they were light infantry and did not have the heavy anti-tank weapons they needed."[8] Even after the initial buildup of U.S. forces in Saudi Arabia, which were effective as a defensive deterrent, offense was still not an option.

The relative force differential is totally unencountered in the Central American cases. While the decisional process began as a crisis response (an unanticipated situation arose, and a limited decisional window was available to make a decision), a crisis intervention was not logistically possible prior to a substantial buildup, giving the occupying Iraqi army ample time to fortify its position.

Unable to launch a crisis response intervention, the crisis decision-making process produced posturing (President George H.W. Bush claiming, "The Invasion Will Not Stand"), a move toward international condemnation and sanctions, and the commencement of a premeditated intervention process. While early intervention plans were conducted in secret, the fact that UN permission was sought and congressional permission was given placed the pending intervention squarely in the public sphere and opened the way to public awareness.

Rare for a post–Cold War intervention, the Gulf War had several strong claims to legitimacy and was easily legitimized at home and abroad. Interests at stake included world oil resources and the defense of international norms regarding sovereignty. The rare "naked aggression" shown by Iraq destroyed any international sympathy for it. Further, removed from the bipolar context of the Cold War, there was no frighteningly powerful "other" in the shadows behind Iraq, dramatically affecting the stakes of interfering with its activities, as had been the case elsewhere in the world. Given these clear and shared interests, the difference between decision-maker motives and claims was very small, leading to easy legitimation and widespread public acceptance.

As mentioned in Chapter 6 (legacy chains), several important legacies informed U.S. Gulf War behavior. First was the Vietnam "overwhelming force" and "imperative to win" legacies. While military planners did prepare a limited offensive option based on the forces in place after the initial defensive buildup in Saudi Arabia, the fact that the joint chiefs did not like that plan kept it from being considered too seriously, and, when the real plans were prepared, the full troop compliment requested was approved. The operation also served as a link in the "War Powers" chain; once UN approval had been given and public support was huge, Congress took advantage of its knowledge of the nonsecret intervention and approved it without ever having been asked, in order to avoid further deterioration of the War Powers Resolution. The Gulf War also provided links in the press legacy chain and the legitimacy through UN/multinational participation legacy chain, as detailed in Chapter 6.

9/11 and Beyond

All of the decisional details of the process resulting in the hunt for Osama bin Laden on Afghan soil are not yet available. Regardless, I suspect that many of my findings regarding the decisional process apply, particularly those having to do with the characteristics of the situation and the roles played by contingency and path dependency. While the lasting legacies of the attacks of 9/11 remain to be seen (and are, as I write, being shaped by the military actions in Afghanistan and in Iraq), one clear legacy is a dramatic shift in the institutional context. One of the major themes of this book has been the impact of the end of the Cold War on the context in which decisions are made, interests are defined, and legitimacy is claimed. The loss of the enemy gave rise to a great deal of ambiguity in that era. With the attacks of 9/11, the United States has an enemy once again. I suspect that the "war against terror," while of unknown duration, is in the process of creating an institutional context for military intervention decision making that is not unlike the Cold War in terms of its certainty and normative force. Were I to write a similar book ten years hence, I suspect that, like the Cold War and the post–Cold War eras, the war against terror will have its own era and its own historically specific set of legacies and contextual effects on the various aspects of the military intervention decision-making process.

Cases of Nonintervention

By their very nature, decisions not to intervene are difficult to identify. Even when they can be picked out, research can be difficult as nondecisions or decisions not to do something are considerably less well documented than positive decisions. That said, even a brief examination of decisions not to intervene can provide a first step toward moving questions at process level questions toward larger questions of governance. Here I review a small selection of decisions not to intervene of which I am aware and briefly examine the discernible reasons for those negative decisions.

First, the decision not to intervene in Kuwait during the "crisis" phase of the Iraqi invasion may seem unremarkable in the face of the ultimate invasion there. Still, it gives evidence of an important limit on military intervention decision making: an intervention for which troops and plans are unavailable, or failure is certain, cannot be launched. It bears repeating that any time the president sits down with his military advisors and they tell him "we cannot do that," the discussion is over for the time being.

In fact, all of the "negative cases" I discovered encountered some kind of barrier during the process. I am sure there are cases where the barrier (either military plausibility, likely diplomatic consequences, or domestic complaint) is so obvious that the notion of intervention is discarded before ever really being considered. These cases, then, are not so completely obvious that they were inconceivable, but, in the last instance, hit a barrier that the president deemed insurmountable or unacceptable. Again, I say "the president" because it is clear from similar situations that what stopped one president would not have stopped another.

Consider, for example, the desire of President Jimmy Carter to put an end to the civil war in Nicaragua. Carter thought to replay the U.S. experience in the Dominican Republic in 1965, where the Organization of American States (OAS) had approved of, and granted considerable legitimacy to, the somewhat questionable intervention. Carter called an emergency meeting of the OAS to urge approval of a primarily U.S. inter-American peacekeeping force after emphasizing Cuba's role in the ongoing conflict.[9] The OAS would have none of it, having had its fill of U.S. military interventions in the region. For Carter, that was enough to drop it. For Reagan, even with Congress expressly forbidding U.S. military activity or funding in Nicaragua, the lack of approval at home or abroad was insufficient to prevent his pursuit of a secret war.[10]

The last negative case I discuss is the U.S. decision not to intervene in Liberia, which was experiencing problems very similar to those experienced by neighboring Somalia roughly contemporaneously. Somalia was the recipient of considerable humanitarian aid and a U.S. peacekeeping force, while Liberia was not. According to Colin L. Powell, during the period when aid and peacekeeping forces were being considered for both countries, the main reason consideration for a Liberian intervention was dropped was the receipt by the Department of State of the so-called "skirts and wigs" video from a U.S. intelligence source.[11] The video depicted a gun battle between two armed factions on a city street. Because of certain tribal beliefs, the members of one faction believed that they were rendered invulnerable by wearing women's dresses; the other faction held a similar belief regarding elaborate women's wigs. The video, then, depicted these two factions in a running gunfight, with each participant equipped for his own protection, according to these beliefs. While not that remarkable if taken in context, taken out of context, the video shows a bunch of African men cross-dressing and having a gunfight. It was widely believed within the Department of State that, if this video or one like it leaked to the press (as it inevitably would), it would seriously damage administration credibility regarding selecting reasonable targets for aid. While this supposition may or may not have been true, it was enough to remove Liberia from consideration as an intervention candidate.

THEORETICAL IMPLICATIONS

Chapter 3 introduced three theories of governance (pluralism, elite theory, and class theory), each seeking to explain at whose behest or in whose interests the United States undertakes military action, and each containing an at least implicit model of how those interests are translated into action. In this section I review those theories in light of the conclusions reached in each of the substantive chapters.

Pluralism, as expected, fares poorly in the face of these findings. As discussed in Chapter 3, the core of pluralism is a belief that in a democracy, strong and organized private interest associations can continually assert influence on the government. Military interventions, especially if decided in secret or in crisis, are not at all exposed to public participation or interest group politics. In the single case that was premeditated in the public eye, Haiti, interest groups did weigh in, but the majority expressed interest did not prevail. Presidents make their decisions based on what they believe to be in the national interest, but, as I discuss in Chapter 4, the calculated presidential national interest is not derived from, or representative of, the public national interest. Outside of pluralism, but also outside of the other major theories of the state, is the tremendous *passive* role played by the public. Pluralism requires *active* public contestation in the policy arena.[12] As the arbiters of legitimacy and the source of the public national interest, public opinion and potential public reaction receive considerable presidential attention, but only in the interest of preserving presidential prestige, popularity, and power. Legitimation, almost wholly concerned with the public, is an important and reflexively undertaken part of the military intervention decision process. While pluralism might be modified to incorporate a powerful passive public role, the idea of power holders pursuing policies to specifically *avoid* public participation and contestation goes against the core principles of polyarchy.

Class theory, whether instrumentalist or structuralist, argues that military interventions either serve the ruling class interest or, at the very least, do not threaten its interests. The latter part of that minimal statement, not threatening capitalist class interests, is a fairly mild requirement. While none of the four cases examined here serve interests opposed to business interests, they are not all clearly in the interests of the business class, either (see the discussion of interests in Chapter 4). Perhaps this is a product of the "smallness" of the cases. Class theory of any flavor predicts that, in an intervention, dominant class interests will not be threatened; if no interests of any kind are at stake, there is no reason that either structuralist or instrumentalists concerns should be involved.

Domhoff's business class dominance approach, though a hybrid, is the most clearly articulated of the class theories I consider.[13] G. William Domhoff's model asserts that business class control of, or influence over, either the decision makers themselves or the process through which policy goals are constructed is sufficient to ensure that policy will always be in the interests of the business class, or, at the very least, not opposed to its interests. Looking at the Dominican Republic case, we find strong evidence supporting this view. Major presidential advisors had ties to the Dominican sugar industry and access to the president, and numerous scholars and historians acknowledge or point out extensive U.S. business involvement and concerns in the Dominican Republic.[14]

The case for Panama is less clear. Panama, specifically the Panama Canal, has a strong traditional claim to being a "vital" U.S. and business interest and was undoubtedly included in the grand area (see Chapter 4). However, given the end of the Cold War and modern developments in transportation technology, the value of the Canal was not as obvious at the time of the invasion. Further, while U.S. investments in Panama were and are considerable, it is unclear the extent to which Noriega was a threat to those interests. Certainly he was a greedy, authoritarian thug involved in the drug trade, but authoritarian thugs are the traditional defenders of U.S. business interests abroad. At the time of the invasion Noriega was very hostile, and tensions between U.S. forces and forces loyal to Noriega were high (not a good situation for business), but that tension was a product of U.S. provocations (an indictment against Noriega and constant provocative military exercises). While Noriega's removal was certainly good for Panamanian democracy and may well have been good for U.S. long-term investments there, it is unclear whether the process of Noriega's removal served U.S. business interests.

Grenada and Haiti are not clearly concerned with business class interests at all. In fact, I would imagine Domhoff would allow that these two cases had nothing really to do with U.S. business interests, but were not at all opposed to U.S. business interests.[15] While this does not impinge particularly at all on Domhoff's assertions, it does fail to explain the decisions to intervene in Grenada or Haiti.

With regard to class theory in general, as I mention above, I found evidence that business interests were at stake in the Dominican Republic and Panama and no particular evidence that they were in the other cases. The complexity I observed at the decision-making level leads me to reject any naively deterministic class approach. On the structuralist side, it is clear that, as Fred Block asserts, the U.S. state is dependent on the health of the U.S. capitalist economy and makes policy within the minimal constraints imposed by that fact.[16] Further, I cannot reject the more instrumentalist careful and empirically well-supported position advanced by Domhoff. While I cannot reject it, I find that it fails to explain state behavior in the two cases of little or no concern to the business class, and I found minimal direct evidence of business class influence in the two cases where interests were present (though his theory does not require that I do so). What I would most like to see in the future is the rigor and attention to detail that Domhoff applies to his scholarship applied to these cases to produce a careful model of how policy is made when it is not in the interests of or at the behest of the ruling class. I hope that this book serves as a step in that direction.

My findings are consonant with the basic premises of most elite theories. Military intervention decisions are ultimately taken by the highest level of decision maker. However, decision making is considerably more constrained than some elite theories would suggest. Path-dependent constraints stem from the behavior of nonelite lower bureaucrats, from the structure of the formal institutions of government, from the results of previous policy, and, as mentioned in the previous chapter (Chapter 7), by the necessity of making decisions that can be legitimated to the public. So, elites do make the decisions, but their decision making is constrained by the decisions and actions of subelites or nonelites. My findings indicate that top decision makers are virtually unaccountable, provided that they take steps to legitimate their decisions (see Chapter 7).

With regard to elite consensus, Chapter 5 explicitly deals with the extent and necessity of consensus within the core decision makers. Here I wish to briefly discuss the extent to which consensus or agreement exists or is required between broader elite groups in society. In the four cases, Haiti was the only case that was conducted in the full public eye over a long enough period so that all groups (elite or otherwise) that wished to participate had a chance to do so. There was considerable disagreement over Haiti throughout the government, particularly in Congress and at middle levels in the executive bureaucracy (see Chapter 2 for details). While this lack of consensus certainly forced the Clinton administration to move with caution and to seek alternatives, it did not ultimately prevent the intervention. In the other three cases, secrecy or temporal urgency prevented elite consensus from being assessed prior to the intervention. Groups that might have objected had no opportunity to do so. While in the Dominican Republic and Panama it may be reasonable to impute *post hoc* elite consensus, we know that in the Grenada case there were considerable objections in the legislature and elsewhere in the government that were silenced by the massive public approval of the operation.

While this suggests that uniform elite agreement is not required for a military intervention, the preintervention history leading up to the invasion of Panama does suggest at least one consensus requirement. As discussed in Chapter 5, the Reagan administration was unable to launch serious policy to remove Noriega because the various executive agency heads did not agree that it was a policy goal, let alone how best to do it. Military intervention as a possible solution could not come onto the table at all until the relevant advisors and agency heads finally agreed that Noriega's ouster was a goal. In sum, while broad elite cohesion and agreement may not be required for minor military interventions, consensus of some kind (and that will depend in part on how the president has organized his cabinet) is required.

Finally, there is the debate on state autonomy within some elite and class theories. Whether or not the four interventions discussed here were undertaken as autonomous state action is not completely clear. As I noted above in the discussion of class theory, one could make a strong argument for the decisions to intervene in the Dominican Republic and in Panama having been influenced by business interests, and thus not being autonomous. While I do not feel that my research on these cases allows me to make a strong statement about state autonomy at the broadest levels, I do have some valuable observations on the issue. First, even if acting in the interests of nonstate societal groups, military intervention decision makers have a great deal of flexibility in how, exactly, to respond. The considerable impact of a president's personal proclivities on the decision process and outcome are clear evidence of some kind of autonomy. Second, and not at all discussed by general state autonomy theorists, is the peculiar "ambassadorial autonomy" I observed. In two of the cases (the Dominican Republic and Grenada; see Chapter 2 for details), the U.S. ambassador to the country or region played an enormous independent role. It is not clear whose ultimate interests these ambassadors acted in, but it was clearly not the interests of a monolithic state, and certainly not directly at the behest of the president whose representatives they were acting as. This very interesting lower-level autonomy deserves attention in the literature and reinforces a point I have made elsewhere rejecting a set of monolithic state interests, looking instead at all relevant agencies and bureaucracies in examining a policy outcome.[17]

The Institutional Context

While my findings are consonant with some aspects of class theory and some aspects of elite theory, none of the existing theories offer a sufficient explanation for state behavior in these military intervention decisions. In Chapter 3 I briefly introduced some constituent elements of a theory of the institutional context. I elaborated on this idea considerably in Chapter 6, and here I wish to finalize my claims in light of the evidence provided throughout the book.

The core of my institutional context argument is that the context of decision making contains and creates constraints on the military intervention decision-making process. The context holds a number of constraints, and more constraints are passed down in a path-dependent manner and held within the institutions of the state and of the society as a whole. These contextual institutions exist at several levels: within the formal legal structures and procedures of the government, in the accepted categories and taken-for-granteds of the decision makers, and in the collective understanding of the American people. Path-dependent constraints are created at many levels: the legacies of previous policy decisions and outcomes, public opinion, and decisions made by decision participants at the top, middle, and bottom.

Within this complex institutional context, decisions, though heavily constrained, are still contingent. Further, many of the events that result in additional path-dependent constraints are the product of highly contingent decisions and behavior by lower-level decision participants. The path dependent constraint of choices puts policy possibilities within a "branch" (if one imagines a policy tree). However, the actual outcome within that branch is highly contingent on further (still path-dependent) events, decisions, and actions at numerous levels of the policy process. Contingent cases build constraints for the future via a process of legacy chains (as discussed in Chapter 6). This model contains a tension between institutional constraints that restrict (but by no means determine) possible outcomes, and contingent factors that are all but impossible to predict which can contribute to the subsequent institutional context. Both aspects of the theory are central, and both contribute to the theory of change implicit in the legacy chains argument.

Structure or Agency?

This view of the institutional context in which decision making takes place contains an implicit view on structure and agency. Consistent with a "choice within constraints" model, I see actors making choices within a context of structured contingency. What is new here is an implicit model of how the context that constrains action changes over time. Chapter 6 lays out a model of legacy chains that contains a model of institutional change. The process looks like this: Actors act within a constraining institutional context; those actions, coupled with contingencies and unforeseen consequences lead to events; the outcomes of these events leave impressions on the institutional context (at a host of different levels), which, in turn, changes the constraints under which actors act. Structure and agency are, indeed, mutually constitutive, with a little bit of caprice sewn in.

Notes

CHAPTER 1

1. James A. Winnefeld, Margaret C. Harrell, Robert D. Howe, Arnold Kanter, Brian Nichiporuk, Paul S. Steinberg, Thomas S. Szayna, and Ashley J. Tellis, *Implications for the Army in the Post–Cold War Era* (Santa Monica, CA: RAND Corporation, 1995), http://www.rand.org/pubs/monograph_reports/2006/MR554.1.pdf.

2. Victor Nee and Mary C. Brinton, "Introduction," in *The New Institutionalism in Sociology,* ed. Mary C. Brinton and Victor Nee (Stanford, CA: Stanford University Press, 1998), xv–xix.

3. C. Edward Paul, "Moving Forward with State Autonomy and Capacity: Example from Two Studies of the Pentagon during W.W.II," *Journal of Political and Military Sociology* 28, no. 1 (Summer 2000): 21–42.

CHAPTER 2

1. Steven Lukes, *Power: A Radical View* (London: The Macmillan Press, Ltd., 1974).

2. Quoted in Abraham F. Lowenthal, *The Dominican Intervention* (Cambridge, MA: Harvard, 1972), 26.

3. Lowenthal, *The Dominican Intervention,* 23–26.

4. Ibid., 9–15.

5. Ibid., 14.

6. John Bartlow Martin, *Overtaken by Events: The Dominican Crisis from the Fall of Trujillo to the Civil War* (New York: Doubleday & Co., 1966).

7. Lowenthal, *The Dominican Intervention,* 29.

8. Richard J. Barnet, *Intervention and Revolution: America's Confrontation with Insurgent Movements around the World* (New York: World Publishing Co., 1968), chap. 8; Fred Goff and Michael Locker, "The Violence of Domination: U.S. Power and the Dominican Republic," in *Latin American Radicalism: A Documentary Report on Left and Nationalist Movements,* ed. Irving Louis Horowitz, Josue Castro, and John Gerassi (New York: Random House, 1969).

9. Martin, *Overtaken by Events,* 645.

10. Lowenthal, *The Dominican Intervention,* 50.

11. Ibid., 63–64.

12. Ibid., 61.

13. Ibid., 66.

14. Santo Domingo cable 20912, General Records of the Department of State (College Park, MD: National Archives at College Park).

15. Lowenthal, *The Dominican Intervention,* 66; Santo Domingo cables 20912 and 20932.

16. Lyndon Baines Johnson, *The Vantage Point: Perspectives of the Presidency, 1963–1969* (New York: Holt, Rinehart & Winston, 1971), 188.

17. Lowenthal, *The Dominican Intervention,* 68.

18. Santo Domingo cable 20959, 4:20 A.M.; Lowenthal, *The Dominican Intervention,* 68.

19. Lowenthal, *The Dominican Intervention,* 70.

20. Ibid., 70–71.

21. Ibid., chap. 3.

22. Ibid.

23. Ibid., 76–77; confirmed in Associated Press, "Dominican Coup Deposes Regime; Rebels Are Split; Some of Military Oppose Plans for the Return of Bosch as President," *New York Times,* April 26, 1965.

24. Lowenthal, *The Dominican Intervention,* 77.

25. Ibid., 77; Associated Press, "Dominican Coup Deposes Regime."

26. Lowenthal, *The Dominican Intervention,* 79.

27. Ibid., chap. 3.

28. Ibid., 83.

29. Johnson, *The Vantage Point,* 191.

30. Tad Szulc, "U.S. to Evacuate Nationals Today in Dominican Crisis," *New York Times,* April 27, 1965.

31. Lowenthal, *The Dominican Intervention,* 84–86; Martin, *Overtaken by Events,* 650–651; Santo Domingo cable 21442.

32. Lowenthal, *The Dominican Intervention,* chap. 3.

33. "Boxer Was in Caribbean," *New York Times,* April 27, 1965.

34. Lowenthal, *The Dominican Intervention,* 89.

35. Ibid., 93; Johnson, *The Vantage Point,* 192; Santo Domingo cable 23304.

36. Santo Domingo cable 23304.

37. Johnson, *The Vantage Point,* 192; Tad Szulc, "Dominican Revolt Fails after a Day of Savage Battle: Hundreds Believed Killed—Accord Calls for a Junta to Rule Till Election, Dominican Forces Put Down Revolt, 1,172 U.S. Citizens Are Evacuated from the Dominican Republic by Navy Task Force," *New York Times,* April 28, 1965.

38. Szulc, "Dominican Revolt Fails."

39. "Transcript of the President's News Conference on Foreign and Domestic Matters," *New York Times,* April 28, 1965.

40. Lowenthal, *The Dominican Intervention,* 95; Santo Domingo cable 23161.

41. Department of State outgoing cable 15215, General Records of the State Department (College Park, MD, National Archives at College Park, 1965).

42. Lowenthal, *The Dominican Intervention,* 95–96; Presidential Daily Diary, *Lyndon B. Johnson Papers* (Lyndon Baines Johnson Library, Austin, TX, 1965).

43. Ibid., 97.

44. Ibid., 99–102.

45. Ibid., 101; Johnson, *The Vantage Point,* 194; Rowland Evans and Robert Novak, *Lyndon B. Johnson: The Exercise of Power* (New York: The New American Library, 1966), 516–517.

46. Martin, *Overtaken by Events,* 656; Santo Domingo cable 24229.

47. Lowenthal, *The Dominican Intervention,* 656; Presidential Daily Diary, *Lyndon B. Johnson Papers.*

48. Lowenthal, *The Dominican Intervention,* 101–102; Santo Domingo cable 24324.

49. Johnson, *The Vantage Point,* 195; Charles Roberts, *LBJ's Inner Circle,* (New York: Delacorte Press, 1965), 204–205; Martin, *Overtaken by Events,* 657; Santo Domingo cable 24340.

50. Lowenthal, *The Dominican Intervention,* 103–104; Johnson, *The Vantage Point,* 195; Roberts, *LBJ's Inner Circle,* 205–206; Martin, *Overtaken by Events,* 657–658; Dean Rusk, *As I Saw It,* ed Daniel Papp and Richard Rusk (New York: W.W. Norton & Co., 1990), 371; Evans and Novak, *Lyndon B. Johnson,* 516–517.

51. Lowenthal, *The Dominican Intervention,* 104; Martin, *Overtaken by Events,* 657.

52. Johnson, *The Vantage Point,* 195.

53. Evans and Novak, *Lyndon B. Johnson,* 517–520; Charles Mohrs, "Johnson's Action on Troops Swift: He Made Decision Himself as Aides Told of Peril," *New York Times,* May 1, 1965.

54. Roberts, *LBJ's Inner Circle,* chap. 8; Lowenthal, *The Dominican Intervention,* 110.

55. Evans and Novak, *Lyndon B. Johnson,* 517.

56. Associated Press, "Envoy Sees Red Plot," *New York Times,* April 29, 1965.

57. Lowenthal, *The Dominican Intervention,* 110–111.

58. Santo Domingo cable 25157.

59. Lowenthal, *The Dominican Intervention,* 107–110.

60. Lowenthal, *The Dominican Intervention,* 110.

61. Roberts, *LBJ's Inner Circle,* asserts communist threat eminent at this meeting; Lowenthal, *The Dominican Intervention,* 110; Department of State cable 16317.

62. Lowenthal, *The Dominican Intervention,* 110.

63. Ibid., 110–111; Presidential Daily Diary, *Lyndon B. Johnson Papers.*

64. Tad Szulc, "2,500 Men Fly In: Two Battalions to Aid 1,700 Marines in Anti-Red Move," *New York Times,* April 30, 1965.

65. Lowenthal, *The Dominican Intervention.*

66. Chris Searle, *Grenada: The Struggle against Destabilization* (London: Writers and Readers Publishing Coop, 1983), 56.

67. Massing, Michael, "Grenada Before and After," *Atlantic Monthly* 1984:80–81)

68. Searle, *Grenada,* 56–60.

69. Ibid., 52–55.

70. Ibid., 52.

71. Reynold A. Burrowes, *Revolution and Rescue in Grenada: An Account of the U.S. Caribbean Invasion* (New York: Greenwood Press, 1988), chap. 2.

72. Statement of the Hon. Ronald V. Dellums, A Representative in Congress from the State of California, in *United States Policy Toward Grenada,* a Hearing before the Subcommittee on Inter-American Affairs of the Committee on Foreign Affairs of the House of Representatives Ninety-Seventh Congress Second Session, June 15, 1982, 17.

73. Editorial desk, "Topics; Hemisphere Diversions," *New York Times,* March 31, 1983.

74. Ambassador Milan Bish, unnumbered cable, October 13, 1983.

75. George P. Shultz, *Turmoil and Triumph: My Years as Secretary of State* (New York: Charles Scribner's Sons, 1993), 326.

76. Fitzroy Ambursley and James Dunkerley, *Grenada: Whose Freedom?* (London: Latin America Bureau Special Brief, 1984), chap. 5.

77. Shultz, *Turmoil and Triumph,* chapter 20.

78. Constantine C. Menges, *Inside the National Security Council: The True Story of the Making and Unmaking of Reagan's Foreign Policy* (New York: Simon and Schuster, 1988), 63.

79. Ibid., 60–62.

80. Burrowes, *Revolution and Rescue,* 137.

81. Presidential Daily Diary, *Ronald Reagan Papers* (Simi Valley, CA: Ronald Reagan Library, 1983).

82. Shultz, *Turmoil and Triumph,* 328.

83. Ambursley and Dunkerley, *Grenada,* 75.

84. Ellen Ray and Bill Schaap, "Grenada—No Bishop, No Revo: U.S. Crushes Caribbean Jewel" *Covert Action* no. 20 (Winter 1984): 10.

85. Ambassador Milan Bish, unnumbered cable, October 13, 1983.

86. Burrowes, *Revolution and Rescue,* chap. 3.

87. Menges, *Inside the National Security Council,* 66.

88. Ibid., 70, not confirmed elsewhere.

89. Ibid., 70.

90. Ibid., 70.

91. Ibid., 72–74.

92. Shultz, *Turmoil and Triumph,* 326–327.

93. Ibid., 331–332.

94. Caspar Weinberger, *Fighting For Peace: Seven Critical Years in the Pentagon* (New York: Warner Books, 1990).

95. Weinberger, *Fighting For Peace,* 109, gives a much different account: "On October 20, the day after Bishop was murdered, I approved General Vessey's recommendation that we turn southward two units—the carrier *Independence* and its Battle Group, and the Marine replacement group that was then under way for normal rotation with units in the Lebanon area—in case they would be needed near Grenada." He makes it sound like he wasn't at the meeting, that it wasn't contested, and that it was Vessey's idea. This might be attributable to recall, but I consider his memoir the most sketchy, followed by Reagan's. Shultz's and Menges's seem considerably more reliable in terms of details (which all cross-check with other sources) and candor.

96. Menges, *Inside the National Security Council,* 78–79.

97. Weinberger, *Fighting For Peace.*

98. Ibid., 111.

99. Ronald Reagan and Robert Lindsey, *An American Life* (New York: Simon and Schuster, 1990), 450–452; Menges, *Inside the National Security Council,* 75–77.

100. William Blum, *Killing Hope: U.S. Military and CIA Interventions since World War II* (Monroe, ME: Common Courage Press, 1995), 270.

101. Seth Mydans, "Caribbean Nations Felt Grenada Threatened Stability," *New York Times,* October 26, 1983.

102. Burrowes, *Revolution and Rescue,* chap. 5.

103. Tad Szulc, "Making The World 'Safe' for Hypocrisy," *New York Times,* October 28, 1983.

104. Menges, *Inside the National Security Council,* 74; Shultz, *Turmoil and Triump,* seems to concur.

105. Menges, *Inside the National Security Council,* 74–76.

106. Bridgetown cable 06490, General Record of the White House (Simi Valley, CA: Ronald Reagan Library, 1983).

107. Bridgetown cable 06514, General Record of the White House (Simi Valley, CA: Ronald Reagan Library, 1983).

108. Presidential Daily Diary, *Ronald Reagan Papers.*

109. Burrowes, *Revolution and Rescue,* 139.

110. Reagan and Lindsey, *An American Life,* 450; Shultz, *Turmoil and Triumph,* 329–330.

111. Menges, *Inside the National Security Council,* 77–79.

112. Ibid., 79.

113. Frank J. Prial, "American Envoys Going to Grenada," *New York Times,* October 23, 1983.

114. Ibid.

115. Shultz, *Turmoil and Triumph,* chap. 20.

116. Reagan and Lindsey, *An American Life,* 453–454.

117. Ambursley and Dunkerley, *Grenada,* 83–88; John T. McQuiston, "School's Chancellor Says Invasion Was Not Necessary to Save Lives," *New York Times,* October 26, 1983.

118. Presidential Daily Diary, *Ronald Reagan Papers.*

119. Reagan and Lindsey, *An American Life;* Menges, *Inside the National Security Council;* Shultz, *Turmoil and Triumph*

120. Ambursley and Dunkerley, *Grenada,* 88.

121. Weinberger, *Fighting For Peace,* 113.

122. Reagan and Lindsey, *An American Life,* 454–455.

123. Shultz, *Turmoil and Triumph,* 335.

124. Menges, *Inside the National Security Council,* 83.

125. Weinberger, *Fighting For Peace,* 114–116.

126. Reuters, "Text of Reagan's Announcement of Invasion," *New York Times,* October 26, 1983.

127. Reagan quoted in Bernard Gwertzman, "Reagan Gains by Grenada, but Mostly on His Own Turf," *New York Times,* November 6, 1983.

128. Blum, *Killing Hope,* 306.

129. Margaret E. Scranton, *The Noriega Years: U.S.–Panamanian Relations, 1981–1990* (Boulder, CO: Lynne Rienner Publishers, 1991), chap. 6.

130. Ibid., 128.

131. Colin L. Powell and Joseph E. Persico, *My American Journey* (New York: Random House, 1995), 416.

132. Scranton, *The Noriega Years,* 105–6.

133. Ibid., 139.

134. Bob Woodward, *The Commanders* (New York: Simon & Schuster, 1991), 85.

135. James A. Baker III and Thomas M. Defrank, *The Politics of Diplomacy: Revolution, War and Peace 1989–1992* (New York: G.P. Putnam's Sons, 1995), 180–181.

136. Woodward, *The Commanders,* 90; Bernard Weinraub, "Denouncing Fraud, Bush Bolsters Force in Panama," *New York Times,* May 12, 1989.

137. Woodward, *The Commanders,* 92; Maureen Dowd, "Bush Hardens Line on Noriega Ouster," *New York Times,* May 14, 1989.

138. Woodward, *The Commanders,* 99; Baker and Defrank, *The Politics of Diplomacy,* 1995.

139. Woodward, *The Commanders,* 100.

140. Ibid., 92.

141. Ibid., 94–95.
142. Ibid., 114.
143. Quoted in Woodward, *The Commanders,* 116.
144. Woodward, *The Commanders,* 119–125; Baker and Defrank, *The Politics of Diplomacy,* 185–186; Scranton, *The Noriega Years,* 185–191; Powell and Persico, *My American Journey,* 417–418.
145. Powell and Persico *My American Journey,* 417–418.
146. Ibid., 418.
147. Ibid., 418.
148. Woodward, *The Commanders,* 119–123; Powell and Persico, *My American Journey,* 418.
149. Woodward, *The Commanders,* 123–125; Andrew Rosenthal, "Noriega Officers Try Coup and Fail: U.S. Knew of Plot," *New York Times,* October 4, 1989.
150. Woodward, *The Commanders,* 128.
151. Ibid., 133.
152. Ibid., 139–140.
153. Scranton, *The Noriega Years,* 197; Reuters, "Opposition Leader in Panama Rejects a Peace Offer from Noriega," *New York Times,* December 17, 1989.
154. Woodward, *The Commanders,* 157–158.
155. Ibid., 158–160.
156. Woodward, *The Commanders.*
157. Powell and Persico, *My American Journey;* Baker and Defrank, *The Politics of Diplomacy.*
158. Scranton, *The Noriega Years,* 199.
159. Woodward, *The Commanders,* 159.
160. Ibid., 159.
161. Ibid., 160–162.
162. Woodward, *The Commanders,* 161–162; Powell and Persico, *My American Journey,* 422.
163. Powell and Persico, *My American Journey,* 423.
164. Woodward, *The Commanders,* 166–167.
165. Ibid., 167.
166. Presidential Daily Diary, *George Bush Papers* (College Station, TX: George Bush Presidential Library, 1989).
167. Specific mention in both Woodward, *The Commanders,* 170, and Powell and Persico, *My American Journey,* 424–425.
168. Woodward, *The Commanders,* 171; Baker and Defrank, *The Politics of Diplomacy,* 189–190; Scranton, *The Noriega Years,* 201; Presidential Daily Diary, *George Bush Papers;* Powell and Persico, *My American Journey,* 425.
169. "Fighting in Panama: Explaining the Attack; Cheney's Reasons for Why the U.S. Struck Now," *New York Times,* December 21, 1989.
170. Woodward, *The Commanders,* 173.
171. Ibid., 175–181.
172. Presidential Daily Diary, *George Bush Papers*
173. Andrew Rosenthal, "President Calls Panama Slaying a Great Outrage," *New York Times,* December 19, 1998.
174. "Excerpts from U.S. Account of Officer's Death in Panama," *New York Times,* December 18, 1989.
175. Scranton, *The Noriega Years,* 201.

176. Scranton, *The Noriega Years,* 201.

177. James Brooke, "Fighting in Panama: Latin America, U.S. Denounced by Nations Touchy about Intervention," *New York Times,* December 21, 1989.

178. Susan F. Rasky, "Fighting in Panama: Legal Case; Administration Says International Agreements Support Its Action," *New York Times,* December 21, 1989.

179. Scranton, *The Noriega Years,* 207–208.

180. Elizabeth D. Gibbons, *The Washington Papers: Sanctions in Haiti—Human Rights and Democracy under Assault* (London: Praeger, 1999), 3.

181. Edward R. Drachman and Alan Shank, *Presidents and Foreign Policy: Countdown to 10 Controversial Decisions* (Albany, NY: SUNY Press, 1997), 315.

182. Kim Ives, "The Unmaking of a President" in *Haiti: Dangerous Crossroads,* ed. Deidre McFadyen and Pierre LaRamee (Boston: South End Press, 1995), 67; Gibbons, *The Washington Papers,* 3–4; John R. Ballard, *Upholding Democracy: The United States Military Campaign in Haiti, 1994–1997* (London: Praeger, 1998), 50.

183. Jim A. Kuypers, *Presidential Crisis Rhetoric and the Press in the Post–Cold War World* (Westport, CT: Praeger, 1997), 112.

184. Drachman and Shank, *Presidents and Foreign Policy,* 331.

185. Kuypers, *Presidential Crisis Rhetoric,* 112; Drachman adn Shank, *Presidents and Foreign Policy,* 315.

186. Drachman and Shank, *Presidents and Foreign Policy,* 316.

187. Kuypers, *Presidential Crisis Rhetoric,* 114.

188. Drachman and Shank, *Presidents and Foreign Policy,* 324.

189. Ives, "The Unmaking of a President," 79.

190. Kuypers, *Presidential Crisis Rhetoric,* 139; Ballard, *Upholding Democracy,* 52; Drachman and Shank, *Presidents and Foreign Policy,* 324.

191. Georges A. Fauriol and Andrew S. Faiola "Chapter 11—Prelude to Intervention" in *Haitian Frustrations: Dilemmas for U.S. Policy: A Report of the CSIS Americas Program,* ed. Georges A. Fauriol (Washington, DC. Center for Strategic & International Studies, 1995), 103.

192. Kuypers, *Presidential Crisis Rhetoric,* 142; Gibbons, *The Washington Papers,* 5–6.

193. Fauriol and Faiola, "Prelude to Intervention," 104.

194. Drachman and Shank, *Presidents and Foreign Policy,* 325–326.

195. Howard W. French, "Aristide Opens Conference with Plea for Help," *New York Times,* January 16, 1994.

196. Kim Ives, "Haiti's Second Occupation" in *Haiti: Dangerous Crossroads,* ed. Deidre McFadyen and Pierre LaRamee (Boston: South End Press, 1995), 109.

197. "Black Caucus Urges Tougher Haiti Policy," *New York Times,* March 23, 1994.

198. "Opponents of Policy on Haiti Begin Fast," *New York Times,* April 13, 1994.

199. Steven Greenhouse, "Clinton Policy Toward Haiti Comes under Growing Fire," *New York Times,* April 15, 1994.

200. Ives, "Haiti's Second Occupation," 109–110; Tim Weiner, "Clinton Forces Out U.S. Envoy to Haiti to Display Resolve," *New York Times,* April 27, 1994.

201. "Haitian Impasse—A Special Report: Failure on Haiti: How U.S. Hopes Faded," *New York Times,* April 29, 1994.

202. Ibid.

203. Ibid.

204. Ibid.

205. Deidre McFadyen, Pierre LaRamee, Mark Fried, and Fred Rosen (NACLA), "Introduction," in *Haiti: Dangerous Crossroads* (Boston: South End Press, 1995), 4.

206. Michael R. Gordon, "Clinton Says Haiti Military Must Go Now," *New York Times,* May 4, 1994.

207. Drachman and Shank, *Presidents and Foreign Policy,* 327.

208. Ballard, *Upholding Democracy,* 75.

209. Steven Greenhouse, "U.S. Shifts Stress to Haiti Sanctions," *New York Times,* June 9, 1994.

210. Ballard, *Upholding Democracy,* 76–77.

211. Ibid., 86.

212. Michael R. Gordon "In Shift, U.S. Will No Longer Admit Haitians at Sea," *New York Times,* July 6, 1994.

213. Steven Greenhouse, "Lawmakers Oppose an Invasion of Haiti Now," *New York Times,* July 7, 1994.

214. Ballard, *Upholding Democracy,* 86.

215. Fauriol and Faiola, "Prelude to Intervention," 114.

216. Ballard, *Upholding Democracy,* 86.

217. Ibid., 87.

218. Ives, "Haiti's Second Occupation," 111; Ballard, *Upholding Democracy,* 87; Gibbons, *The Washington Papers,* 6.

219. Drachman and Shank, *Presidents and Foreign Policy,* 327.

220. Ibid., 327; Elaine Sciolino, "Top U.S. Officials Divided in Debate on Invading Haiti," *New York Times,* August 4, 1994.

221. Sciolino, "Top U.S. Officials Divided in Debate on Invading Haiti."

222. Ibid.

223. Drachman and Shank, *Presidents and Foreign Policy,* 327.

224. Fauriol and Faiola, "Prelude to Intervention," 114.

225. Drachman and Shank, *Presidents and Foreign Policy,* 327.

226. Ibid., 328.

227. Evan Thomas, "Under the Gun," *Newsweek* 124, no. 14 (October 3, 1994): 28.

228. Ibid.

229. Ibid.

230. Thomas H. Henriksen, *Clinton's Foreign Policy in Somalia, Bosnia, Haiti, and North Korea* (Stanford: Hoover Institution, 1996), 27.

CHAPTER 3

1. Pluralists—e.g., Robert A. Dahl, *Who Governs? Democracy and Power in an American City* (New Haven: Yale University Press, 1961; and Robert A. Dahl, *Polyarchy: Participation and Opposition* (New Haven: Yale University Press, 1971); class theorists—e.g., Ralph Miliband, *The State in Capitalist Society* (London: Weidenfeld and Nicholson, 1969); G. William Domhoff, *Who Really Rules? New Haven and Community Power Reexamined* (New Brunswick, NJ: Transaction Books, 1978), G. William Domhoff, *The Power Elite and the State: How Policy Is Made in America* (New York: Aldine DeGruyter, 1990), G. William Domhoff, *State Autonomy or Class Dominance? Case Studies on Policy Making in America* (New York: Aldine DeGruyter, 1996); Fred Block, "State Theory in Context," in *Revising State Theory: Essays in Politics and Postindustrialism,* ed. Fred Block (Philadelphia: Temple University Press, 1987);

elite theorist—e.g., C. Wright Mills, *The Power Elite* (New York: Oxford University Press, 1956); Thomas Dye, *Who's Running America? The Clinton Years* (New Jersey: Prentice-Hall, 1995); Theda Skocpol, *States & Social Revolutions: A Comparative Analysis of France, Russia, & China,* (1979).

2. Dahl, *Polyarchy: Participation and Opposition.*

3. Marvin E. Olsen, *Participatory Pluralism: Political Participation and Influence in the United States and Sweden* (Chicago: Nelson-Hall, 1982).

4. See the famous Miliband/Poulantzas debate. Miliband, *The State in Capitalist Society,* and Nicos Poulantzas, "The Problem of the Capitalist State," in *New Left Review* no. 58 (1969).

5. Domhoff, *Who Really Rules?* Domhoff, *The Power Elite and the State;* and Domhoff, *State Autonomy.*

6. Block, "State Theory in Context."

7. Gaetano Mosca, *The Ruling Class (Elementi di Scienza Politica),* trans. Hannah D. Kahn, ed. and rev. with an Introduction by Arthur Livingston (New York and London: McGraw-Hill, Inc., 1939).

8. Mills, *The Power Elite.*

9. Alice H. Amsden, "The State and Taiwan's Economic Development," in *Bringing the State Back In,* ed. Peter B. Evans, Dietrich Rueschemeyer, and Theda Skocpol (Cambridge: Cambridge University Press, 1985); Michael Mann, *States, War and Capitalism* (Oxford: Blackwell, 1984); Charles Tilly, "War Making and State Making As Organized Crime," in *Bringing the State Back In,* ed. Peter B. Evans, Dietrich Rueschemeyer, and Theda Skocpol (Cambridge: Cambridge University Press, 1985); Theda Skocpol, "Introduction," in *Bringing the State Back In,* ed. Peter B. Evans, Dietrich Rueschemeyer, and Theda Skocpol (Cambridge: Cambridge University Press, 1985); Theda Skocpol, "The Potential Autonomy of the State," in *Power in Modern Societies,* ed. Marvin Elliott Olsen and Martin N. Marger (Boulder, CO: Westview Press, 1993).

10. See John M. Hobson, *The State and International Relations* (Cambridge: Cambridge University Press, 2000) for a critique of many state autonomy theorists who, while allowing what Hobson calls "domestic agential power" (autonomy), fail to allow the state any "international agential power" (autonomy in behavior within the international domain).

11. John Higley and Michael Burton, "The Elite Variable in Democratic Transitions and Breakdowns," *American Sociological Review* 54, no. 1 (1989).

12. Karl Marx and Friedrich Engles, "The 18th Brumaire of Louis Bonaparte," *Collected Works* vol. XI (London: Lawrence & Wishart, 1975), 103–104.

13. David Dessler, "What's at Stake in the Agent-Structure Debate?" *International Organization* 43, no. 3 (1989): 443.

14. See Miliband, *The State in Capitalist Society;* and Poulantzas, "The Problem of the Capitalist State."

15. Victor Nee and Mary C. Brinton, "Introduction," in *The New Institutionalism in Sociology,* ed. Mary C. Brinton and Victor Nee (Stanford, CA: Stanford University Press, 1998).

16. As identified by John L. Campbell, "Institutional Analysis and the Role of Ideas in Political Economy," *Theory and Society* 27 (1998): 377–409; see John W. Meyer, John Boli, George M. Thomas, and Francisco O. Ramirez, "World Society and the Nation-State," *American Journal of Sociology* 103, no 1 (1997): 144–181; Paul J. DiMaggio and Walter W. Powell, "Introduction," in *The New Institutionalism in Organizational Analysis,* ed. Paul J. Powell and Walter W. DiMaggio (Chicago: University of Chicago Press, 1991), 1–38.

17. Ann Swidler, "Culture in Action: Symbols and Strategies," *American Sociological Review* 51 (April 1986), 273–286; Campbell, "Institutional Analysis," 377–409.

18. For more on state autonomy in this way, see C. Edward Paul, "Moving Forward with State Autonomy and Capacity: Example from Two Studies of the Pentagon During W.W.II. ," *Journal of Political and Military Sociology* 28, no. 1 (Summer 2000): 21–42.

19. Victor Nee and Paul Ingram, "Embeddedness and Beyond: Institutions, Exchange, and Social Structure," in *The New Institutionalism in Sociology,* ed. Mary C. Brinton and Victor Nee (Stanford, CA: Stanford University Press, 1998), 19.

20. Patrick J. Haney, *Organizing for Foreign Policy Crises: Presidents, Advisers, and the Management of Decision Making* (Ann Arbor: University of Michigan Press, 1997), 17.

21. Michael Mann, *The Sources of Social Power, v.2: The Rise of Classes and Nation-States, 1760–1914* (Cambridge: Cambridge University Press, 1993), 52.

22. Kenneth Finegold and Theda Skocpol, *State and Party in America's New Deal* (Madison: The University of Wisconsin Press, 1995); Mann, *The Sources of Social Power.*

23. Mann, *The Sources of Social Power,* 54.

24. Block, "State Theory in Context."

25. Former President George H.W. Bush does not have (by choice, according to an archivist at the Bush library) a memoir or autobiography per se; instead, he has a co-authored book of reflections on policy, entitled *A World Transformed.*

CHAPTER 4

1. Alexander L. George, *Presidential Decisionmaking in Foreign Policy: The Effective Use of Information and Advice* (Boulder, CO: Westview, 1980), 218.

2. Michael G. Roskin, *National Interest: From Abstraction to Strategy* (Carlisle, PA: U.S. Army War College, Strategic Studies Institute, 1994).

3. Uniting and Strengthening America by Providing Appropriate Tools Required to Intercept and Obstruct Terrorism (USA Patriot Act) Act of 2001, Public Law 107–56, 107th Congress, October 26, 2001, 171–172; in the discussion of the role played by "those groups who hold the power" in the maintenance of national prestige I contend that, while business elites are likely to include business interests in the national interest, they are also likely to encourage a definition of the national interests that includes the broader interests of the nation.

4. Peter L. Berger and Thomas Luckmann, *The Social Construction of Reality: A Treatise its the Sociology of Knowledge* (Garden City, New York: Anchor Books, 1966).

5. G. William Domhoff, *The Power Elite and the State: How Policy Is Made in America* (New York: Aldine DeGruyter, 1990), chap. 5, the argument is that ruling class elites are interested in business interests first, and the interests of the nation at large after that. Drawing on Max Weber, *From Max Weber: Essays in Sociology,* ed. Hans .H. Gerth and C. Wright Mills (New York: Oxford University Press, 1946).

6. Derek Miller, "Towards a Theory of Media Pressure: A Literature Review on Effects of Media Technology on National Security Decisionmaking" (Unpublished, 1999).

7. Miroslav Nincic, "The National Interest and Its Interpretation," *Review of Politics* 61, no. 1 (Winter 1999): 29.

8. John M. Hobson, *The State and International Relations* (Cambridge: Cambridge University Press, 2000).

9. For a more complete discussion of IR theories, see Hobson, *The State and International Relations.*

10. Nincic, "The National Interest."
11. Ibid.
12. Ibid.
13. Ibid.
14. Stephan Krasner, *Defending the National Interest* (Princeton, NJ: Princeton University Press, 1978), 13.
15. Nincic, "The National Interest."
16. Domhoff, *The Power Elite and the State.*
17. Ibid., chap. 5.
18. Krasner, *Defending the National Interest,* 15.
19. Samuel P. Huntington, "The Erosion of American National Interests," in *The Domestic Sources of American Foreign Policy: Insights and Evidence,* ed. Eugene R. Wittkopf and James M. McCormick (New York: Rowman & Littlefield, 1999), 12.
20. Domhoff, *The Power Elite and the State,* chap. 5. This grand area included the Western Hemisphere, the United Kingdom and the remainder of the British Commonwealth, and significant portions of the Far East.
21. Ibid., 137.
22. Ibid., chap. 5.
23. Krasner, *Defending the National Interest,* 298.
24. Deborah Welch Larson, *Origins of Containment: A Psychological ExplanationI* (Princeton, NJ: Princeton University Press, 1985), 329.
25. Christina Jacqueline Johns and P. Ward Johnson, *State Crime, The Media, and The Invasion of Panama* (Westport: Praeger, 1994), 5.
26. Ibid., 7.
27. Gaddis Smith, "Haiti: From Intervention to Intervasion," *Current History* 94, no. 589 (February 1995): 56.
28. M. Berkowitz, P.G. Bock, and Vincent J. Fuccillo, *The Politics of American Foreign Policy* (Edgewood Cliffs, NJ: Prentice-Hall, 1977), 299.
29. Ronald H. Hinckley, *People, Polls, and Policymakers: American Public Opinion and National Security* (New York: Lexington Books, 1992); Fredrik Logevall, *Choosing War: The Lost Chance for Peace and the Escalation of War in Vietnam* (Los Angeles: University of California Press, 1999).
30. Quoted in Huntington, "The Erosion of American National Interests," 13.
31. See, for example, Arnold Kanter, "Intervention Decisionmaking in the Bush Administration," in *U.S. and Russian Policymaking with Respect to the Use of Force* (Santa Monica, CA: RAND Corporation, 1996).
32. James Chace, "The National Interest," *World Policy Journal* 10, no. 4 (Winter 1993): 109.
33. Robert Ellsworth, Andrew Goodpaster, and Rita Hauser, Co-Chairs, *America's National Interests: A Report from The Commission on America's National Interests,* Graham T. Allison, Dimitri K. Simes, and James Thomson, Executive Directors (Boston, MA: Belfer Center for Science and International Affairs, Harvard, 2000), 3.
34. Krasner, *Defending the National Interest,* 291.
35. Abraham F. Lowenthal, *The Dominican Intervention* (Cambridge, MA: Harvard, 1972), chap. 3; Department of State outgoing Ccables 13901 and 16317, General Records of the State Department (College Park, MD: National Archives at College Park, 1965).
36. Richard J. Barnet, *Intervention and Revolution: America's Confrontation with Insurgent Movements Around the World* (New York: World Publishing Co., 1968), 177; Lowenthal,

The Dominican Intervention, 14; North American Congress on Latin America (NACLA), "NACLA'S Latin American & Empire Report—Smoldering Conflict: Dominican Republic 1965–1975," vol. IX, no. 3 (New York: North American Congress on Latin America, April 1975), 9.

37. Fred Goff and Michael Locker, "The Violence of Domination: U.S. Power and the Dominican Republic," in *Latin American Radicalism: A Documentary Report on Left and Nationalist Movements,* ed. Irving Louis Horowitz, Josue Castro, and John Gerassi (New York: Random Hose, 1969), 280.

38. Presidential Daily Diary, *Lyndon B. Johnson Papers* (Austin, TX: Lyndon Baines Johnson Library, 1965).

39. Dean Rusk, "If there was a mistake in the crisis, it was the way in which we presented our actions to the American people and the world," quoted in *As I Saw It,* ed. Daniel Papp and Richard Rusk (New York: W.W. Norton & Co., 1990), 373.

40. Michael J. Kryzanek, "The Grenada Invasion: Approaches to Understanding" in *United States Policy in Latin America: A Decade of Crisis and Challenge,* ed. John D. Martz. (Lincoln: University of Nebraska Press, 1995), 60.

40. Statement of the Hon. Ronald V. Dellums, A Representative in Congress from the State of California, in *United States Policy Toward Grenada,* a Hearing before the Subcommittee on Inter-American Affairs of the Committee on Foreign Affairs of the House of Representatives Ninety-Seventh Congress Second Session, June 15, 1982, 17.

41. Samuel Kernell, *Going Public: New Strategies of Presidential Leadership* (Washington, DC. CQ Press., 1986), 148.

42. Colin L. Powell and Joseph E. Persico, *My American Journey* (New York: Random House, 1995).

43. Georges A. Fauriol and Andrew S. Faiola "Chapter 11—Prelude to Intervention," in *Haitian Frustrations: Dilemmas for U.S. Policy: A Report of the CSIS Americas Program,* ed. Georges A. Fauriol (Washington, DC. Center for Strategic & International Studies, 1995), 113.

44. Peter Viggo Jakobsen, "National Interest, Humanitarianism or CNN: What Triggers UN Peace Enforcement After the Cold War?" *Journal of Peace Research* 33, no. 2 (1996): 211.

45. Jim A. Kuypers, *Presidential Crisis Rhetoric and the Press in the Post–Cold War World* (Westport, CT: Praeger, 1997), 3.

CHAPTER 5

1. Peter Bachrach and Morton J. Baratz, "Decisions and Non-Decisions," *American Political Science Review* 57 (September 1963).

2. For other definitions of crisis in foreign policy, see Richard C. Snyder, "Introduction," in *Foreign Policy Decision-Making: An Approach to the Study of International Politics,* ed. Richard Snyder, H.W. Bruck, and Burton Sapin (Glencoe, ON: The Free Press, 1962), 14; Ole Holsti, "Crisis Decision Making," in *Behavior, Society, and Nuclear War,* ed. Philip E. Tetlock, Jo L. Husbandsm, Robert Jervis, Paul C. Stern, and Charles Tilly (New York: Oxford University Press, 1989), 12; Margaret E. Scranton, *The Noriega Years: U.S.–Panamanian Relations, 1981–1990* (Boulder, CO: Lynne Rienner Publishers, 1991), 34; Richard E. Neustadt, *Presidential Power and the Modern Presidents: The Politics of Leadership from Roosevelt to Reagan* (New York: The Free Press, 1990), 66; or Jim A. Kuypers, *Presidential Crisis Rhetoric and the Press in the Post–Cold War World* (Westport, CT: Praeger, 1997), 8.

3. Note that a situation that is a crisis (that is, is surprising and time pressing) can result in a premeditated military intervention. This can occur when a crisis intervention is not possible. For example, the President George H.W. Bush would very much have liked to launch a defense of Kuwait when the Iraqis first occupied it. However, the U.S. forces available in the area were inadequate to mount an effective operation at that time. Crisis decision making quickly encountered this roadblock, and the process turned into (in every respect) a premeditated intervention.

4. Lester W. Milbrath, "Interest Groups and Foreign Policy," in *Domestic Sources of Foreign Policy,* ed. James N. Rosenau (New York: The Free Press, 1967), 235.

5. Neustadt, *Presidential Power and the Modern Presidents,* 191.

6. Theodore J. Lowi, "Making Democracy Safe for the World," in *Domestic Sources of Foreign Policy,* ed. James N. Rosenau (New York: The Free Press, 1967), 301.

7. Lowi is using the word "institution" where I would use the word "organization." Following William G. Roy, *Socializing Capital: The Rise of the Large Industrial Corporation in America* (Princeton, NJ: Princeton University Press, 1997), 14: "By social institution I mean the matrix of organizations, taken-for-granted categories, and the agreed-upon modes of relationship among those organizations that administer a major social task." This definition of institution is much broader than an organization or department. I wish to use organization with the standard English denotation of an administrative and functional structure and the associated personnel, which is what Lowi seems to mean with his use of "institutions."

8. To be fair, one of Lowi's important arguments regards the extent to which various institutional *interests* and internal politicking are subsumed in crisis, leaving only "the national interest." I also believe this is true to some extent, though, again, not the extent that Lowi seems to argue.

9. Lowi, "Making Democracy Safe for the World," 301.

10. Yes, this was caprice rather than calculation. The coup makers did not choose to launch their insurrection based on the ambassador's absence. In fact, they were forced to begin several days early when the head of the Dominican government got wind of their plot and sent a loyal colonel to arrest several of the key plotters. The officers the colonel chose to take with him turned out to be part of the plot (so he went from being the arrester to being the arrestee), but the plotters' plans were exposed and they had no choice but to begin immediately Abraham F. Lowenthal, *The Dominican Intervention* (Cambridge, MA: Harvard, 1972), 61.

11. This view is consonant with a "choice within constraints" framework/resolution of the structure/agency debate. I discuss this topic more completely in chapter 6 on legacy chains.

12. Charles Roberts, *LBJ's Inner Circle* (New York: Delacorte Press, 1965), 211; confirmed with Presidential Daily Diary, *Lyndon B. Johnson Papers* (Austin, TX: Lyndon Baines Johnson Library, 1965).

13. "President's Speech on Military Spending and a New Defense," *New York Times,* March 24, 1983.

14. Fitzroy Ambursley and James Dunkerley, *Grenada: Whose Freedom?* (London: Latin America Bureau Special Brief, 1984), chap. 5; Reynold A. Burrowes, *Revolution and Rescue in Grenada: An Account of the U.S. Caribbean Invasion* (New York: Greenwood Press, 1988), 83.

15. See, for example, Scranton, "The Noriega Years"; and Patrick J. Haney, *Organizing for Foreign Policy Crises: Presidents, Advisers, and the Management of Decision Making* (Ann Arbor: University of Michigan Press, 1997).

16. Bob Woodward, *The Commanders* (New York: Simon & Schuster, 1991); Colin L. Powell and Joseph E. Persico, *My American Journey* (New York: Random House, 1995),

chap. 16; James A. Baker III and Thomas M. Defrank, *The Politics of Diplomacy: Revolution, War and Peace 1989–1992* (New York: G.P. Putnam's Sons, 1995), chap. 11.

17. Elizabeth D. Gibbons, *The Washington Papers: Sanctions in Haiti—Human Rights and Democracy under Assault* (London: Praeger, 1999), 3.

18. Ronald Reagan and Robert Lindsey, *An American Life* (New York: Simon and Schuster, 1990), 451; Presidential Daily Diary, *Ronald Reagan Papers* (Simi Valley, CA: Ronald Reagan Library, 1983).

19. For example, Stephan, Krasner, *Defending the National Interest* (Princeton, NJ: Princeton University Press, 1978).

20. Jame A. Winnefeld, Margaret C. Harrel, Robert D. Howe, Arnold Kanter, Brian Nichiporuk, Paul S. Steinberg, Thomas S. Szayna, and Ashley J. Tellis, *Intervention in Intrastate Conflict: Implications for the Army in the Post–Cold War Era* (Santa Monica, CA: RAND Corporation, 1995).

21. Ibid., *Intervention in Intrastate Conflict.*

22. I do not wish to argue a strong distinction in quality or importance of participation in the lower bureaucracy. I make reference to different "tiers" for holistic/narrative clarity only. Empirically, "tier" corresponds roughly with steps down the formal government hierarchy, with the president and his cabinet being the first tier, their subordinates being second tier, and so forth.

23. Constantine C. Menges, *Inside the National Security Council: The True Story of the Making and Unmaking of Reagan's Foreign Policy* (New York: Simon and Schuster, 1988), chap. 2.

24. Ibid.

25. Neustadt, *Presidential Power and the Modern Presidents,* 29.

26. Ronald H. Hinckley, *People, Polls, and Policymakers: American Public Opinion and National Security* (New York: Lexington Books, 1992), 108.

27. For example, see George P. Shultz, *Turmoil and Triumph: My Years as Secretary of State* (New York: Charles Scribner's Sons, 1993), 331–332.

28. Menges, *Inside the National Security Council,* 4.

29. Evan Thomas, "Under the Gun," *Newsweek* 124, no. 14 (October 3, 1994).

30. John R. Ballard, *Upholding Democracy: The United States Military Campaign in Haiti, 1994–1997* (London: Praeger, 1998), 63.

31. Ibid.

32. Woodward, *The Commanders.*

33. Dean Acheson, *Present at the Creation: My Years in the State Department* (New York: W. W. Norton and Co., 1969), 266.

34. Holsti, "Crisis Decision Making," 17.

35. Woodward, *The Commanders,* 139–140.

36. Ibid., 159.

37. Lauren Holland, "The U.S. Decision to Launch Operation Desert Storm: A Bureaucratic Politics Analysis," *Armed Forces & Society* 25, no. 2 (Winter 1999): 219–242.

38. Neustadt, *Presidential Power and the Modern Presidents,* 38; Menges, *Inside the National Security Council,* implicitly agrees.

39. "Haitian Impasse—A Special Report; Failure on Haiti: How U.S. Hopes Faded," *New York Times,* April 29, 1994.

40. Georges A. Fauriol and Andrew S. Faiola "Chapter 11—Prelude to Intervention," in *Haitian Frustrations: Dilemmas for U.S. Policy: A Report of the CSIS Americas Program,* Georges A. Fauriol (Washington, DC: Center for Strategic & International Studies, 1995), 105.

41. Ibid., 115.

42. Michael Mann, *The Sources of Social Power, v. 2: The Rise of Classes and Nation-States, 1760–1914* (Cambridge: Cambridge University Press, 1993), 53.

43. Lowenthal, *The Dominican Intervention,* 63–64.

44. Santo Domingo cable 24100, General Records of the Department of State (College Park, MD: National Archives at College Park).

45. Lyndon Baines Johnson, *The Vantage Point: Perspectives of the Presidency, 1963–1969* (New York: Holt, Rinehart & Winston, 1971), 193.

46. Ibid., 195; Roberts, *LBJ's Inner Circle,* 204–205; John Bartlow Martin, *Overtaken by Events: The Dominican Crisis from the Fall of Trujillo to the Civil War* (New York: Doubleday & Co., 1966), 657; Santo Domingo cable 24340.

47. Lyndon Baines Johnson, "Statement by President Johnson, May 2, 1965," Department of State Bulletin, May 17, 1965.

48. Lowenthal, *The Dominican Intervention,* 103.

49. Shultz, *Turmoil and Triumph,* 327.

50. Bachrach and Morton J. Baratz, "Decisions and Non-Decisions."

51. Fauriol and Faiola, "Prelude to Intervention," 115; George Stephanopoulos, *All Too Human: A Political Education* (Boston: Little, Brown and Co., 1999), 313.

52. Thomas, "Under the Gun."

53. Neustadt, *Presidential Power and the Modern Presidents.*

54. Geoffrey Kemp, "Presidential Management of the Executive Bureaucracy," in *The Domestic Sources of American Foreign Policy: Insights and Evidence,* ed. Eugene R. Wittkopf and James M. McCormick (New York: Rowman & Littlefield, 1999).

55. Presidential Daily Diary, *Lyndon B. Johnson Papers,* especially phone call records.

56. Menges, *Inside the National Security Council,* 63.

57. Quoted in Bob Woodward, *The Commanders* (New York: Simon & Schuster, 1991), 116.

58. Irving L. Janis, *Victims of Groupthink: A Psychological Study of Foreign-Policy Decisions and Fiascoes* (Boston: Houghton Mifflin, 1967), 13.

59. Glenn Hastedt and Anthony Eksterowicz, "Presidential Leadership and American Foreign Policy: Implications for a New Era," in *The Domestic Sources of American Foreign Policy: Insights and Evidence,* ed. Eugene R. Wittkopf and James M. McCormick (New York: Rowman & Littlefield, 1999); Kemp, "Presidential Management of the Executive Bureaucracy; or see Haney, *Organizing for Foreign Policy Crises,* for an example and a review of other authors' work on the topic.

60. Steven B. Redd, "The Influence of Advisers on Foreign Policy Decision Making: An Experimental Study," *Journal of Conflict Resolution* 46 no. 3 (2002): 335–364.

61. Powell and Persico, *My American Journey,* 418.

62. Menges, *Inside the National Security Council,* 66–68.

CHAPTER 6

1. For "schemas" see William H. Sewell Jr., "A Theory of Structure: Duality, Agency, and Transformation," *American Journal of Sociology* vol. 98, no. 1, (1992), 1–29.

2. Kenneth Finegold and Theda Skocpol, *State and Party in America's New Deal* (Madison: The University of Wisconsin Press, 1995), 222.

3. Finegold and Skocpol, *State and Party,* 224.

4. Robin Stryker, "Beyond History Versus Theory: Strategic Narrative and Sociological Explanation," *Sociological Methods & Research* 24, no. 3,(1996): 307.

5. John David Skrentny, "State Capacity, Policy Feedbacks and Affirmative Action for Blacks, Women, and Latinos," *Research in Political Sociology* 8 (1998): 282.

6. Ronald Aminzade, "Historical Sociology and Time," *Sociological Methods & Research* 20, no. 4 (1992): 463.

7. For a full discussion, see Christopher Paul and James Kim, *Reporters on the Battlefield: The Embedded Press System in Historical Context* (Santa Monica, CA: RAND Corporation, 2004), 4.

8. See, for example, Richard E. Neustadt and Ernest R. May, *Thinking in Time: The Uses of History for Decision-Makers* (New York: The Free Press, 1986).

9. Yuen Foong Khong, *Analogies at War: Korea, Munich, Dien Bien Phu, and the Vietnam Decisions of 1965* (Princeton, NJ: Princeton University Press, 1992), 13.

10. Khong, *Analogies at War.*

11. Ann Swidler, "Culture in Action: Symbols and Strategies," *American Sociological Review* 51, (April 1986): 273–286; Sewell, Jr., "A Theory of Structure," 992; see also Paul J. DiMaggio and Walter W. Powell, "Introduction," in *The New Institutionalism in Organizational Analysis,* ed. Paul J. Powell and Walter W. DiMaggio (Chicago: University of Chicago Press, 1991), 1–3.

12. Aminzade, "Historical Sociology and Time," 463.

13. For example see DiMaggio and Powell, *The New Institutionalism in Organizational Analysis.*

14. John Prados, *Presidents' Secret Wars: CIA and Pentagon Covert Operations from World War II through the Persian Gulf* (Chicago: Elephant, 1986).

15. DiMaggio and Powell, *The New Institutionalism in Organizational Analysis;* Skrentny, "State Capacity, Policy Feedbacks and Affirmative Action"; Robin H. Rogers-Dillon and John David Skrentny, "Administering Success: The Legitimacy Imperative and the Implementation of Welfare Reform," *Social Problems* 46, no. 1 (1999): 13–29.

16. Skrentny, "State Capacity, Policy Feedbacks and Affirmative Action."

17. See Richard E. Neustadt, *Presidential Power and the Modern Presidents: The Politics of Leadership from Roosevelt to Reagan* (New York: The Free Press, 1990) for some examples.

18. Sewell, Jr., "A Theory of Structure," 19.

19. Swidler, "Culture in Action; John L. Campbell, "Institutional Analysis and the Role of Ideas in Political Economy," *Theory and Society* 27 (1998).

20. For more on state autonomy in this way, see C. Edward Paul, "Moving Forward with State Autonomy and Capacity: Example from Two Studies of the Pentagon During W.W.II.," *Journal of Political and Military Sociology* 28, no. 1 (Summer 2000): 21–42.

21. See Andrew Abbott, "Conceptions of Time and Events in Social Science Methods: Causal and Narrative Approaches," *Historical Methods* 23, no. 4 (1990): 140–150; Aminzade, "Historical Sociology and Time"; Stryker, "Beyond History Versus Theory," for various discussions.

22. Stryker, "Beyond History Versus Theory."

23. Aminzade, "Historical Sociology and Time," 457.

24. Abbott, "Conceptions of Time and Eve," 141.

25. Stryker, "Beyond History Versus Theory."

26. Michael Mann, *The Sources of Social Power: Volume 1, A History of Power from the Beginning to AD 1760* (Cambridge: Cambridge University Press, 1986); and Michael Mann,

The Sources of Social Power, v. 2: The Rise of Classes and Nation-States, 1760–1914 (Cambridge: Cambridge University Press, 1993).

27. Philip Geyelin, "Vietnam and the Press: Limited War and an Open Society," in *The Legacy of Vietnam: The War, American Society and the Future of American Foreign Policy,* ed. Anthony Lake (New York: Council on Foreign Relations, 1976), 76.

28. Lloyd Gardner, "America's War in Vietnam: The End of Exceptionalism?" in *The Legacy: The Vietnam War in the American Imagination,* ed. D. Michael Shafer (Boston: Beacon Press, 1990), 21.

29. Ibid., 21.

30. Barbara Tischler, "Promise and Paradox: The 1960s and American Optimism," in *The Legacy: The Vietnam War in the American Imagination,* ed. D. Michael Shafer (Boston: Beacon Press, 1990), 47.

31. Common Ground, Program 9828, "Media vs. Military," Guest: Warren Strobel, author, *Late Breaking Foreign Policy,* 1998, air date: July 14, 1998.

32. Michael X. Delli Carpini, "Vietnam and the Press," in *The Legacy: The Vietnam War in the American Imagination,* ed. D. Michael Shafer (Boston: Beacon Press, 1990), 151.

33. Caspar Weinberger, *Fighting For Peace: Seven Critical Years in the Pentagon* (New York: Warner Books, 1990).

34. Ronald Reagan and Robert Lindsey, *An American Life* (New York: Simon and Schuster, 1990), 451.

35. David Benjamin, "Censorship in the Gulf," 1995, http://web1.duc.auburn.edu/~benjadp/gulf/gulf.html

36. Ibid.

37. Common Ground, "Media vs. Military."

38. Benjamin, "Censorship in the Gulf."

39. Colin L. Powell and Joseph E. Persico, *My American Journey* (New York: Random House, 1995), 431.

40. Ibid., 431.

41. Benjamin, "Censorship in the Gulf."

42. Ibid.

43. Douglas Porch, "Media/Military Relations in the United States," *Partnership for Democratic Governance & Security,* Occasional Paper # 10, July 2001, http://www.pdgs.org./main-site.htm.

44. Anne Holohan, "Haiti 1990–6: Older and Younger Journalists in the Post–Cold War World," *Media, Culture & Society* 25, no. 6 (2003): 706.

45. Paul and James Kim, *Reporters on the Battlefield.*

46. Ibid.

47. Ibid.

48. For a more detailed treatment of the War Powers legacy chain, see Christopher Paul, "US Presidential War Powers: Legacy Chains in Military Intervention Decisionmaking," forthcoming in *Journal of Peace Research,* 45, no. 5 (2008).

49. Irving Kristol, "Consensus and Dissent in U.S. Foreign Policy," in *The Legacy of Vietnam: The War, American Society and the Future of American Foreign Policy,* ed. Anthony Lake (New York: Council on Foreign Relations, 1976), 83.

50. Louis Fisher, "Without Restraint: Presidential Military Initiatives from Korea to Bosnia," in *The Domestic Sources of American Foreign Policy: Insights and Evidence,* ed. Eugene R. Wittkopf and James M. McCormick (New York: Rowman & Littlefield, 1999), 141.

51. Reagan and Lindsey, *An American Life,* 451.

52. George P. Shultz, *Turmoil and Triumph: My Years as Secretary of State* (New York: Charles Scribner's Sons, 1993), 335.

53. Ellen Ray and Bill Schaap, "Grenada—No Bishop, No Revo: U.S. Crushes Caribbean Jewel," *Covert Action* no. 20 (Winter 1984): 17.

54. Edward R. Drachman and Alan Shank, *Presidents and Foreign Policy: Countdown to 10 Controversial Decisions* (Albany, NY: SUNY Press, 1997), 325.

55. George Stephanopoulos, *All Too Human: A Political Education* (Boston: Little, Brown and Co., 1999), 306.

56. George W. Bush, "Letter to Congressional Leaders Transmitting a Report on Iraq, June 13, 2003," *Public Papers of the Presidents,* 2003; Ron Fournier, "Bush Says U.S. Troops Making Progress: President Formally Notifies Congress of Use of Force,"*Associated Press,* 2003.

57. William Blum, *Killing Hope: U.S. Military and CIA Interventions Since World War II* (Monroe, ME: Common Courage Press, 1995), 48.

58. Fred Goff and Michael Locker, "The Violence of Domination: U.S. Power and the Dominican Republic," in *Latin American Radicalism: A Documentary Report on Left and Nationalist Movements,* ed. Irving Louis Horowitz, Josue Castro, and John Gerassi (New York: Random House, 1969).

59. Note the temporal overlap of the Dominican Republic intervention and American involvement in Vietnam. The Dominican Republic intervention, which took place wholly during the Vietnam war, was accorded less international legitimacy than either Korea or Lebanon, but received considerably more international approval than U.S. involvement in Vietnam.

60. I do mean to distinguish international legitimacy from domestic legitimacy. Many policies (especially in this sphere) are very popular and highly legitimate within the United States, but receive intense criticism and no legitimacy in international public opinion and on the UN floor; take the U.S. invasion of Panama, for example (also see chapter 7 for a full discussion of legitimacy).

61. See, for example, Bob Woodward, *Shadow: Five Presidents and the Legacy of Watergate* (New York: Simon & Schuster, 1999).

62. Pastor, "Chapter 8—The Caribbean Basin."

63. Roberts, *LBJ's Inner Circle,* 208.

64. Lowenthal, *The Dominican Intervention,* 85.

65. See Larson, *Origins of Containment,* for a full discussion.

66. Harry S. Truman, Presidential Address before Congress, March 12, 1947.

67. Gardner, "America's War in Vietnam," 16.

68. Ibid., 17.

69. Krasner, *Defending the National Interest,* 298.

70. Smith, "Haiti: From Intervention to Intervasion."

71. Blum, *Killing Hope,* 45.

72. Ibid., chap. 10.

73. Higgins, *The Perfect Failure.*

74. Blum, *Killing Hope,* chap. 10.

75. Higgins, *The Perfect Failure.*

76. Higgins, *The Perfect Failure;* Hinckle and Turner, *The Fish Is Red,* 41.

77. Smith, "Haiti: From Intervention to Intervasion," 56.

78. Evans and Novak, *Lyndon B. Johnson,* 516.

79. See, for example, Janis, *Victims of Groupthink.*

80. Hinckle and Turner, *The Fish Is Red,* 41; Higgins, *The Perfect Failure.*
81. Pastor, "Chapter 8—The Caribbean Basin."
82. Higgins, *The Perfect Failure,* 78.
83. Ibid., 75.
84. Hinckle and Turner, *The Fish Is Red.*
85. Prados, *Presidents' Secret Wars.*
86. Lowenthal, *The Dominican Intervention,* 107.
87. Thomson Jr., "How Could Vietnam Happen?" 241.
88. Gardner, "America's War in Vietnam."
89. Smith, "Haiti: From Intervention to Intervasion," 58; Grose, *Continuing the Inquiry;* Buchan, "The Indochina War," 16.
90. Roche, "The Impact of Dissent on Foreign Policy, 129.
91. Shultz, *Turmoil and Triumph,* 343.
92. Gardner, "America's War in Vietnam," 21; Blum, *Killing Hope,* 183.
93. Delli Carpini, "Vietnam and the Press," 152; Geyelin, "Vietnam and the Press," 76; Tischler, "Promise and Paradox, 47.
94. Kristol, "Consensus and Dissent"; Barber, "The Importance of Remembering."
95. Kristol, "Consensus and Dissent," 83.
96. Ronald H. Hinckley, *People, Polls, and Policymakers: American Public Opinion and National Security* (New York: Lexington Books, 1992), 113.
97. Smith, "Haiti: From Intervention to Intervasion," 58.
98. Lowenthal, *The Dominican Intervention,* 26.
99. Blum, *Killing Hope,* 175.
100. Lowenthal, *The Dominican Intervention;* Santo Domingo cable 24324, General Records of the Department of State (College Park, MD: National Archives at College Park).
101. Lowenthal, *The Dominican Intervention,* 107.
102. Agee, *Inside the Company,* 421.
103. Neustadt and May, *Thinking in Time,* 79.
104. Barnet, *Intervention and Revolution,* 174.
105. Roberts, *LBJ's Inner Circle,* 208.
106. Goff and Locker, "The Violence of Domination."
107. Millett, "Chapter 9—Panama and Haiti,"
108. Sick, *All Fall Down.*
109. Ibid.
110. Ibid.
111. For example, Weinberger, *Fighting For Peace,* 112.
112. Kelly, "Chapter 6—Lebanon: 1982–1984."
113. Ibid.
114. Weinberger, *Fighting For Peace,* 151.
115. Larson, *Casualties and Consensus.*
116. Powell and Persico, *My American Journey,* 558.
117. Kryzanek, "The Grenada Invasion," 60.
118. Reagan and Lindsey, *An American Life,* 451.
119. Shultz, *Turmoil and Triumph,* 343.
120. Weinberger, *Fighting for Peace,* 112.
121. Ibid., 107; Shultz, *Turmoil and Triumph,* 328; Reagan and Lindsey, *An American Life,* 450).

122. Burrowes, *Revolution and Rescue in Grenada;* Brown, "The U.S. Invasion of Grenada."

123. Fitzroy Ambursley and James Dunkerley, *Grenada: Whose Freedom?* (London: Latin America Bureau Special Brief, 1984), chap. 5.

124. Woodward, *The Commanders,* 141.

125. Powell and Persico, *My American Journey,* 430.

126. Woodward, *The Commanders,* 163.

127. Fisher, "Without Restraint," 141.

128. Kansteiner, "Chapter 7—U.S. Policy in Africa in the 1990s."

129. Powell and Persico, *My American Journey,* 565.

130. Over 500 Somalis were killed, with an additional 800–1,000 wounded. While many were unambiguously militiamen, many were equally unambiguously civilian noncombatants. A significant fraction of the Somali casualties were incurred by persons who were ostensibly noncombatants (unarmed civilians) who engaged in military or semimilitary activities (acting as human shields, pointing out the concealed position of U.S. soldiers to armed Somalis, and so forth) in a way that makes their proper categorization problematic. See Mark Bowden, *Black Hawk Down: A Story of Modern War* (New York, NY: Atlantic Monthly Press); and Rick Atkinson, "Night of a Thousand Casualties: Battle Triggered U.S. Decision to Withdraw from Somalia," *Washington Post,* January 31, 1994, for more details.

131. Kansteiner, "Chapter 7—U.S. Policy in Africa in the 1990s."

132. Powell and Persico, *My American Journey,* 565; Henriksen, *Clinton's Foreign Policy.*

133. Dandeker and Gow, "The Future of Peace Support Operations," 329.

134. Larson, *Casualties and Consensus.*

135. Henriksen, *Clinton's Foreign Policy.*

136. Fauriol and Faiola, " Chapter 11—Prelude to Intervention," 115.

137. Ballard, *Upholding Democracy.*

138. Henriksen, *Clinton's Foreign Policy,* 23.

139. Zimmermann, "Chapter 11—Yugoslavia: 1989–1996."

140. Ibid.

141. Powell and Persico, *My American Journey,* 558.

CHAPTER 7

1. This is the difference between the calculated presidential national interest and what is seen to be in the public national interest. See chapter 4 for a full discussion.

2. Jonathan Waskan, "De facto Legitimacy and Popular Will," *Social Theory and Practice* 24, no. 1 (Spring 1998): 25.

3. There is an interesting strand of research on legitimacy that focuses on the difference between *acceptance of* and *passive consent to* (pragmatic acceptance of) governance, finding a distinction between behavior and belief to be worthy of consideration, particularly on the fringes when legitimacy starts to break down (see, for example, Arthur J. Vidich and Ronald M. Glassman, "Introduction," in *Conflict and Control: Challenge to Legitimacy of Modern Governments,* ed. Arthur J. Vidich and Ronald M. Glassman (London: Sage, 1979).

4. Morris Zelditch Jr., "Theories of Legitimacy," in *The Psychology of Legitimacy: Emerging Perspectives on Ideology, Justice, and Intergroup Relations,* ed. John T. Jost and Brenda Major (Cambridge: Cambridge University Press, 2001), 33–53; Morris Zelditch Jr. and Henry A. Walker, "Legitimacy and the Stability of Authority," in *Status, Power and Legitimacy: Strategies & Theories,*

ed. Joseph Berger and Morris Zelditch (New Brunswick, NJ: Transaction, 1998), 315–338; Morris Zelditch Jr. and Anthony S. Floyd, "Consensus, Dissensus, and Justification," in *Status, Power and Legitimacy: Strategies & Theories,* ed. Joseph Berger and Morris Zelditch (New Brunswick, NJ: Transaction, 1998), 339–370.

5. For an earlier discussion of propriety and validity, see Sanford M. Dornbusch and W. Richard Scott, *Evaluation and the Exercise of Authority* (San Francisco: Jossey-Bass, 1975).

6. Max Weber, in *The Theory of Social and Economic Organization,* ed. Talcott Parsons (New York: The Free Press, 1947), 327.

7. Joseph Bensman, "Max Weber's Concept of Legitimacy: An Evaluation," in *Conflict and Control: Challenge to Legitimacy of Modern Governments,* ed. Arthur J. Vidich and Ronald M. Glassman (London: Sage, 1979), 19.

8. Zelditch Jr. and Floyd, "Consensus, Dissensus, and Justification," 340.

9. See Tom R. Tyler, "A Psychological Perspective on the Legitimacy of Institutions and Authority," in *The Psychology of Legitimacy: Emerging Perspectives on Ideology, Justice, and Intergroup Relations,*ed. John T. Jost and Brenda Major (Cambridge: Cambridge University Press, 2001), 416–436, as an example of a scholar making this sort of "procedural justice" argument about legitimacy).

10. There is, of course, the notable exception of mass protest and the social movements of the 1960s. However, these movements still targeted legal change and were largely conducted through legal, nonviolent protest assemblies and carefully (rationally) chosen acts of civil disobedience.

11. Herbert C. Kelman, "Reflections on Social and Psychological Process of Legitimization and Delegitimzation," in *The Psychology of Legitimacy: Emerging Perspectives on Ideology, Justice, and Intergroup Relations,* ed. John T. Jost and Brenda Major (Cambridge: Cambridge University Press, 2001), 54–73.

12. Alice H. Amsden, "The State and Taiwan's Economic Development," in *Bringing the State Back In,* ed. Peter B. Evans, Dietrich Rueschemeyer, and Theda Skocpol (Cambridge: Cambridge University Press, 1985); Michael Mann, *The Sources of Social Power, v. 2: The Rise of Classes and Nation-States, 1760–1914* (Cambridge: Cambridge University Press, 1993); Charles Tilly, "War Making and State Making as Organized Crime," in *Bringing the State Back In,* ed. Peter B. Evans, Dietrich Rueschemeyer, and Theda Skocpol (Cambridge: Cambridge University Press, 1985); Theda Skocpol, "Introduction," in *Bringing the State Back In,* ed. Peter B. Evans, Dietrich Rueschemeyer, and Theda Skocpol (Cambridge: Cambridge University Press, 1985); Theda Skocpol, "The Potential Autonomy of the State," in *Power in Modern Societies,* ed. Marvin Elliott Olsen and Martin N. Marger (Boulder, CO: Westview Press, 1993); Fred Block, "State Theory in Context," in *Revising State Theory: Essays in Politics and Postindustrialism,* ed. Fred Block (Philadelphia, PA: Temple University Press, 1987).

13. Mann, *The Sources of Social Power, v. 2,* 70–75.

14. Again, with the exception of immigrants or expatriates for the country intervened in, their ancestors or sympathizers, or cases in which salience has been increased by dramatic events, such as the attacks of 9/11.

15. If not more; see the "rally to the flag" effect as discussed in Ronald H. Hinckley, *People, Polls, and Policymakers: American Public Opinion and National Security* (New York: Lexington Books, 1992), 108.

16. Paul L. Rosen, "Legitimacy, Domination, and Ego Displacement," in *Conflict and Control: Challenge to Legitimacy of Modern Governments,* ed. Arthur J. Vidich and Ronald M. Glassman (London: Sage, 1979), 76.

17. Richard E. Neustadt, *Presidential Power and the Modern Presidents: The Politics of Leadership from Roosevelt to Reagan* (New York: The Free Press, 1990).

18. Andrew S. Faiola, "Chapter 8: Refugee Policy: The 1994 Crisis," in *Haitian Frustrations: Dilemmas for U.S. Policy: A Report of the CSIS Americas Program,* ed. Georges A. Fauriol (Washington, DC: Center for Strategic & International Studies, 1995).

19. With regard to the ongoing (at this writing) U.S. military action in Afghanistan, there is likely to be a reasonably strong concurrence between motives and claims. However, there are still "unclaimed" decisions involved, such as which countries allow or have allowed terrorist training camps will be publicly chided for this activity, and which among those will be targets of military action. The attacks of 9/11 left a sufficient normative claim to justify just about anything up to complete open season on "bad men." The early choice to focus all attention on bin Laden, regardless of his established complicity in the attacks, was certainly a calculated choice.

20. Abraham F. Lowenthal, *The Dominican Intervention* (Cambridge, MA: Harvard, 1972), 86; John Bartlow Martin, *Overtaken by Events: The Dominican Crisis from the Fall of Trujillo to the Civil War* (New York: Doubleday & Co., 1966).

21. Martin, *Overtaken by Events;* Department of State outgoing cable 17082, General Records of the Department of State (College Park, MD: National Archives at College Park, 1965).

22. Rowland Evans and Robert Novak, *Lyndon B. Johnson: The Exercise of Power* (New York: The New American Library, 1966), 517–520; Charles Mohrs, "Johnson's Action on Troops Swift; He Made Decision Himself as Aides Told of Peril," *New York Times,* May 1, 1965.

23. Charles Roberts, *LBJ's Inner Circle* (New York: Delacorte Press); Lowenthal, *The Dominican Intervention,* 104.

24. Reuters, "Text Of Reagan's Announcement of Invasion," *New York Times,* October 26, 1983.

25. Reagan quoted in Bernard Gwertzman, "Reagan Gains by Grenada, but Mostly on His Own Turf," *New York Times,* November 6, 1983.

26. William Blum, *Killing Hope: U.S. Military and CIA Interventions since World War II* (Monroe, ME: Common Courage Press), 269.

27. Christina Jacqueline Johns and P. Ward Johnson, *State Crime, The Media, and The Invasion of Panama* (Westport: Praeger, 1994), 14.

28. John and Johnson, *State Crime.*

29. Colin L. Powell and Joseph E. Persico, *My American Journey* (New York: Random House, 1995), 425.

30. Bob Woodward, *The Commanders* (New York: Simon & Schuster, 1991).

31. Powell and Persico, *My American Journey;* James A. Baker III with Thomas M. Defrank, *The Politics of Diplomacy: Revolution, War and Peace 1989–1992* (New York: G.P. Putnam's Sons, 1995).

32. Margaret E. Scranton, *The Noriega Years: U.S.–Panamanian Relations, 1981–1990* (Boulder, CO: Lynne Rienner Publishers, 1991), 199.

33. Christian S. Crandall and Ryan K. Beasley, "A Perceptual Theory of Legitimacy: Politics, Prejudice, Social Institutions, and Moral Value," in *The Psychology of Legitimacy: Emerging Perspectives on Ideology, Justice, and Intergroup Relations,* ed. John T. Jost and Brenda Major (Cambridge: Cambridge University Press, 2001), 77–102.

34. Robert J. Robinson and Laura Kray, "Status versus Quo: Naïve Realism and the Search for Social Change and Perceived Legitimacy," in *The Psychology of Legitimacy: Emerging*

Perspectives on Ideology, Justice, and Intergroup Relations, ed. John T. Jost and Brenda Major (Cambridge: Cambridge University Press), 135– 154.

35. Noam Chomsky, "Democracy Enhancement: Part II: The Case of Haiti," *Z Magazine* (July/August 1994).

36. Samuel Kernell, *Going Public: New Strategies of Presidential Leadership* (Washington, DC: CQ Press, 1986), 148.

37. Neustadt, *Presidential Power and the Modern Presidents.*

38. Waskan, "De facto Legitimacy and Popular Will," 25.

39. Blum, *Killing Hope,* 276.

40. Thomas M. Franck, "Legitimacy in the International System," *American Journal of International Law* 82, no. 4 (October 1988): 705.

41. Richard J. Barnet, *Intervention and Revolution: America's Confrontation with Insurgent Movements around the World* (New York: World Publishing Co., 1968), 174.

42. Charles W. Kegley Jr. and Eugene R. Wittkopf, "Americans' Values, Beliefs, and Preferences: Political Culture and Public Opinion in American Foreign Policy," in *American Foreign Policy: Pattern and Process* (New York: St. Martin's Press, 1996), 264.

43. Jim A. Kuypers, *Presidential Crisis Rhetoric and the Press in the Post–Cold War World* (Westport, CT: Praeger, 1997), 3.

44. John and Johnson, *State Crime,* 8.

45. Gaddis Smith, "Haiti: From Intervention to Intervasion," *Current History* 94, no. 589 (February 1995).

46. Georges A. Fauriol and Andrew S. Faiola, "Chapter 11—Prelude to Intervention," in *Haitian Frustrations: Dilemmas for U.S. Policy: A Report of the CSIS Americas Program,* ed. Georges A. Fauriol (Washington, DC: Center for Strategic & International Studies, 1995).

47. As quoted in Woodward, *The Commanders,* 154.

48. Baker, with Defrank, *The Politics of Diplomacy,* 187.

49. Constantine C. Menges, *Inside the National Security Council: The True Story of the Making and Unmaking of Reagan's Foreign Policy* (New York: Simon and Schuster, 1988), 83.

50. Dean Rusk, *As I Saw It,* ed. Daniel Papp and Richard Rusk (New York: W.W. Norton & Co., 1990), 373.

51. Kegley and Wittkopf, "Americans' Values, Beliefs, and Preferences, 288.

52. George Stephanopoulos, *All Too Human: A Political Education* (Boston: Little, Brown and Co., 1999).

53. Lowenthal, *The Dominican Intervention,* 104.

54. John Mueller, "Public Opinion and Foreign Policy: The People's 'Common Sense'" in *The Domestic Sources of American Foreign Policy: Insights and Evidence,* ed. Eugene R. Wittkopf and James M. McCormick (New York: Rowman & Littlefield., 1999).

55. Deidre McFadyen and Pierre LaRamee with Mark Fried and Fred Rosen (NACLA), "Introduction," in *Haiti:Dangerous Crossroads* (Boston: South End Press), 5.

56. Woodward, *The Commanders.*

57. John and Johnson, *State Crime.*

58. Dana Bash, "White House Pressed on 'Mission Accomplished' Sign," *CNN.com/Inside Politics,* October 29, 2003, http://www.cnn.com/2003/ALLPOLITICS/10/28/mission.accomplished/.

59. Hinckley, *People, Polls, and Policymakers,* 108.

60. Kuypers, *Presidential Crisis Rhetoric,* 8.

61. Note that the Grenada intervention was almost universally condemned by Cold War allies and opponents alike, primarily as a result of rejection of the tiny nation to threats of any vital interests of any kind.

62. Robert Pastor, "Chapter 8—The Caribbean Basin," in *Conference Report, U.S. and Russian Policymaking with Respect to the Use of Force,* ed. Jeremy R. Azrael and Emil A. Payin, RAND Report No. CF-129-CRES (Santa Monica, CA: RAND, 1996).

63. Kim Ives, "Haiti's Second Occupation," in *Haiti: Dangerous Crossroads,* ed. Deidre McFadyen and Pierre LaRamee (Boston: South End Press, 1995), 110.

64. Lowenthal, *The Dominican Intervention;* Evans and Novak, *Lyndon B. Johnson,* 517.

65. Ronald Reagan and Robert Lindsey, *An American Life* (New York: Simon and Schuster, 1990), 450–452.

66. Blum, *Killing Hope,* 270.

67. Jame A. Winnefeld, Margaret C. Harrel, Robert D. Howe, Arnold Kanter, Brian Nichiporuk, Paul S. Steinberg, Thomas S. Szayna, and Ashley J. Tellis, *Intervention in Intrastate Conflict: Implications for the Army in the Post–Cold War Era* (Santa Monica, CA: RAND Corporation, 1995).

68. Ives, "Haiti's Second Occupation"; John R. Ballard, *Upholding Democracy: The United States Military Campaign in Haiti, 1994–1997* (London: Praeger, 1998); Elizabeth D. Gibbons, *The Washington Papers: Sanctions in Haiti—Human Rights and Democracy Under Assault* (London: Praeger, 1999).

69. Edward R. Drachman and Alan Shank, *Presidents and Foreign Policy: Countdown to 10 Controversial Decisions* (Albany, NY: SUNY Press, 1997).

70. Lowenthal, *The Dominican Intervention;* Department of State cable 24324.

71. Blum, *Killing Hope,* 270.

72. Mueller, "Public Opinion and Foreign Policy."

73. Stephanopoulos, *All Too Human,* 309.

74. Eric V. Larson, *Casualties and Consensus* (Santa Monica: RAND, 1996).

75. Eric Schmitt, "Legislators in U.S. Differ over Haiti," *New York Times,* September 1, 1994.

76. George P. Shultz, *Turmoil and Triumph: My Years as Secretary of State* (New York: Charles Scribner's Sons, 1993), 335.

77. Kernell, *Going Public,* 148.

78. Ives, "Haiti's Second Occupation," 109–110; Tim Weiner, "Clinton Forces out U.S. Envoy to Haiti to Display Resolve," *New York Times,* April 27, 1994.

CHAPTER 8

1. Victor Nee and Paul Ingram, "Embeddedness and Beyond: Institutions, Exchange, and Social Structure," in *The New Institutionalism in Sociology,* ed. Mary C. Brinton & Victor Nee (Stanford, CA: Stanford University Press, 1998), 19.

2. Kenneth Finegold and Theda Skocpol, *State and Party in America's New Deal* (Madison: The University of Wisconsin Press, 1995), 224.

3. Fredrik Logevall, *Choosing War: The Lost Chance for Peace and the Escalation of War in Vietnam* (Los Angeles: University of California Press, 1999), xiii.

4. Logevall, *Choosing War.*

5. Leslie Gelb and Richard Betts, *The Irony of Vietnam: The System Worked* (Washington, DC: Brookings, 1978), 244.

6. Robert Dallek, *Flawed Giant: Lyndon Johnson and His Times, 1961–1973,* (New York: Oxford University Press, 1998).

7. Norman Schwarzkopf, interviewed during "The Gulf War," report on *PBS Frontline,* January 9, 1996, http://www.pbs.org/wgbh/pages/frontline/gulf/oral/commanders.html.

8. Ibid.

9. Walter LaFeber, *Inevitable Revolutions: The United States in Central America* (New York: W.W. Norton & Co., 1983), 234.

10. John Prados, *Presidents' Secret Wars: CIA and Pentagon Covert Operations from World War II through the Persian Gulf* (Chicago: Elephant, 1986).

11. Colin L. Powell and Joseph E. Persico, *My American Journey* (New York: Random House, 1995).

12. Robert A. Dahl, *Polyarchy: Participation and Opposition* (New Haven: Yale University Press, 1971).

13. G. William Domhoff, *State Autonomy or Class Dominance? Case Studies on Policy Making in America* (New York: Aldine DeGruyter, 1996).

14. Fred Goff and Michael Locker, "The Violence of Domination: U.S. Power and the Dominican Republic," in *Latin American Radicalism: A Documentary Report on Left and Nationalist Movements,* ed. Irving Louis Horowitz, Josue Castro, and John Gerassi (New York: Random House, 1969); Richard J. Barnet, *Intervention and Revolution: America's Confrontation with Insurgent Movements around the World* (New York: World Publishing Co., 1968); North American Congress on Latin America (NACLA), "NACLA'S Latin American & Empire Report—Smoldering Conflict: Dominican Republic 1965–1975," vol. IX, no. 3 (New York: North American Congress on Latin America, April 1975), for example.

15. Or, he would launch an impressive empirical probe ultimately showing some interesting but previously not obvious interest or influence.

16. Fred Block, "State Theory in Context," in *Revising State Theory: Essays in Politics and Postindustrialism,* ed. Fred Block (Philadelphia, PA: Temple University Press, 1987).

17. C. Edward Paul, "Moving Forward with State Autonomy and Capacity: Example from Two Studies of the Pentagon During W.W.II.," *Journal of Political and Military Sociology* 28, no. 1 (Summer 2000).

References

Acheson, Dean. *Present at the Creation: My Years in the State Department.* New York: W.W. Norton and Co., 1969.

Agee, Philip. *Inside the Company: CIA Diary.* Baltimore: Penguin Books, 1975.

Allison, Graham. *Essence of Decision: Explaining the Cuban Missile Crisis.* Boston: Little, Brown and Co., 1971.

Ambursley, Fitzroy, and James Dunkerley. *Grenada: Whose Freedom?* London: Latin America Bureau Special Brief, 1984.

Amsden, Alice H. "The State and Taiwan's Economic Development." In *Bringing the State Back In,* edited by Peter B. Evans, Dietrich Rueschemeyer, and Theda Skocpol. Cambridge: Cambridge University Press, 1985.

Bachrach, Peter, and Morton J. Baratz. "Decisions and Non-Decisions." *American Political Science Review* 57 (September 1963).

Baker, James A. III, with Thomas M. Defrank. *The Politics of Diplomacy: Revolution, War and Peace 1989–1992.* New York: G.P. Putnam's Sons, 1995.

Ballard, John R. *Upholding Democracy: The United States Military Campaign in Haiti, 1994–1997.* London: Praeger, 1998.

Barber, Benjamin R. "The Importance of Remembering: The Vietnam Legacy's Challenge to American Democracy." In *The Legacy: The Vietnam War in the American Imagination,* edited by D. Michael Shafer. Boston: Beacon Press, 1990.

Barnet, Richard J. *Intervention and Revolution: America's Confrontation with Insurgent Movements around the World.* New York: World Publishing Co., 1968.

Benjamin, David. "Censorship in the Gulf." 1995. http://web1.duc.auburn.edu/~benjadp/gulf/gulf.html.

Bensman, Joseph. "Max Weber's Concept of Legitimacy: An Evaluation." In *Conflict and Control: Challenge to Legitimacy of Modern Governments,* edited by Arthur J. Vidich and R. Glassman. London: SAGE, 1979.

Berger, Peter L., and Thomas Luckmann. *The Social Construction of Reality: A Treatise in the Sociology of Knowledge.* Garden City, NY: Anchor Books, 1966.

Berkowitz, M., P.G. Bock, and Vincent J. Fuccillo. *The Politics of American Foreign Policy.* Edgewood Cliffs, NJ: Prentice-Hall, 1977.

Block, Fred. "State Theory in Context." In *Revising State Theory: Essays in Politics and Postindustrialism,* edited by Fred Block. Philadelphia: Temple University Press, 1987.

———. "The Ruling Class Does Not Rule." *Socialist Revolution* 33 (1977).

Blum, William. *Killing Hope: U.S. Military and CIA Interventions since World War II.* Monroe, ME: Common Courage Press, 1995.

Bowden, Mark. *Black Hawk Down: A Story of Modern War.* New York: Atlantic Monthly Press, 1999.

Bridgetown Cables 06490, 06514, 6547. General Record of the White House. Simi Valley, CA: Ronald Reagan Library, 1983.

Brown, Mozilla N. "The U.S. Invasion of Grenada During the Reagan Administration: A Re-Evaluation." Naval Academy Foreign Affairs Conference: Keeping the Peace, 1999.

Buchan, Alistair. "The Indochina War and the Changing Pattern of World Politics." In *The Legacy of Vietnam: The War, American Society and the Future of American Foreign Policy,* edited by Anthony Lake. New York: Council on Foreign Relations, 1976.

Burrowes, Reynold A. *Revolution and Rescue in Grenada: An Account of the U.S. Caribbean Invasion.* New York: Greenwood Press, 1988.

Bush, George, and Brent Scowcroft. *A World Transformed.* New York: Alfred A. Knopf, 1998.

Campbell, John L. "Institutional Analysis and the Role of Ideas in Political Economy." *Theory and Society* 27 (1998): 377–409.

Chace, James. "The National Interest." *World Policy Journal* 10, no. 4 (Winter 1993): 109.

Chomsky, Noam. "Democracy Enhancement: Part II: The Case of Haiti." *Z Magazine* (July/August 1994).

Cohen, Bernard C. *The Press and Foreign Policy.* Princeton: Princeton University Press, 1963.

Common Ground. Program 9828, "MEDIA VS. MILITARY." Guest: Warren Strobel, author, Late Breaking Foreign Policy. Air Date: July 14, 1998.

Connolly, William E. "On 'Interests' in Politics." *Politics and Society* 2, no. 4 (1972).

Crandall, Christian S., and Ryan K. Beasly. "A Perceptual Theory of Legitimacy: Politics, Prejudice, Social Institutions, and Moral Value." In *The Psychology of Legitimacy: Emerging Perspectives on Ideology, Justice, and Intergroup Relations* edited by John T. Jost and Brenda Major, 77–102. Cambridge: Cambridge University Press, 2001.

Dahl, Robert A. *Polyarchy: Participation and Opposition.* New Haven: Yale University Press, 1991.

———. *Pluralist Democracy in the United States: Conflict and Consensus.* Chicago: Rand McNally, 1967.

———. *Who Governs? Democracy and Power in an American City.* New Haven: Yale University Press, 1961.

Dallek, Robert. *Flawed Giant: Lyndon Johnson and His Times, 1961–1973.* New York: Oxford University Press, 1998.

Dandeker, Christopher, and James Gow. "The Future of Peace Support Operations: Strategic Peacekeeping and Success." *Armed Forces & Society* 23, no. 3 (Spring 1997): 327–348.

Della Fave, L. Richard. "Toward an Explication of the Legitimation Process." *Social Forces* 65, no. 2 (1984): 476–500.

Delli Carpini, Michael X. "Vietnam and the Press." In *The Legacy: The Vietnam War in the American Imagination,* edited by D. Michael Shafer. Boston: Beacon Press, 1990.

Dellums, the Hon. Ronald V., Statement of. A Representative in Congress from the State of California. In *United States Policy Toward Grenada,* pp. 15–21, a Hearing before the

Subcommittee on Inter-American Affairs of the Committee on Foreign Affairs of the House of Representatives Ninety-Seventh Congress Second Session, June 15, 1982.

Dessler, David. "What's at Stake in the Agent-Structure Debate?" *International Organization* 43, no 3 (1989): 441–473.

Domhoff, G. William. *Who Rules America? Power and Politics in the Year 2000.* 3rd ed. Mountain View, CA: Mayfield Publishing Co., 1998.

———. *State Autonomy or Class Dominance? Case Studies on Policy Making in America.* New York: Aldine DeGruyter, 1996.

———. *The Power Elite and the State: How Policy Is Made in America.* New York: Aldine DeGruyter, 1990.

———. *Who Really Rules? New Haven and Community Power Reexamined.* New Brunswick, NJ: Transaction Books, 1978.

Dornbusch, S.M., and W.R. Scott. *Evaluation and the Exercise of Authority.* San Francisco: Jossey-Bass, 1975.

Drachman, Edward R., and Alan Shank. *Presidents and Foreign Policy: Countdown to 10 Controversial Decisions.* Albany: SUNY Press, 1997.

Dye, Thomas. *Top Down Policymaking.* New York: Chatham House, 2001.

———. *Who's Running America? The Clinton Years.* New Jersey: Prentice-Hall, 1995.

Elliott, Michael. "Yes, There IS a National Interest." *Newsweek* 124, no. 12 (September 19, 1994): 43.

Ellsworth, Robert, Andrew Goodpaster, and Rita Hauser, Co-Chairs. *America's National Interests: A Report from The Commission on America's National Interests.* Graham T. Allison, Dimitri K. Simes, and James Thomson, Executive Directors. Cambridge, MA: Belfer Center for Science and International Affairs, 2000.

Elsbach, Kimberly D. "The Architecture of Legitimacy: Constructing Accounts of Organizational Controversies." In *The Psychology of Legitimacy: Emerging Perspectives on Ideology, Justice, and Intergroup Relations,* edited by John T. Jost and Brenda Major, 391–415. Cambridge: Cambridge University Press, 2001.

Evans, Rowland, and Robert Novak. *Lyndon B. Johnson: The Exercise of Power.* New York: The New American Library, 1966.

Faiola, Andrew S. "Chapter 8: Refugee Policy: The 1994 Crisis." In *Haitian Frustrations: Dilemmas for U.S. Policy: A Report of the CSIS Americas Program,* edited by in Georges A. Fauriol. Washington, DC: Center for Strategic & International Studies, 1995.

Fauriol, Georges A., and Andrew S. Faiola. "Chapter 11—Prelude to Intervention." In *Haitian Frustrations: Dilemmas for U.S. Policy: A Report of the CSIS Americas Program,* edited by in Georges A. Fauriol. Washington, DC: Center for Strategic & International Studies, 1995.

Finegold, Kenneth, and Theda Skocpol. *State and Party in America's New Deal.* Madison: The University of Wisconsin Press, 1995.

Finnemore, Martha. "Norms, Culture, and World Politics: Insights from Sociology's Institutionalism." *International Organization* 50, no. 2 (1996): 325–47

Fisher, Louis. "Without Restraint: Presidential Military Initiatives from Korea to Bosnia." In *The Domestic Sources of American Foreign Policy: Insights and Evidence,* edited by Eugene R. Wittkopf and James M. McCormick. New York: Rowman & Littlefield, 1999.

Franck, Thomas M. "Legitimacy in the International System." *American Journal of International Law* 82, no. 4 (October 1988): 705–759.

Gardner, Lloyd. "America's War in Vietnam: The End of Exceptionalism?" In *The Legacy: The Vietnam War in the American Imagination,* edited by in Shafer, D. Michael. Boston: Beacon Press, 1990.

Gelb, Leslie, and Richard Betts. *The Irony of Vietnam: The System Worked.* Washington, DC: Brookings, 1978.

George, Alexander L. *Presidential Decisionmaking in Foreign Policy: The Effective Use of Information and Advice.* Boulder, CO: Westview, 1980.

Gerth, H.H., and C. Wright Mills. *From Max Weber: Essays in Sociology.* New York: Oxford University Press, 1946.

Geyelin, Philip. "Vietnam and the Press: Limited War and an Open Society." In *The Legacy of Vietnam: The War, American Society and the Future of American Foreign Policy,* edited by Anthony Lake. New York: Council on Foreign Relations, 1976.

Gibbons, Elizabeth D. *The Washington Papers: Sanctions in Haiti—Human Rights and Democracy under Assault.* London: Praeger, 1999.

Gilboa, Eytan. "The Panama Invasion Revisited: Lessons for the Use of Force in the Post Cold War Era." *Political Science Quarterly* 110, no. 4 (Winter 1995).

Goff, Fred, and Michael Locker. "The Violence of Domination: U.S. Power and the Dominican Republic." In *Latin American Radicalism: A Documentary Report on Left and Nationalist Movements,* edited by Irving Louis Horowitz, Josue Castro, and John Gerassi. New York: Random House, 1969.

Gowa, Joanne. "State Power, State Policy: Explaining the Decision to Close the Gold Window." *Politics and Society* 13 (1984).

Grose, Peter. *Continuing the Inquiry: The Council on Foreign Relations from 1921 to 1996.* New York: Council on Foreign Relations, 1996.

Haney, Patrick J. *Organizing for Foreign Policy Crises: Presidents, Advisers, and the Management of Decision Making.* Ann Arbor: University of Michigan Press, 1997.

Hastedt, Glenn, and Anthony Eksterowicz. "Presidential Leadership and American Foreign Policy: Implications for a New Era." In *The Domestic Sources of American Foreign Policy: Insights and Evidence,* edited by Eugene R. Wittkopf and James M. McCormick. New York: Rowman & Littlefield, 1999.

Henriksen, Thomas H. *Clinton's Foreign Policy In Somalia, Bosnia, Haiti, and North Korea.* Stanford, CA: Hoover Institution, 1996.

Herek, Gregory M., Irving L. Janis, and Paul Huth. "Decision Making during International Crises: Is Quality of Process Related to Outcome?" *Journal of Conflict Resolution* 31, no. 2 (June 1987): 203–226.

Higgins, Trumbull. *The Perfect Failure: Kennedy, Eisenhower, and the CIA at the Bay of Pigs.* New York: W.W. Norton & Co., 1987

Higley, John, and Michael Burton. "The Elite Variable in Democratic Transitions and Breakdowns." *American Sociological Review* 54, no. 1 (1989).

Hinckle, Warren, and William W. Turner. *The Fish Is Red: The Story of the Secret War against Castro.* New York: Harper & Row, 1981.

Hinckley, Ronald H. *People, Polls, and Policymakers: American Public Opinion and National Security.* New York: Lexington Books, 1992.

Hobson, John M. *The State and International Relations.* Cambridge: Cambridge University Press, 2000.

Holland, Lauren. "The U.S. Decision to Launch Operation Desert Storm: A Bureaucratic Politics Analysis." *Armed Forces & Society* 25, no. 2 (Winter 1999): 219–242.

Holsti, Ole. "Crisis Decision Making." In *Behavior, Society, and Nuclear War,* edited by Philip E. Tetlock, Jo L. Husbands, Robert Jervis, Paul C. Stern, and Charles Tilly. New York: Oxford University Press, 1989.

Huntington, Samuel P. "The Erosion of American National Interests." In *The Domestic Sources of American Foreign Policy: Insights and Evidence,* edited by Eugene R. Wittkopf and James M. McCormick. New York: Rowman & Littlefield, 1999.

Ives, Kim. "The Unmaking of a President." In *Haiti: Dangerous Crossroads,* edited by Deidre McFadyen and Pierre LaRamee. Boston: South End Press, 1995.

———. 1995b. "Haiti's Second Occupation." In *Haiti: Dangerous Crossroads,* edited by Deidre McFadyen and Pierre LaRamee. Boston: South End Press, 1995.

Jakobsen, Peter Viggo. "National Interest, Humanitarianism or CNN: What Triggers UN Peace Enforcement after the Cold War?" *Journal of Peace Research* 33, no. 2 (1996): 205–215.

Janis, Irving L. *Victims of Groupthink: A Psychological Study of Foreign-Policy Decisions and Fiascoes.* Boston: Houghton Mifflin, 1967.

Janis, Irving L., and Leon Mann. *Decision Making: A Psychological Analysis of Conflict, Choice, and Commitment.* New York: The Free Press, 1977.

Johns, Christina Jacqueline, and P. Ward Johnson. *State Crime, The Media, and The Invasion of Panama.* Westport, CT: Praeger, 1994.

Johnson, Lyndon Baines. *The Vantage Point: Perspectives of the Presidency, 1963–1969.* New York: Holt, Rinehart & Winston, 1971.

———. "Statement by President Johnson, May 2, 1965." Department of State Bulletin. May 17, 1965.

Kansteiner, Walter H. "Chapter 7—U.S. Policy in Africa in the 1990s." In *Conference Report, U.S. and Russian Policymaking with Respect to the Use of Force* edited by Jeremy R. Azrael and Emil A. Payin. RAND Report No. CF-129-CRES. Santa Monica, CA: RAND.

Kegley, Charles W., Jr., and Eugene R. Wittkopf. "Americans' Values, Beliefs, and Preferences: Political Culture and Public Opinion in American Foreign Policy." In *American Foreign Policy: Pattern and Process.* New York: St. Martin's Press, 1996.

Kelly, John H. "Chapter 6—Lebanon: 1982–1984." In *Conference Report, U.S. and Russian Policymaking with Respect to the Use of Force,* edited by Jeremy R. Azrael and Emil A. Payin. RAND Report No. CF-129-CRES. Santa Monica, CA: RAND.

Kelman, Herbert C. "Reflections on Social and Psychological Process of Legitimization and Delegitimzation." In *The Psychology of Legitimacy: Emerging Perspectives on Ideology, Justice, and Intergroup Relations* edited by John T. Jost and Brenda Major, 54–73. Cambridge: Cambridge University Press, 2001.

Kemp, Geoffrey. "Presidential Management of the Executive Bureaucracy." In *The Domestic Sources of American Foreign Policy: Insights and Evidence,* edited by Eugene R. Wittkopf and James M. McCormick. New York: Rowman & Littlefield, 1999.

Kernell, Samuel. *Going Public: New Strategies of Presidential Leadership.* Washington, DC: CQ Press, 1986.

Khong, Yuen Foong. *Analogies at War: Korea, Munich, Dien Bien Phu, and the Vietnam Decisions of 1965.* Princeton, NJ: Princeton University Press, 1992.

Kozak, David C. "The Bureaucratic Politics Approach: The Evolution of the Paradigm." In *Bureaucratic Politics and National Security: Theory and Practice,* edited by David C. Kozak and James M. Keagle. Boulder, CO: Lynne Rienner Publishers, 1988.

Krasner, Stephen D. "Sovereignty: An Institutional Perspective." *Comparative Political Studies* 21, no. 1 (April 1988): 66–94.

———. *Defending the National Interest.* Princeton: Princeton University Press, 1978.

Kristol, Irving. "Consensus and Dissent in U.S. Foreign Policy." In *The Legacy of Vietnam: The War, American Society and the Future of American Foreign Policy,* edited by Anthony Lake. New York: Council on Foreign Relations, 1976.

Kryzanek, Michael J. "The Grenada Invasion: Approaches to Understanding." In *United States Policy in Latin America: A Decade of Crisis and Challenge,* edited by in John D. Martz. Lincoln: University of Nebraska Press, 1995.

Kuypers, Jim A. *Presidential Crisis Rhetoric and the Press in the Post-Cold War World.* Westport, CT: Praeger, 1997.

LaFeber, Walter. *Inevitable Revolutions: The United States in Central America.* New York: W.W. Norton & Co., 1983

Larson, Deborah Welch. *Origins of Containment: A Psychological Explanation.* Princeton, NJ: Princeton University Press, 1985.

Larson, Eric V. *Casualties and Consensus.* Santa Monica, CA: RAND, 1996.

Logevall, Fredrik. *Choosing War: The Lost Chance for Peace and the Escalation of War in Vietnam.* Los Angeles: University of California Press, 1999.

Lowenthal, Abraham F. *The Dominican Intervention.* Cambridge, MA: Harvard, 1972.

Lowi, Theodore, J. "Making Democracy Safe for the World." In *Domestic Sources of Foreign Policy,* edited by James N. Rosenau. New York: The Free Press, 1967.

Lukes, Steven. *Power: A Radical View.* London: The Macmillan Press, Ltd., 1974

Mann, Michael. *The Sources of Social Power, v. 2: The Rise of Classes and Nation-States, 1760–1914.* Cambridge: Cambridge University Press, 1993.

———. "The Autonomous Power of the State." In *Power in Modern Societies.* Boulder, CO: Westview Press, 1993.

———. *States, War and Capitalism.* Oxford, United Kingdom: Blackwell, 1984.

Margolis, Michael, and Gary A. Mauser. "Introduction: Public Opinion as a Dependent Variable." In *Manipulating Public Opinion: Essays on Public Opinion as a Dependent Variable,* edited by Michael Margolis and Gary A. Mauser. Pacific Grove, CA: Brooks/Cole, 1989.

Martin, John Bartlow. *Overtaken by Events: The Dominican Crisis from the Fall of Trujillo to the Civil War.* New York: Doubleday & Co., 1966.

Marx, Karl, and Friedrich Engles. "The 18th Brumaire of Louis Bonaparte." *Collected Works,* Vol. XI. London: Lawrence & Wishart, 1975.

Massing, Michael. "Grenada Before and After." *Atlantic Monthly* (February 1984, 80–81).

McFadyen, Deidre, and Pierre LaRamee with Mark Fried and Fred Rosen (NACLA). "Introduction." In *Haiti: Dangerous Crossroads.* Boston: South End Press, 1995.

Menges, Constantine C. *Inside the National Security Council: The True Story of the Making and Unmaking of Reagan's Foreign Policy.* New York: Simon and Schuster, 1988.

Meyer, John W., John Boli, George M. Thomas, and Francisco O. Ramirez. "World Society and the Nation-State." *American Journal of Sociology* 103, no. 1 (1997): 144–181.

Milbrath, Lester W. "Interest Groups and Foreign Policy." In *Domestic Sources of Foreign Policy,* edited by James N. Rosenau. New York: The Free Press, 1967.

Miliband, Ralph. *The State in Capitalist Society.* London: Weidenfeld and Nicholson, 1969.

Miller, Derek. "Towards a Theory of Media Pressure: A Literature Review on Effects of Media Technology on National Security Decisionmaking." Unpublished, 1999.

Millett, Richard L. "Chapter 9—Panama and Haiti." In *Conference Report: U.S. and Russian Policymaking with Respect to the Use of Force,* edited by Jeremy R. Azrael and Emil A. Payin. RAND Report No. CF-129-CRES. Santa Monica, CA: RAND, 1996.

Mills, C. Wright. *The Power Elite.* New York: Oxford University Press, 1956.

Morgenthau, Hans J. *The Impasse of American Foreign Policy.* Chicago: University of Chicago Press, 1962.

Mueller, John. "Public Opinion and Foreign Policy: The People's 'Common Sense'" In *The Domestic Sources of American Foreign Policy: Insights and Evidence,* edited by Eugene R. Wittkopf and James M. McCormick. New York: Rowman & Littlefield, 1999.

Nee, Victor, and Mary C. Brinton. "Introduction." In *The New Institutionalism in Sociology,* edited by Mary C. Brinton and Victor Nee, xv–xix. Stanford, CA: Stanford University Press, 1998.

Nee, Victor, and Paul Ingram. "Embeddedness and Beyond: Institutions, Exchange, and Social Structure." In *The New Institutionalism in Sociology,* edited by Mary C. Brinton and Victor Nee, 19–45. Stanford: Stanford University Press, 1998.

Neustadt, Richard E. *Presidential Power and the Modern Presidents: The Politics of Leadership from Roosevelt to Reagan.* New York: The Free Press, 1990.

Neustadt, Richard E., and Ernest R. May. *Thinking in Time: The Uses of History for Decision-Makers.* New York: The Free Press, 1986.

New York Times. New York: The New York Times Company.

Nincic, Miroslav. "The National Interest and Its Interpretation." *Review of Politics* 61, no. 1 (Winter 1999): 29.

North American Congress on Latin America (NACLA). "NACLA's Latin American & Empire Report—Smoldering Conflict: Dominican Republic 1965–1975." IX, no. 3, April. New York: North American Congress on Latin America, 1975.

Olsen, Marvin E. *Participatory Pluralism: Political Participation and Influence in the United States and Sweden.* Chicago: Nelson-Hal, 1982l.

Pastor, Robert. "Chapter 8—The Caribbean Basin." In *Conference Report: U.S. and Russian Policymaking with Respect to the Use of Force,* edited by in Jeremy R. Azrael and Emil A. Payin. RAND Report No. CF-129-CRES. Santa Monica, CA: RAND, 1996.

Paul, C. Edward. "Moving Forward with State Autonomy and Capacity: Example from Two Studies of the Pentagon During W.W. II." *Journal of Political and Military Sociology* 28, no. 1 (Summer 2000): 21–42.

Poulantzas, Nicos. "The Problem of the Capitalist State." *New Left Review* no. 58 (1969).

Powell, Colin L., with Joseph E. Persico. *My American Journey.* New York: Random House, 1995.

Prados, John. *Presidents' Secret Wars: CIA and Pentagon Covert Operations From World War II Through the Persian Gulf.* Chicago: Elephant, 1986.

Presidential Daily Diary. George Bush Papers. College Station, TX: George Bush Presidential Library, 1989.

Presidential Daily Diary. Ronald Reagan Papers. Simi Valley, CA: Ronald Reagan Library, 1983.

Presidential Daily Diary. Lyndon B. Johnson Papers. Austin, TX: Lyndon Baines Johnson Library, 1965.

Ray, Ellen, and Bill Schaap. "Grenada—No Bishop, No Revo: U.S. Crushes Caribbean Jewel." *Covert Action* no. 20 (Winter 1984).

Reagan, Ronald, with Robert Lindsey. *An American Life.* New York: Simon and Schuster, 1990.

Redd, Steven B. "The Influence of Advisers on Foreign Policy Decision Making: An Experimental Study." *Journal of Conflict Resolution* 46, no. 3 (2002: 335–364.

Roberts, Charles. *LBJ's Inner Circle.* New York: Delacorte Press, 1965.

Robinson, Robert J., and Laura Kray. "Status versus Quo: Naïve Realism and the Search for Social Change and Perceived Legitimacy." In *The Psychology of Legitimacy: Emerging Perspectives on Ideology, Justice, and Intergroup Relations,* edited by John T. Jost and Brenda Major, 135–154. Cambridge: Cambridge University Press, 2001.

Roche, John P. "The Impact of Dissent on Foreign Policy: Past and Future." In *The Legacy of Vietnam: The War, American Society and the Future of American Foreign Policy,* edited by Anthony Lake. New York: Council on Foreign Relations, 1976.

Rosen, Paul L. "Legitimacy, Domination, and Ego Displacement." In *Conflict and Control: Challenge to Legitimacy of Modern Governments,* edited by Arthur J. Vidich and Ronald M. Glassman. London: SAGE, 1979.

Roskin, Michael G. *National Interest: From Abstraction to Strategy.* Carlisle, PA: U.S. Army War College, Strategic Studies Institute, 1994.

Roy, William G. *Socializing Capital: The Rise of the Large Industrial Corporation in America.* Princeton, NJ: Princeton University Press, 1997.

Rusk, Dean. *As I Saw It,* edited by Daniel Papp and Richard Rusk. New York: W.W. Norton & Co., 1990.

Santo Domingo Cables 20912, 20932, 20959, 21313, 21442, 23304, 23630, 24100, 24229, 24324, 24340, 24640, and 25157. College Park, MD: General Records of the State Department. National Archives at College Park, 1965.

Schwarzkopf, Norman. Originally aired 01/09/1996 on *Frontline* as part of "The Gulf War" report. http://www.pbs.org/wgbh/pages/frontline/gulf/oral/commanders.html.

Scranton, Margaret E. *The Noriega Years: U.S.–Panamanian Relations, 1981–1990.* Boulder, CO: Lynne Rienner Publishers, 1991.

Searle, Chris. *Grenada: The Struggle Against Destabilization.* London: Writers and Readers Publishing Cooperative, 1983.

Shultz, George P. *Turmoil and Triumph: My Years as Secretary of State.* New York: Charles Scribner's Sons, 1993.

Sick, Gary. *All Fall Down: America's Tragic Encounter with Iran.* New York: Penguin, 1986.

Skocpol, Theda. *Protecting Soldiers and Mothers: The Political Origins of Social Policy in the United States.* Cambridge: The Belknap Press of Harvard University Press, 1992.

———. "Introduction." In *Bringing the State Back In,* edited by in Peter B. Evans, Dietrich Rueschemeyer, and Theda Skocpol. Cambridge: Cambridge University Press, 1985.

———. *States & Social Revolutions: A Comparative Analysis of France, Russia, & China.* Cambridge: Cambridge University Press, 1979.

Smith, Gaddis. "Haiti: From Intervention to Intervasion." *Current History* 94, no. 589 (February 1995): 54.

Snyder, Richard C. "Introduction." In *Foreign Policy Decision-Making: An Approach to the Study of International Politics,* edited by R. Snyder, H.W. Bruck, and Burton Sapin. Glencoe, ON: The Free Press, 1962.

State Department Outgoing Cables 13901, 16317. College Park, MD: General Records of the State Department. National Archives at College Park, 1965.

Stephanopoulos, George. *All Too Human: A Political Education.* Boston: Little, Brown and Co., 1999.

Strobel, Warren. "The CNN Effect: Myth or Reality?" In *The Domestic Sources of American Foreign Policy: Insights and Evidence,* edited by Eugene R. Wittkopf and James M. McCormick. New York: Rowman & Littlefield, 1999.

Swidler, Ann. "Culture in Action: Symbols and Strategies." *American Sociological Review* 51, (April 1986): 273–286.

Thomas, Evan. "Under The Gun." *Newsweek* 124, no. 14 (October 3, 1994): 28.

Thomson, James Jr. "How Could Vietnam Happen? An Autopsy." In *The Domestic Sources of American Foreign Policy: Insights and Evidence,* edited by Eugene R. Wittkopf and James M. McCormick. New York: Rowman & Littlefield, 1999.

Tilly, Charles. "War Making and State Making As Organized Crime." In *Bringing the State Back In,* edited by Peter B. Evans, Dietrich Rueschemeyer, and Theda Skocpol. Cambridge: Cambridge University Press, 1985.

Tischler, Barbara. "Promise and Paradox: The 1960s and American Optimism." In *The Legacy: The Vietnam War in the American Imagination,* edited by D. Michael Shafer. Boston: Beacon Press 1990.

Tyler, Tom R. "A Psychological Perspective on the Legitimacy of Institutions and Authority." In *The Psychology of Legitimacy: Emerging Perspectives on Ideology, Justice, and Intergroup Relations,* edited by John T. Jost and Brenda Major, 416–436. Cambridge: Cambridge University Press.

Vidich, Arthur J., and Ronald M. Glassman. "Introduction." In *Conflict and Control: Challenge to Legitimacy of Modern Governments,* edited by Arthur J. Vidich and Ronald M. Glassman. London: SAGE, 1979.

Waskan, Jonathan. "De Facto Legitimacy and Popular Will." *Social Theory and Practice* 24, no. 1 (Spring 1998): 25.

Weber, Max. *The Theory of Social and Economic Organization,* edited by Talcott Parsons. New York: The Free Press, 1947.

Weinberger, Caspar. *Fighting for Peace: Seven Critical Years in the Pentagon.* New York: Warner Books, 1990.

Wendt, Alexander E. "The Agent-Structure Problem in International Relations Theory." *International Organization* 41, no. 3 (1987): 335–370.

Winnefeld J.A., M.C. Harrel, R.D. Howe, A. Kanter, B. Nichiporuk, P.S. Steinberg, T.S. Szayna, and A.J. Tellis. *Intervention in Intrastate Conflict: Implications for the Army in the Post-Cold War Era.* RAND Report No. MR-554/1-A Santa Monica, CA: RAND, 1995.

Woodward, Bob. *Shadow: Five Presidents and the Legacy of Watergate.* New York: Simon & Schuster, 1999.

———. *The Commanders.* New York: Simon & Schuster, 1991.

Zelditch, Morris Jr. "Theories of Legitimacy." In *The Psychology of Legitimacy: Emerging Perspectives on Ideology, Justice, and Intergroup Relations,* edited by John T. Jost and Brenda Major, 33–53. Cambridge: Cambridge University Press, 2001.

Zelditch, Morris Jr., and Anthony S. Floyd. "Consensus, Dissensus, and Justification." In *Status, Power and Legitimacy: Strategies & Theories,* edited by Joseph Berger and Morris Zelditch, 339–370. New Brunswick: Transaction, 1998

Zelditch, Morris Jr., and Henry A. Walker. "Legitimacy and the Stability of Authority." In *Status, Power and Legitimacy: Strategies & Theories,* edited by Joseph Berger and Morris Zelditch, 315–338. New Brunswick, NJ: Transaction.

Zimmermann, Walter. "Chapter 11—Yugoslavia: 1989–1996." In *Conference Report: U.S. and Russian Policymaking with Respect to the Use of Force,* edited by Jeremy R. Azrael and Emil A. Payin. RAND Report No. CF-129-CRES. Santa Monica, CA: RAND, 1996.

Index

ABOUT THE AUTHOR

CHRISTOPHER PAUL is a social scientist working out of RAND's Pittsburgh office. He received his Ph.D. in sociology from UCLA in 2001. His current research interests include military influence operations, integration of air and naval forces, simulation training, press-military relations, counterterrorism, and military operations on urban terrain. He is the author of *Information Operations* (Praeger Security International, 2008).